AF560267

# KASHMIR
## Return of Democracy

# KASHMIR
## Return of Democracy

*Edited by*
**Yudhishtar Kahol**

ANMOL PUBLICATIONS PVT. LTD.
NEW DELHI - 110002 (INDIA)

**ANMOL PUBLICATIONS PVT. LTD.**
4374/4B, Ansari Road, Daryaganj
New Delhi - 110 002
Ph.: 23261597, 23278000
Visit us at: www.anmolpublications.com

*Kashmir: Return of Democracy*


First Edition, 2003

ISBN 81-261-1438-X

[The responsibility for the facts stated, conclusions reached and plagiarism, if any, in this work is entirely that of the Editor. And the Publisher bears no responsibility for them, whatsoever.]

PRINTED IN INDIA

Published by J.L. Kumar for Anmol Publications Pvt. Ltd., New Delhi - 110 002 and Printed at Mehra Offset Press, Delhi.

# Contents

## Part VIII
## JAMMU'S STATUS



## Part VIII
## SIGNIFICANT PEOPLE

# Preface

Kashmir Valley experienced a wave of fresh air, recently. A historic, fair and free election — first after the Independence took place in the State of Jammu and Kashmir.

The election results were really startling, though not quite unexpected. The verdict of people overthrew the rule of one dynasty and paved way for people's rule. It was rightly termed as 'the return of democracy'.

Mufti Mohammad Saeed, the veteran leader took reins of the State Government, replacing Dr. Farooq Abdullah and disappointing Omar Abdullah. The loss of National Conference appeared to be the gain of People's Democratic Party. It seemed to be so simple.

In fact, it was not so simple. It was not easy to analyse the outcome of the general elections. The defeat of the ruling National Conference cannot be attributed to the anti-incumbency factor alone. The voter clearly disapproved of its opportunistic attitude and lust of power.

People's Democratic Party (PDP) emerged as the new power while Congress shared power in a fairly conducted election. The PDP received a mandate in the Valley and the Congress performed well in Jammu area.

The political pundits concluded the election verdict as a vote for change — change for better in the hope for the best. The real winner, however, was the collective desire and will of people fatigued of violence. The Kashmiris showed both wisdom and fortitude in standing up against the tyranny and violence.

The international community also recognised that the elections in Jammu and Kashmir were fair and by and large free. Being a witness to India's commitment to democracy they expressed hope that justice would prevail and democracy would succeed in Jammu and Kashmir, as all political combinations of whatever hue and colour, barring the disgruntled All Parties Hurriyat Conference had stood against undemocratic means to grab power.

Let's salute people of Kashmir, who braved all seasons and helped materialise the positive development, now accepted by all as 'the Return of Democracy'.

Hopefully, this modest work would succeed in accounting the historic events for the record and prove to be a living tribute to the people of Kashmir.

**—Editor**

**New Delhi**
2002

# Introduction

This was rathet rich coming from someone who was widely seen to have practised an unacceptably immoral and irresponsible governance for six years. That his statement was made within a short span of inaugurating a tournament at Srinagar's posh new Golf Course — and barely 3 km from it — only multiplied the irony.

Hypocrisy and sanctimoniousness were writ large in the manner in which Farooq Abdullah resigned on October 17, 2002 as the caretaker Chief Minister of Jammu and Kashmir, thus precipitating Governor's Rule in the State just as it eagerly waited for a popular government. The ground Abdullah cited for his decision would have sounded less incredible had it not been couched in moralising terms while citing the Constitution of Jammu and Kashmir. "I do not have the moral right," he said, "to continue as Chief Minister since the Assembly by virtue of which my government was in office would cease to exist tonight."

For the people of Jammu and Kashmir, the Rs.32-crore Golf Course is nothing but a symbol of obscenely warped priorities in public spending, and a monument to malgovernance in a State whose economic and social indicators have steadily declined since 1996.

One needs not go as far in lambasting Abdullah as the People's Democratic Party (PDP) general secretary Tariq Hameed Qarrah did when he said Abdullah had been "sitting on our head for the past six years without a mandate", and "now he refuses to continue for four more days", thus creating a constitutional crisis. But there can be little doubt that

Abdullah waited till the very last day of the term of the Assembly to announce his decision, and then took another 10 hours finally to convey it to the Governor — too late for the National Conference's (NC) rivals to prepare another course of action on October 17.

Had a certain reading of the Constitution of Jammu and Kashmir alone determined Abdullah's decision, he couid have rejected Governor Girish Chandra Saxena's request to act as caretaker immediately after the Assembly election results came in on October 10. He could have told the Governor that his interpretation of the Constitution would not allow him to continue even as caretaker Chief Minister beyond October 17- (It is another matter that this would have given a wholly bizarre meaning to the "caretaker" concept.)

Indeed, Abdullah had a chance to do this one whole day earlier when the Governor formally declared that he would give the main political parties time till October 21 to produce evidence of majority support — pending which caretaker arrangements would continue. Questions about Abdullah's motives became all the more relevant because he has been under pressure from within the NC and some of his own advisers to make a bid for power in case the Congress (I) and the PDP do not form a government together.

The Governor too should have expected Abdullah's move after his press conference at 11-30 a.m. and taken such "incidental and consequential" measures as he is empowered to do virtually un-fetteted under Article 92 of the State Constitution. It is regrettable that he allowed Abdullah to spring a crisis on the State in this manner.

The effect of the imposition of Governor's Rule is hard to predict. It can either mount greater pressure on the Congress(I) and the PDP, the two main winners of the elections, to agree to a coalition arrangement. It certainly gives them time to do so well beyond October 21.

Or, it can defuse the momentum for political negotiations and lead to widespread cynicism and further erosion of the Kashmiri people's faith in the political system. One can only hope the second possibility does not become a reality. It would be a shame if the historic opportunity for a political breakthrough in Kashmir that has been opened up by the elections, is lost amidst crassly manipulative politics and cynicism. The mandate is uniquely subtle and nuanced. To start with, the polls themselves were largely fair, probably the fairesi since 1977, although they were not quite free.

No election can be fully free which takes place under conditions of violence and intimidation, in which the voter cannot feel that she or he can exercise an unfettered choice. Such conditions have long characterised Jammu and Kashmir, for which both *jehadi* militants and the Indian security forces are responsible. Nevertheless, the Election Commission deserves full credit for judiciously deploying forces and personnel to minimise interference with the voter's choice, and generally for demonstrating remarkable independence and boldness.

Even the most critical of independent citizens' groups monitoring the elections concede that the EC's role on the whole was praiseworthy. They include the Coalition of Civil Society, formed by nongovernmental organisations (NGOs) from the Valley and other parts of India, whose detailed reports do not mince words on the (limited) coercion deployed by sections of the security forces.

The credibility of the elections was enhanced by significant popular participation in rallies, each drawing 8000 to 10000-strong crowds. There was even an "election fever" in rural Kashmir, where the turnout was 55 per cent. There was little stuffing of ballot boxes or impersonation (although many names were missing from the hurriedly revised electoral rolls).

The outcome would have been more representative had the hawks in New Delhi not vetoed a pre-poll dialogue with the Hurriyat and had National Democratic Alliance leaders not snubbed groups such as Shabir Ahmed Shah's.

The very fact that the NC was reduced to half its strength in the last Assembly, and that the Bharatiya Janata Party was all but wiped out, should once and for all put paid to the idea that the New Delhi and Srinagar governments rigged the elections so their nominees could win.

The NC was severely punished for its thoroughly opportunist alliance with the BJP, its monumental corruption, its betrayal of its own "autonomy" platform, its malgovernance and its unresponsiveness to the people's basic needs. The BJP's defeat is particularly important because it marks the rejection by Jammu region's predominantly Hindu voters of the regional and religious-chauvinist platform.

It is disingenuous for the central leadership of the BJP to argue, as it does, that the party fared badly because of the division of its votes owing to the Rashtriya Swayamsewak Sangh's sponsorship of the Jammu State Morcha. On the ground, there was good coordination and seat adjustment between the two. It is heartening that Jammu's electorate voted against the BJP after the Akshardham incident in Gujarat. That event, the BJP had predicted, would turn the tide in its favour. This only goes to show that the people of Jammu and Kashmir, who know what it is to live under the shadow of violence, are far from gullible and are highly discriminating.

Among the other big losers were the *jehadis* who had said the elections were an affront to the people of Jammu and Kashmir who, they predicted, would boycott them *en masse*.

The next loser was the Hurriyat itself, some of whose leaders feel chastened and privately concede that the election boycott was a "mistake". There is strong evidence that the Jamaat-e-Islami, a major constituent of the Hurriyat, and with an organisational base in the Valley, secretly campaigned against the NC, and for the PDF, especially in southern Kashmir.

That said, however, it would be thoroughly mistaken to regard the verdict as an endorsement of New Delhi's Kashmir policy and its "anti-terrorist" measures, or a vote for a categorical "integration" of Jammu and Kashmir with the Indian "mainstream". More than anything else, the Kashmiris showed a strong urge for a return to more peaceful, less violent, normal life, and for the restitution of human rights and the rule of law.

Political leaders and civil liberties activists such as Yusuf Tarigami — the Communist Party of India (Marxist) MLA who has emerged as an outstanding leader — and Kumar Wanchoo are agreed that the Kashmiri people "unmistakably voted for an unconditional dialogue with all shades of opinion in the State, the scrapping of draconian laws, including the Prevention of Terrorism Act (POTA), and the release of detenus languishing in jails". The electors' main intent was to install a new administration that would be more responsive to their immediate needs related to issues such as water supply and provision of jobs, roads and hostels.

That is where the formation of a government with a popular mandate becomes crucial. The Congress (I) (20 seats) and the PDP (16 seats) are ideally suited to form the core of such a government. They have pledges of support from the independent Democratic People's Forum (six MLAs), the CPI(M) (two), the Panthers Party (four), and some other groups, totalling well over the majority figure of 44 in the Assembly.

The PDP leadership has so far been the main obstacle in the formation of such an alliance. It advances the rank regionalist argument that it must lead the alliance, and not the Congress (I), because it alone represents the people of the Valley, to which all its 16 MLAs belong, whereas the Congress Legislature Party leader, Ghulam Nabi Azad, is from Doda in the Jammu region.

This reasoning is specious. Azad is a Kashmiri settled in Doda. Although Doda is on the other side of the Banihal Pass, it has historically been culturally close to the Valley. Besides, the PDP's argument amounts to an attempt to resurrect regional chauvinism that was so strongly rejected by the electorate in Jammu and the Valley. Nor can the PDP claim to be the exclusive or principal representative of the Valley. It holds barely a third of the region's seats. (The NC has three more than its 16). Independents and others hold a sizeable chunk too.

In reality, PDP leader Mufti Mohammed Sayeed seems to be advancing the regional argument because he is allied with forces both at the Centre and in the Valley who are pursuing a parochial agenda and want to keep "national" parties (barring the BJP) out of power in Srinagar.

The Congress (I), for its part, is reluctant to make Mufti Chief Minister out of fear that he would play into the hands of the Union Home Ministry hawks and, at the same time, encourage Kashmiri-chauvinist forces in the Valley. The Congress (I) has declared its commitment to the repeal of repressive laws like POTA, to the release of political prisoners, to strengthening the State Human Rights Commission, and to disbanding the Special Task Force/Special Operations Group of "surrendered" militants that has committed excesses under the NC's patronage. Sonia Gandhi in her (well-noticed) public speeches in Jammu and Kashmir said so in so many words, while endorsing a dialogue with all currents of opinion. However, the Congress (I) would like to negotiate the pace and timing of these moves.

The Congress (I) and the PDP must resolve these differences through mutual negotiation, and if necessary, external political mediation, for example, through V.P. Singh. If they fail to form a coalition in consonance with the electoral mandate, they will earn popular anger and disgust.

Nothing that has happened in Jammu and Kashmir is a substitute for a genuine broad-based dialogue with all shades of opinion in the State, and with Pakistan. The case for a dialogue unscarred by violence both from the State and militant groups remains overwhelmingly powerful.

A setback to democratisation at this delicate stage will cause enormous damage in Jammu and Kashmir. Domestically, a historic opportunity to begin the process of healing and reconciliation could be lost. Internationally, the gains from the credible elections would be frittered away. A fateful opportunity to find a long-term solution to the Kashmir issue will slam shut.

Kashmir is delicately, perilously poised. Any resort to knee-jerk habits of crass *realpolitik* and parochialism will send it back into the abyss.

PART — I

# A Chance for Kashmir

Chapter 1

# A Verdict Pegged on Hope

In Jammu and Kashmir, a historic, fair and free election — first after independence took place in Jammu & Kashmir. It was always tempting to identify the winners and the losers. The loss of the National Conference cannot be attributed to the anti-incumbency factor alone. The voter clearly disapproved of its opportunistic attitude and lust of power.

The vote against the National Conference recognised, the utter failure of the government of the National Conference the verdict was a rejection of the ineffective policies of the NC in dealing with increasing terrorist activity in the aftermath of May 11, 1998. No amount of obfuscation by the National Conference in relying on vote percentages detracted from the enormity of the defeat.

## Vote for Change

The PDF considered that it received a mandate in the Valley. The Congress performed well in the Jammu area by winning in 15 constituencies. This was a verdict for change. It is also a verdict pegged on hope.

The real winner, however, was the collective desire of a people fatigued of violence who showed both wisdom and fortitude in standing up against terrorism. The people of Kashmir sent a message to both the harbingers and perpetrators of terrorism that they embraced democracy and peace.

The people of Kashmir demonstrated that the breeding ground of terrorism was across the Line of Control. The ordinary voter, during the four phases of the election, in the midst of the sound of the gunshots, proved that the power of the ballot was far stronger than the threat of the bullet. The voter also demonstrated that the representative will of the people could only emerge by embracing the democratic process.

The international community also recognised that the election in Jammu and Kashmir were fair and by and large, free. Being witness to India's commitment to democracy it expressed hope that infiltration and perpetration of cross-border terrorism will be brought to a halt. In fact, all political combinations of whatever hue and colour, barring the disgruntled Hurriyat Conference, stood united against terrorism.

Those who broke away from the Hurriyat and fought as representatives of Abdul Gani Lone's People's Conference succeeded, in the victory of one of their representatives, Ghulam Mohiuddin, also in a sense preferred participation as means to a possible solution. Now, the Hurriyat will find it difficult to have its voice heard having chosen to stay away from the elections fearing that the process itself will neither be fair nor free. That charge has been debunked as baseless. So far so good.

However, now, the more difficult pail is for the new dispensation to carve out a road map for the resurrection of the spirit of Kashmiris. This can only happen when the problems of the people of Kashmir starts getting addressed and this is not an easy task.

The PDF is committed to the revocation of POTA, releasing prisoners detained without trial, disbanding the Special

Operations Group and commence an unconditional dialogue with those who are 'alienated'.

The Congress has certain compulsions, being part of the national mainstream, to adopt a more circumspect approach. These teething problems must be addressed. A common minimum programme, if possible, with dialogue at its centrality, is the way forward.

## A Gloomy Picture

The inarch of history has shown the hopelessness of the situation, which the people of Kashmir have landed themselves in. The growth rate of the state economy was 8.47 per cent in the nineties. Today, it is only 4.5 per cent. Living standards have declined. The government's finances are in a mess. The fiscal deficit which was Rs 574 million ten years ago, now stands at Rs 9.4 billion. The rise of militancy has had a devastating effect on state finances. While expenditure has tripled since the nineties, all sources of revenue have dried up. The public sector is a parasite on the budget, suffering continuous losses. Revenue income from power tariff and sales tax is seldom realised. The Centre has not reimbursed the state security expenses. Only, the agriculture and horticulture are the backbone of the economy.

Peace is a precondition for prosperity to take root and flourish; and peace can only be brought about if the day-do-day problems of the people of Kashmir arc addressed. Kashmir will not attract investment nor will trade and commerce flourish till there is an acceptable resolution of die complex problems of the Kashmiri psyche.

A political dialogue is the need of the hour. Now, that Pakistan stands isolated and terrorists stand rejected, the atmosphere is conducive for the commencement of such a dialogue. Can the Government now, allow, Kashmiris to build the state by laying the foundations of stability, embarking upon an enterprise which will make Kashmir a true symbol of secular India?

## A Chance for Kashmir

Let us remember that Kashmir cannot lay the foundations of an egalitarian society through State funding alone and resurrect an emaciated people sapped of their energy and spirit of enterprise. The people of Kashmir must have the right to choose from a variety of opportunities that should be made available to them. Investment in the social sector alone will arm the people of Kashmir with the requisite wherewithal to meet the challenges of the future. The nation must commit itself to Kashmir: what is urgently required is the development of its infrastructure, telecommunications and the like. If the nation and the state move in that direction, then alone will an alternative dispensation be successful. But if those who come to power consider this yet another opportunity to temporarily share in its spoils, the battle would be lost before it had begun. Therein lies the challenge.

## A Turning Point

Jonathan Power's article suggests a simplistic and surreal solution to the Kashmir problem. Unless the origin of the problem is understood, there is a liability of addressing the issue from a tangent, well removed from reality. Actually, the origin of the problem itself shows the way to arriving at a solution!

In brief, Jawaharlal Nehru promised Mohammed Ali Jinnah a portion of Jammu and Kashmir and true to his word, he effectively stymied the operations of the Indian armed forces when war broke out with Pakistan in 1947. However, the Indian army, through its high professionalism, not only stabilised the front but pushed the aggressors back, regaining the initiative after a successful link-up at Poonch. Our troops' debouching for Muzzafarabad, the capture of which would have put paid to Jinnah's plot altogether, was scuppered by Nehru's Machiavellian ceasefire and referral of the issue to the United Nations against every patriot's advice.

This help through Nehru allowed Jinnah to consolidate whatever part of Kashmir he had seized. Thus Pakistan-Occupied Kashmir as we know it today came into being and has remained under that country's occupation. Factually, POK was Nehru's gift to Jinnah. Since the latter could not secure the whole of Kashmir which he had wanted to, he had.to be content with, "half a loaf being better than no bread!"

Over the years, it has become apparent that neither Pakistan nor India is keen to solve the Kashmir problem as keeping it alive is much more profitable for both. It gives Islamabad a readymade ploy for fighting India: supporting Kashmiri "independence" but with the ultimate objective of garnering the Valley. Hence any compromise on this by agreeing to a solution to the Kashmir problem would leave Pakistan's rulers on thin ice. They would forfeit the ever available leeway for diverting the people's attention from-inadequacies of governance in that country.

The Taliban movement has been of great advantage to Islamabad in this regard and, as-the election results show, religious thehards have got a foothold in Pakistan's governing machinery.

On New Delhi's part, a similar cause prevails for shifting the public's focus away from its misgovernance. Operation Parakrarna is a shining example of this sleight of hand. This apart, Nehru had bestowed the rostrum of a superior status to the Kashmiris via Article 370 that any ruling clique in Srinagar would hate to give up. This status is only viable so long as the Kashmir problem prevails. This truism was evident at Shimla — and in a fashion at Tashkent — where our Kashmiri caucus forced New Delhi to surrender to Islamabad during post-ceasefire negotiations despite our holding the trumps. It boggles any rationale as to how an outright victor in the 1971 Indo-Pakistani conflict, to wit India, opted for an "agreement" with its thoroughly vanquished adversary, to wit Pakistan, instead of ensuring that Pakistan could never trouble India again. Obviously, our motive had ulterior intentions. This duplicity has been Kashmir's and. India's tragedy. Nirad Chaudhuri had verily commented that India's history is replete with case stuthes where any military victory achieved by its armed forces has been sold out to the enemy by our own political leaders of the time. Shimla glaringly exemplified this.

Compounding the political affairs, New Delhi has painted a picture that Pakistan is illegally occupying PoK and the only acceptable solution would be for Pakistan to vacate the area, knowing well enough that this was for the birds. It was indeed amusing to listen to our erstwhile foreign minister state this in the BBC's *Hardtalk* programme some while back. For good measure, he should have added that China too must vacate Aksai Chin in a sweeping gesture of Hindi-Chini Bhai Bhai! Two respective parliamentary resolutions have been passed to this effect.

If such resolutions solved national problems, why don't we pass one more seeking reunification of the subcontinent? Also, New Delhi's rendering that Kashmir is exemplar of our tradition of secularism is periodically intoned for everyone's benefit.

Unfortunately, all this bunkum is swallowed by our naive citizens hook, line and sinker.

Dr Mahbub-ul-Huq's solution for Kashmir as highlighted by Jonathan Power as one sample of surrealism. Such view's have been aired by our intellectuals too, without considering practicalities. Why should Pakistan do anything that could jeopardise its holding on to PoK, specifically as PoK was gifted to it? There is no justification for Islamabad to play ducks and drakes with such a gift. No government in Islamabad, be it civil or military, can survive if it even thinks on Huq's lines.

Similarly, any attempt by New Delhi to reconcile Kashmir will be strongly opposed by the Kashmiris themselves as they do not want to lose out on their "God's own" status. The present NDA government realised this and quietly dropped its manifesto leader of scrapping Article 370. Even the incumbent PDF-Congress regime in Jammu and Kashmir will never bring itself around to integrating the state with the rest of the country. Granting autonomy would be inviting treason because at the first opportunity, the state government will enact the highly partisan and dangerous Jammu and Kashmir Migrants Resettlement Act and flood the area with ISI and Lashkar operatives. Thank goodness the Supreme Court has stayed this unholy piece of legislature.

Jonathan Power should create an awareness in international circles that the only sensible solution to 'Kashmir would be to implement the old Ayub-Cariappa *modus vivencli* of converting the Line of Control into a formal international border between the two nations, based on an 'as is where is' arrangement.

This is in consonance with the ceasefire scene of 1947-48. However, neither nation will give in easily to this because each has its own axe to grind.

Ideally, an Iraq-like UN diktat with the uncompromising threat of. severe sanctions if India and Pakistan did not comply, could do the trick. It would not be a bad idea for George W

Bush in his post midterm incarnation to concentrate on Kashmir after he settles with Iraq. He has given a new lease of life to Afghanistan. Likewise, he could 'deliver an *entente cordiale* to the Indian sub-continent that would reshape Asia's regional dialectics of "live and let live" in a manner unborn.

Postscript: In his capacity as an outstanding columnist, Mr Power could render invaluable service by investigating and expanding on the following aspects:

- Why did India not deploy its full military might against Pakistan in the 1947-48 J&K operations to include a convincing explanation for the unwarranted ceasefire?
- Why did India throw in the towel at Tashkent and Shimla from a position of strength?
- Why has India not adopted a comprehensive counter-terrorism doctrine in Jammu and Kashmir in spite of several top rate action plans being suggested by various bothes?
- Why shouldn't the UN demand a public White Paper on how Srinagar has spent the money given it by New Delhi over the past 55 years, golf courses inclusive?

## After the Elections

The recently concluded elections in Jammu and Kashmir have very appropriately been hailed as the triumph of democracy. More than that, they also signify a triumph of the political sagacity and courage of the Kashmiris and an emphatic assertion of their preference for a peaceful settlement of the Kashmir issue within a democratic framework.

Democracy produces a strange alchemy of astounding value and significance. In the case of India, in several hopeless situations when everything seemed to be falling apart, it has pulled us back from the precipice and opened the door to sanity. Democracy has proved to be indispensable for holding our society together. Whether it would continue to do so in the future will depend upon the way we practice it and uphold democratic values.

The Election Commission must be congratulated for holding the freest and fairest elections in Jammu and Kashmir in two decades and in conditions more adverse than ever before. One hopes the successful manner in which the elections were completed will come as a chastisement to those who cast aspersions on the Election Commission and dragged it into a totally unnecessary constitutional controversy.

The most likely scenario seems to be that a coalition of the Congress, the People's Democratic Party (PDF) and Independents will form the government in the State. They have first to get over the hurdle of electing a Chief Minister. If political reality is to be taken into account, it is quite legitimate for the party with the maximum number of seats in the coalition to stake claim for leading the government. On the other hand, there is also a case for the PDF to head the government as it represents the sentiments of the people in the Kashmir Valley more comprehensively than the Congress.

If the PDF heads the government, the most likely choice for the Chief Minister's post is going to be Mufti Mohammad Sayeed, the party leader who has the requisite seniority and administrative experience. However, if one looks at the issue in the perspective of the overall national interest, the coalition should select Mehbooba Mufti as the Chief Minister. For, no one in the coalition, or for that matter very few in the entire State, has echoed the hurt, anguish and the sufferings of the people of Kashmir as forcefully and has identified with their cause as sincerely as she has done. Besides, India has reasons to be grateful to her for building a popular movement in the form of the PDF which, while respecting the sentiments of the people, stands for a change in a peaceful and orderly fashion.

The election results have a few positive external fallouts for India. They have equipped us to deal with Pakistan with greater confidence and fineness than before. They will also enable us to hold our own against the pressures that have been exerted on us by external forces. But much more important than the external consequences, the elections have once again opened, after almost six years, the window of opportunity for the nation to come to terms with the aspirations of the Kashmiri people. The last time we had such an opportunity was in 1996 when Farooq Abdullah came to power on the platform of autonomy. Unfortunately, that opportunity was frittered away because of the exclusive pre-occupation of the then United Front Government with the problem of its survival and because the National Conference was blinded by the immediate gain of power and became complacent to the objective of negotiating autonomy which called for political courage and involved risks including that of loss of power. The events will not be allowed to take such an ungainly turn this time because the PDF attaches the highest priority to a political settlement of the Kashmir issue through talks with the militants. Though the Congress will suffer from the constraints that generally hinder the action of a national political party, during its election campaign it expressed full sympathy for the plight of the Kashmiri people and commited itself to a dialogue. All political forces in the State must be involved in the dialogue which, one hopes, would begin soon after the new government assumes charge. In particular, the dialogue must include the Hurriyat which, in its own way, reflects genuine Kashmiri aspirations. Besides, it has very close links with the militants with whom the dialogue would be held. The National Conference is also destined to play a very important role. It is the single largest party in the newly-elected Assembly and has stood for the unity and integrity of India in the most adverse circumstances. Besides, once in the Opposition, it is bound to take up the cause of autonomy with vigour and sincerity because this is the only way it can recapture lost ground in the State.

The most critical factor is going to be the Central Government's attitude. In this connection, the Prime Minister's statement in Copenhagen that "the Centre would work in close cooperation with the elected representatives in Srinagar to fulfil the aspirations of the people", provides a good opening. The statement does not exactly commit the government to parleys on autonomy which is quite understandable at this stage, The *Sangh Parivar* hardliners will do their utmost to prevent the government from granting any form of *azadi* to the Kashmiris. However, the Centre will have to recognise the drastic change in the political situation in the State brought about by the elections. It will have to deal with a government which is bound to be committed to a Common Minimum Programme which will include as its main element the demand for meeting the aspirations of the Kashmiri people, and to contend with an Opposition in the Assembly which will be more sharply focussed on its demand for autonomy. One also expects the Congress not to remain mired in its policy of the recent past in favour of a status quo. After all, the two historic agreements for granting special status to the Kashmiris were negotiated by a Congress Government in power at the Centre. One hopes the Congress will rise to the occasion and play a major role in fashioning another pact for ensuring the continued association of the Kashmiri people with the Indian Union, which is fully in keeping with their dignity and aspirations.

Next to the demand for autonomy, the election results also constitute a mandate for providing good governance. The results reflect a longing of the people for peace, safety and security. It is true that the State's people will not feel safe as long as the militants continue their violent activities and Pakistan continues to support them. But for carrying on their day-to-day activities they want a corruption-free government and the State to cease to be an instrument of harassment, torture and oppression.

Mufti Mohammad Sayeed has asked for an economic package from the Centre. What the State needs is not the traditional economic package consisting of mega projects resurrected from the past —which have long been promised but never implemented. Instead, it needs genuine decentralisation of development activities whereby people at the grassroots level can directly receive resources for development and are empowered to formulate, approve and implement development projects. Jammu and Kashmir has a legislation on decentralisation pre-dating the adoption of the 73rd and 74th Amendments to the Indian Constitution. But many parts of it are archaic and need to be updated, incorporating the best elements of the 73rd and 74th Amendments. Happily, with the outcome of the elections, the idea of the trifurcation of the State has been rejected. Nevertheless, a solution will have to be found for meeting the aspirations of the people of Jammu and Ladakh for local self-governance. They do not want to look up to the government in Srinagar for meeting all their needs. An effective devolution of governance to the grass-roots level is the best means of meeting their aspirations.

## Chapter 2

# Half Baked Mandate

The latest round of elections was not a sham as in most of the earlier rounds, but it did not reflect the popular will as did the elections of 1977 and 1983. Beneath the hung Assembly of 2002 lies a fractured verdict, itself the result of a fractured process.

The elections to the Jammu and Kashmir Assembly raise three questions — with regard to their quality, their true verdict, and their political impact. Kashmir has a long history of rigged elections, bar the one in 1977. In the 1951 elections to the Constituent Assembly, which drafted the State's Constitution, 73 of the 75 seats were won by Prime Minister Sheikh Abdullah's National Conference (NC) "unopposed". In the other two elections, the NC defeated Independents. On October 18, 1951, Prime Minister Jawaharlal Nehru said that the results showed that the people "were with the National Conference and with India". It set the pattern for half a century. In 2002, Prime Minister Atal Behari Vajpayee sings the same old tune.

In 1957, of the 75 seats 43 — of which 41 were from the Kashmir Valley — went to Bakshi Ghulam Mohammed's NC without a contest. The Sheikh was behind bars since 1953. The technique now used was rejection of nomination papers on flimsy grounds. The NC won 68 seats, the Praja Parishad won five.

In 1962, the NC won unopposed 32 seats in the Valley and seven in Jammu. G.M. Sadiq, the Chief Minister in 1967, heading a Congress regime, used a different technique. Coupled with the rejection of nomination papers was the arrest of Opposition leaders and cadres. Twenty-two unopposed returns and rejection of nomination papers in 17 others instances ensured an easy win of 39 seats. In 1972, Opposition workers were arrested. The Sheikh and his colleague M.A. Beg were interned in Delhi. Congress Chief Minister Mir Qasim later admitted the rigging in his memoirs, *My Life and Times*. The Congress secured a cool 57 seats, the Opposition was graciously allowed 17.

Sadiq and Mir Qasim had wound up the NC and joined the Congress. Their governments, elected through rigged elections, consented to the erosion of Article 370 of the Constitution by abuse of this very provision guaranteeing J&K's autonomy. *(Article 370: Law and Politics; Frontline,* September 29, 2000)

The Indira Gandhi-Sheikh Abdullah Accord of 1975 brought the Sheikh back to power. He revived the NC to her dismay. In the 1977 elections the NC won 47 seats. The Congress won 11. Of the electorate, 67.7 per cent voted. In 1983, Farooq Abdullah led the NC to victory, bagging 46 seats to the Congress' 26. In both the cases the electorate defied the Central government. Toppled in 1984, he warmed his way to power in a shot-gun marriage with the Congress in November 1986.

In 1987, blatant rigging was compounded with the arrest, assault and even imprisonment of defeated candidates. Syed Salahuddin, now the Hizbul Mujahideen chief, trounced Ghulam Mohiuddin Shah. Yet Shah was declared the winner. A majority of the leaders of the militancy that followed had participated in this democratic exercise. The NC won 39 seats; the Congress (I) 24, the Muslim United Front four, the Bharatiya Janata Party two, and Independents four.

The 1996 elections ensured Farooq Abdullah's return as Chief Minister. He secured 57 seats and 34.7 per cent of the vote. The BJP won eight, the Congress seven. It was a farce. Farooq Abdullah himself thanked the surrendered militants for the results.

Through al! these years most of the media were complicit. Rather like the un-faithful husband who denies the present affair while admitting a previous one, the media would certify every new round of elections to be fair "in contrast" to earlier ones. Some sections of the media are at it even now. Beneath the hung Assembly of 2002 lies a fractured verdict, itself the result of a fractured process. The fractures inflicted by the governments at the Centre and in the State were ones which not even the best Section Commission of India has seen since Sukumar Sen was the Chief Election Commissionet (CEC) 50 years ago, J.M. Lyngdoh, the present CEC, and his two colleagues deserve praise. Not a single aspersion has been cast on their integrity or competence from any quarter. Ironically, while the past rigging sought to cover up popular alienation, the honest exercise reveals it glaringly. The fractured process demands a nuanced verdict based on close analysis.

If Prime Minister Atal Behari Vajpayee meant to fulfil his pledges of "free and fair" elections, he would have healed the fractures before holding the elections. Two of the tallest leaders of the Opposition, Syed Ali Shah Geelani and Yaseen Malik, are in prison, besides Sheik Aziz. So is Iftikhar Geelani whose documented analyses of the election process one sorely misses today. In 1999, leaders of the All Parties Hurriyat Conference (APHC) were imprisoned for exercising their democratic right to advocate a boycott of the parliamentary elections. They were teleased a few months later. The APHC has been more cautious now.

Kashmir must be the only place in the world where elections are held though civil liberties are denied and the political process is not permitted. "We are not allowed to hold political rallies, talk to our people, to hold political programmes," Mirwaiz Maulvi Omar Farooq has complained. Arbitrary arrests, a host of special laws and repression over the years created a clime of fear. Fear of militants who threatened to punish those who voted did the rest. The election was not a sham like the ones of 1951, 1952, 1957, 1962,1967,1972,1987 and 1996. Neither did it reflect the popular will as did the ones of 1977 and 1983. The mechanics, put in place by the E.C.'s devoted labours, were competent. Missing was the political lubrication which would have ensured its proper working.

It worked in places where the people wanted to vote for reasons of their own. To cite two critics, the Mirwaiz himself noted the turnout in Kupwara, Handwara and Budgam and attributed it to local factors. Two responsible dailies from the State put thing in perspective. *Greater Kashmir,* published from Srinagar, said (September 18): "For starters, let us make a frontal admission that a good number of voters in the far-off country-side — good only by the standards of Kashmir — participated willingly in the exercise. In areas of larger population concentration they vengefully avoided polls. And it was at many such places the security forces took to their now infamous drill of forcibly dragging people out of polling booths.

*Kashmir Times,* published from Jammu, made (September 20) the following points. Voters were intimidated by the gun, wielded not only by the militants but also by the security forces. There was a total boycott in places such as Sopore, Baramulla and Sengrama. Enthusiasm in some places was due to "local issues". "The polls dearly had nothing to do with the political aspirations of the people, but were only linked to their day-to-day needs.... The people of Kashmir have not exercised their vote in favour of either India or Pakistan,.. The Centre is politicising the polls and using it as a tool to project a false notion of success before the international community. This could only deepen further the alienation of the people."

We have reports of four institutes of repute to draw on. The Director of the Institute of Social Sciences (1SS), New Delhi, Dr. George Mathew, released on October 9 a report by the ISS' 47-member study team, titled "Fair Elections Under the Shadow of Fear". Dr. Mathew said that the polls endorsed the importance of the democratic process but cautioned against "taking this election as a plebiscite" *(The Hindu,* October 10). He is astute enough to know that it would be so projected. While the detailed analyses of the poll process and the voting behaviour are awaited, the study team has come out with certain conclusions. The team comprised social scientists, journalists, civil rights activists and concerned citizens besides the ISS' faculty members and researchers.

The study covers all the 14 districts. The team visited 56 constituencies and oversaw the voting in about 450 polling stations. The team received full cooperation from the E.C. Forty-six individual reports and group reports by teams were analysed to come to certain conclusions.

The elections were "fair but not necessarily free". It holds that "the majority of Kashmiri people are in favour of *azadi;* but they are not very clear about the nature of the *azadi* they desire. To some *azadi,* is a cry for good politics and good governance; to others it is freedom from both India and Pakistan." This is very glib. *Azadi,* a simple Urdu word, means freedom and has been a slogan in common use since 1989. No one has had any doubts as to what it spelt. Least of all, the security forces.

The press release on the report notes: "Coercion by the security forces is a complaint members of the study team who visited the Valley frequently heard. In several places people complained that they were forced to vote by the security forces. In Sopore town, our team reported that they landed in a big demonstration of people in the New Colony, face-to-face with gun-toting BSF, with armoured cars standing in position. People told them that at 3 p.m. on the voting day (September 16) the BSF had announced from the mosque that only one hour was left and people should go to vote. It was reported to the team that when people did not vote, the security forces went door-to-door asking them to come out. 'Some women showed us scratches on their shoulder, some men beating signs, one bleeding from teeth,' said the report. Since nobody saw the security forces beating the people we have to leave these statements as it is, entirely to the credibility of those who said it." But, surely, the team itself could assess credibility.

And, is it any consolation that the forces merely demanded that the people vote and did not favour any political party? The turnout was the desired goal, combating the APHCs boycott and popular apathy. In 1996 it was the NC's victory. The assertion that "coercion will be marginal to the outcome is not shared by others, as we shall see. It is a useful document, nonetheless.

What one would like its fuller version to note is that the *modus operandi* of the security forces was the very one the team reported — loudspeakers blaring from mosques at the instance of the security forces with an air of menace. *Greater Kashmir* of October 9 reported from Srinagar:

"Mediapersons witnessed unwilling people being forced by persons to vote. At Hall Maidan, announcement was made on mosques loudspeakers asking people to immediately come out for voting."

Next comes the report by the Rural Litigation and Entitlement kendra, Dehra Dun, titled "J & K elections 2002: How free how fair", by a 22-member multinational team. Its conclusion was nearly the same as the ISS': "The extent of freedom to vote that people could exercise is debatable."

There is also the joint survey conducted by the Centre for the Study of Developing Societies, New Delhi and the Department of Political Science, University of Jammu. It was supervised and coordinated by Prof. Rekha Choudhury of the university. A preliminary report which Yogendra Yadav and she wrote in *The Indian Express* (October 9) makes important points. The polls were "substantially fair" but were not "free". Militants apart, "the security forces also contributed to making the people's choice unfree". There was, however, in all respects a definite improvement on the 1996 polls.

They write: "Notwithstanding the many warnings given by the Election Commission, the security forces engaged in many irregular activities. Our investigators recorded in 20 out of the 44 constituencies surveyed in the Valley that security forces were forcing people to come out to vote. It is not clear how much this use of force influenced the final turnout figure. The turnout in these 20 booths was merely 21 per cent as compared to 35 per cent in the remaining booths in the Valley. There were many cases of security forces entering polling booths very often, something they were not supposed to do. We also came across instances of security forces checking rhe finger mark after polling was over. But it must also be recorded that our investigators did not come across a single case of security forces asking the voters to vóte in favour of a particular candidate." It bears mention here that an Associated

Press correspondent in Baramula (September 17} saw "solthers walking door to door urging people to vote".

The three Interim Reports on the three phases of the elections by the J & K coalition of civil society have been little unnoticed in the national media. It comprised, among others, Parvez Imroz, a lawyer dedicated to human rights, other noted lawyers, journalists and academics. Their remit was two-fold. "Use of coercion" and "interaction with electorate to find out why they participated or abstained". The first report found "widespread coercion by the security forces on the people to cast their vote... in many instances, announcements were made from the village mosques at the instances of the security forces — asking people to go out and cast their vote". This reveals a pattern, and the pattern betrays decision at a fairly high level to the security forces to secure a turnout for face-saving. It is no consolation that their object was not to save the Abdullahs' skin. Specific instances are cited. "A large number of those who voted told the members of the team that they did so with absolutely no prejudice to their respective positions on the way forward to seeking a just solution to the future of Kashmir." The team witnessed Army personnel of the Rashtriya Rifles taking people to a polling booth. Minors aiso voted. The report on the second phase found the same feature. "Those who went to cast their vote voluntarily and affirmatively said that they were doing so either to defeat the National Conference or to back a candidate who they believed would address long-standing local issues."

Among the outstanding individual reports is one by Kalpana Sharma in *The Hindu* (October 6) on an aspect that tends to be ignored: Why the women voted. "Many of the women openly told us that they would vote. They knew the name of the candidate they wanted to support, they said they wanted him not just to win but to become a Minister so that he could really do something for their area. And what were their needs? 'Water, health care and education', in that order,.. What is evident from conversations with ordinary voters is that they wanted to have a say in local governance and that they saw no contradiction between voting in an election and at the same time demanding *azadi*"

*The Hindu's* conclusion would come as news only to those who refuse to face the truth known to the wide world. "If there is one thing the elections have shown us, it is that the Indian government has lost the battle for the heards and minds of the people of Kashmir. Election turnouts and voting figures do not tell the real story of what has been happening in that State during this past month." So deep is the alienation.

Reports in the national and international media confirm these observations. But assessments are shaped by faulty perceptions. A noted television correspondent who covers Kashmir found it "paradoxical" that people should cast their votes in Handwara and yet cry *azadi* . Rather like a British reporter who once found it "paradoxical" that Congress leaders like Nehru, Patel, Pant and Rajaji took power under the Government of India Acts, 1919 and 1935; took an oath of loyalty to the King-Emperor and remained nationalists, ready to the for India's freedom. In both cases the ignorance underlying the perception of a "paradox" was colossal. Supporters of Qazi Mohammad Afzal, who defeated Omar Abdullah in Ganderbal, shouted "Pakistan Zindabad", *(The Asian Age,* October 11).

Anjali Modi reported in *The Hindu* (September 29): ".. ,in places where people stood in long queues to cast their vote, and the turnout was well over 40 per cent, voters also wanted the media to 'tell the truth... we are voting... but we want *azadi.* She added: "This has been a steady undercurrent in an election that New Delhi insists is a befitting rebuff to Pakistan." According to a senior Srinagar-based journalist, "it is nothing of the sort. If New Delhi believes this is a vote for India it is living in a fool's paradise."

What emerges from all the reports shows how utterly false are the conclusions which Prime Minister Vajpayee and Deputy Prime Minister L.K. Advani, drew. Vajpayee said in Nicosia on October 8, two days before the counting began; "People of Kashmir have made their wishes known in these elections that they will be with us at any cost." Advani said on October 13 that "the real winner in this election has been India" and its democracy. He promised to hold talks on devolution of power to the State; not on restoration of its autonomy. Talks would be held with the militants "if they shun violence," he said (October 9). No such conditions are imposed on Naga militants.

Even Foreign Secretary Kanwal Sibal, an able professional, said on October 4: "Our hope is that they (Pakistan) will see reason, accept the results of these elections, cease cross-border terrorism and see whether a way can be opened to a resumption." Thus, New Delhi screams "victory" and offers surrender terms to both Pakistan and the separatists. This validates the Hurriyat's stand. Had it participated in the polls, New Delhi would have bound it to the oath — unlike the British rulers — and argued that the Kashmir issue was settled. That self-styled Indian practitioners of the so-called track two should have thought to get the APHC to participate in the polls is understandable.

They simply wanted to promote themselves and were merely acting at New Delhi's behest. The foreigners, official or others, who tried to pressurise the APHC, sought to earn brownie points with New Delhi and betrayed crass ignorance of the actual situation, especially of the Government of India's mindset and their own impertinence. Both sets had dick own axes to grind. The agenda was New Delhi, not the lot of the Kashmiris.

*Kashmir Times,* founded by the veteran socialist Ved Bhasin, is no separatist, only a realist. Its verdict is damning. "The participation of a sizeable section of the voters in the polling despite threats, was hailed by the leaders in New Delhi as their rejection of the demand for *azadi,* their faith in India and their rebuff to Pakistan and the militants from across the border. It is also being hailed as the marginalisation, if not elimination, of Hurriyat Conference and others engaged in the ongoing struggle for *azadi....* The hawks are already shouting for blood and raising their jingoistic slogans as if New Delhi has already won the hearts and minds of the estranged people of Kashmir. The demands are already being made to take military action against Pakistan and pursue stronger and more ruthless measures in Kashmir to put down violence. The election to the State Assembly for them is a pan of their jingoism," (October 5). The stark reality is that the Rashtriya Swayamsewak Sangh driven-Bharatiya Janata Party government has no hand to play at all, nothing to offer to win an alienated populace to the Union.

The Congress (I) has not much to offer either. Ghulam Nabi Azad said: "We are not for pre-1953 status." He stands put on the 1975 accord. The Congress (I)'s 1991 election Manifesto criticised the "shameful violation of human rights".

The 1999 manifesto was silent on that. It said: "The Congress is open to dialogue and discussion with any group within the Framework of the Constitution," Advani would heartily agree.

The People's Democratic Party's (PDP) manifesto is different. Mehbooba Mufti rules out plebiscite but advocates talks with the militants and conciliation with Pakistan. The manifesto promises dismantling of the apparatus of a repressive state. How far will the Congress go along with that? Unless the Congress and the PDP forge a coalition, along with the dedicated Mohammed Yusuf Tarigami of the Communist Party of India (Marxist), to provide a truly caring government, the prospects for the people of the State are bleak. Farooq Abdullah sought to hinder India-Pakistan rapprochement. The new government should encourage it.

Contrary to the Congress (I)'s stand, on October 11 Mehbooba Mufti said: "If we are in the coalition, our first thing would be for the negotiations with the people of Kashmir to settle the Kashmir issue with order and dignity. The militant groups and the political leaderships as well as other leaderships should be involved".

## An Incomplete Job

The defeat of the National Conference has opened up the possibility of a cathartic new beginning for Jammu and Kashmir. A new discourse of politics has emerged in a place where this was once thought impossible. The furtive negotiations between rival aspirants for the top job and the whiff of horse-trading — which elsewhere in India seem sordid and distasteful — appear deeply liberating in Kashmir.

The NC failed to provide dignity or development to the people of the state and they have now been voted out. The free and fair vote was definitely a victory for the government of India, which has earned the goodwill of the Kashmiris. However, a surprisingly large number of people in the valley— including People's Democratic Party activists — insist the real test of the Centre's sincerity comes now. Most people voted to get respite from their day-to-day problems and not because they thought the *masla-e-Kashmir*, or 'Kashmir Problem' would be resolved by pressing a button on an electronic voting machine. But they were energised by the promises made by the PDP, the independents and even the Congress that progress would be made towards establishing peace with the militants. How the new government — and the Centre — work towards this objective will determine the ending of this promising new chapter in the political history of Kashmir.

## Equations: Don't add up?

At the state level, the biggest problem will be managing regional contradictions between Kashmir, on the one hand, and Jammu and Ladakh on the other. The BJP may have been decisively defeated in the Jammu region and the advocates of communal trifurcation like the RSS-backed Jammu State Morcha largely ignored, but the strong showing by the Panthers' Party and some independents is evidence that the regional autonomy issue remains a live one. Were Congress chief Ghulam Nabi Azad to become CM, this could go a long way towards managing contradictions not only between Jammu and Kashmir but also between Doda (where he hails from) and Jammu, says Prof. Rekha Chaudhary of Jammu University. She feels if the PDP insists on the top job for itself, "this will only confirm the view that a person from Jammu can never be chief minister". In such a situation, the trifurcationists and Jammu chauvinists can only grow in strength.

Aside from the regional issue, there is also the question of how the new coalition government deals with the aspirations of people in Kashmir for a political solution to the problem of militancy.

The PDP advocates an approach which the Congress may well find unpalatable: Revoking the Prevention of Terrorism Act and Armed Forces (Special Powers) Act, releasing prisoners held without trial, disbanding the Special Task Force (STF). PDP supporters and ordinary Kashmiris expect the new government to take bold steps towards a dialogue process with militant groups. PDP leader Mufti Mohammed Sayeed himself is conscious of the fact that as a national party, the Congress view will differ from that of the PDP. "But I think it is possible for a common minimum programme on the question of restoration of peace with dignity to the state," he says. .

When it comes to relations between J&K and the Centre, a lot depends on the maturity with which the NDA government acts. The Centre's rejection of Farooq Abdullah's autonomy demands — and Farooq's meek acceptance of this rebuff helped put the final nail into NC's coffin. New Delhi should now work with the prospective Congress-PDP alliance towards issuing an unconditional call for a ceasefire and dialogue with militant groups in the state, says a senior official. "We have nothing to lose."

## Militancy: End in sight?

Not by a long shot. Within the security forces and intelligence community, opinions are divided on whether the new government - - which is expected to advocate a 'softer line' on counter-insurgency — will make the battle against militancy harder.

According to a senior army officer, the PDP's call for the STF to be disbanded would have a "devastating effect" on anti-terrorist operations in the valley. But an intelligence official is confident the STF it issue would be resolved amicably "Once terrorists start targeting PDP workers, Mehhooba Mufti will find she needs agencies like STF".

At the popular level, however, there is an expectation the PDP will disband the task force. "This is one promise we expect Mufti Sahab to deliver on." said a group of young men in Ganderbal, the town which defeated Omar Abdullah. "It is only because of the *zulm* of the task force that NC lost. If any boys are still picking up the gun, it is because of the STF."

But apart from internal factors like alienation — which the PDP and Congress say they will address — militancy also depends on Pakistan. What will Islamabad now do? "Of course the polls have been a setback to Musharraf," said a top army officer. "But I think he will continue taking cheeky singles. Infiltration is not going to stop."

The only way to break this logjam is for a political dialogue to start with Islamabad, perhaps once the new government takes power there. Otherwise, the current situation of no war, no peace looks set to continue indefinitely.

## Economy: Top Priority?

Ordinary people in Kashmir certainly want development — jobs, roads, electricity, water and sanitation facilities — but a lot will depend on the Centre's generosity and the degree to which the new set of ministers resist the temptation to feather their own nest. In Ganderbal, people said they voted against the NC "only because" of *taraqqiyati masail* (development problems).

"This does not mean, we have changed our views on the fundamental problem of Kashmir, which is that we should have independence," said a salesman of tin sheets. "But there are no public toilets here, no jobs, Farqoq's representatives used to take money and not deliver. So we said enough. And if PDP doesn't deliver, we will choose someone else."

"All politicians make promises to get elected," said a woman running a *puri-halwa* stall in Charar-e-Sharif. "But I don't think they will deliver." Nevertheless, she said, the defeat of the NC had given her *aadhi azadi* (half-freedom) and that was good enough for now.

## Significant Events

During the partition of India in 1947, Jinnah had hoped that Kashmiri Muslims would revolt against Maharaja Hari Singh of Jammu and Kashmir, resulting in the State's accession to Pakistan. When the Pakistani hopes did not materialise, it organized a tribal invasion of Kashmir valley. Maharaja Hari Singh acceded the State of Jammu and Kashmir to the Indian Union and signed the legal and constitutional Instrument of Accession. Seeing the failure of tribal invasion, Pakistan decided to employ its regular forces. The Indian army was hastily moved in to neutralise the Pakistani aggression. When the Pakistanis were on the run Pt Nehru, much against the advice of his advisors, chose to take the problem to the UN.

The undeclared war in Kashmir, which started in October 1947, continued until January 1, 1949, when a truce was arranged through UN mediation; negotiations between India and Pakistan began and lasted until 1954, without resolving the Kashmir problem. Since 1949, Pakistan has controlled part of the area, PoK or Azad (Free) Kashmir, as also Northern Areas, while India has held most of the other territory.

Taking of Kashmir issue to the UN resulted in the conversion of Kashmir issue into a power politics issue and Kashmir became a disputed territory.

The blueprint of aggression to annex Kashmir, which was drawn in 1947-48, continues to be followed as policy even today. Attacks by infiltration in 1965, which led to the second Indo-Pak war, Pakistan's proxy war since 1988, and the Kargil offensive of 1999 confirm that Pakistan prefers to follow a policy of confrontation in Kashmir. In 1988-89, Pakistan began expanding its operation to sponsor and promote separatism and terrorism primarily in Kashmir, as part of long-term strategic programme, as also its effort to avenge the loss of Bangladesh.

## Major Developments

**1953:** Sheikh Abdullah is dismissed and sent to jail. From a temporary measure, he demands perpetual status for Article 370, flirts with Pakistan, toys with *azadi.* Riots break out. The Centre extends jurisdiction over J&K.

**1964:** Sheikh Abdullah is released from prison, sent to Pakistan as emissary to negotiate peace. But Nehru thes in interim period. J&K loses its chance of peace. Nomenclature of Prime Minister is changed to Chief Minister.

**1975:** Sheikh Abdullah signs accord with Indira Gandhi. This reaffirms the relevance of Article 370 but rejects the demand that pre-1953 autonomy be returned. Sheikh becomes Chief Minister again.

**1983:** Sheikh Abdullah thes, son Farooq takes over as Chief Minister. Loses job in Congress-backed palace coup.

**1987:** Rajiv-Farooq pact leads to dubious poll win. Farooq discredited.

**1989:** Militancy begins. Mufti Mohd Sayeed's daughter Rubaiyya is released in exchange for terrorists.

**1990-2000:** Dark decade of guns. The 1993 hold-up at Hazrat-bal, burning of Charar-e-Sharif, massacres.

**2000:** Centre begins talks with Hizbul.

**June 2000:** Autonomy bill passed by JK Assembly.

Chapter 3

# The New Guard

The real began to intrude on the possible in the hours before Mufti Mohammad Sayeed became the Jammu and Kashmir Chief Minister on November 2. A day earlier, his daughter Rubaiya Sayeed had returned to Srinagar to witness the swearing-in. Shaukat Bakshi, the terrorist who had kidnapped her in 1989, also returned to his home, having been released on bail after 12 years. Three hours before the swearing-in, suspected members of one of the same terrorist groups with which Mufti Mohammad Sayeed has promised negotiations, fired rifle grenades at his home. The attack came after the al-Umar chief Mushtaq Zargar, released from jail in December 1999 in return for the safety of the hostages on board Indian Airlines Flight 1C 814, warned the People's Democratic Party (PDF) against entering into any alliance with the Congress(l). A little later, Sikandar Khan, a Congress(I) candidate who narrowly lost the Karnah Assembly seat, was shot dead along with his security guards while shopping in a Srinagar market. The new Jammu and Kashmir seems as depressingly surreal as the old.

All this did little to puncture the curious political reverie in Srinagar, perhaps because the circumstances of the new government's birth have done not a little to affirm the faith that the impossible can be willed into existence. Until October 21, the Congress(I)'s mediator with the PDF, former Union Finance Minister Manmohan Singh, had failed to arrive at even a minimum understanding with Sayeed. Manmohan Singh even offered Sayeed a rotating chief ministership deal, which, sources say, was rejected out of hand, On his return to New Delhi, the Congress(I) began to consider staking a claim to power on its own. Senior Congress(I) leaders in Srinagar believed that they would be able to manage a majority with the aid of PDF rebels. As the prospect of a split in the PDF accelerated, Sayeed backed down from his hardline stand, and flew to New Delhi for talks with Congress(I) president Sonia Gandhi on October 25. Former Prime Minister V.P. Singh, Congress(I) insiders say, played a key role in moving Sonia Gandhi to hold back on her party's plans to break the PDF and resume a dialogue with Sayeed.

Sayeed was now willing to accept Manmohan Singh's rotating chiefministership plan, but with key caveats. First, the PDF would have the first shot at the top job. Second, it would hold it for all of three years, half the length of the Jammu and Kashmir Assembly's tenure. Congress(I) MLAs found both proposals unacceptable, but Sonia Gandhi thought it best to override the State party unit. Senior Congress(I) leaders like Arjun Singh persuaded her that a Congress(I)-led government would end in disaster. A fractious alliance, with only tenuous support from maverick figures like Panther's Party leader Bhim Singh, would be more busy fighting internal fires to get on with governance. The Congress(I) would be blamed for encouraging the factions, Arjun Singh is believed to have argued, and would be criticised if and when an unstable alliance fell apart. Sonia Gandhi also held broad consultations with several intellectuals, who insisted that blocking Sayeed's rise to power would fuel popular alienation in Kashmir. Speaking to journalists after the deal with the PDF was inked on October 26, Sonia Gandhi made this concern explicit: the decision, she said, was made "in the larger interests of the people of the Valley". Outraged Congress(I) and Independent MLAs responded with unprecedented public protests, and threatened to boycott the swearing-in. The Congress (I) MLA from Uri, Taj Mohiuddin, described Sonia

Gandhi's decision as a betrayal. A group of 14 MLAs held a series of meetings through October 27 to consider their course of action. The three-year term given to Sayeed was unacceptable, they argued, since there were no guarantees that he would not bring the government down after that time. In any case, the Valley-based MLAs in the group of 14 said, the decision to accept Sayeed's claims to represent the Valley amounted to political suicide. Key MLAs from Jammu like Yogesh Sawhney also made known their view that the decision would cost the party dear in that region. The newly elected Congress(I) Legislature Party leader, Ghulam Nabi Azad, tried to quell the rebellion on the phone from New Delhi. But it took a visit by him the next afternoon, and generous promises of significant ministerial representation, to avert a break in the Congress(I)'s ranks.

Sonia Gandhi's notion of the "Valley's larger interest" needs examination, since it is widely shared by much of New Delhi's intelligentsia. Effusive newpaper editorial writers who have greeted the rise of the PDF as something of a latter-day resurrection might have done well to spend a little time with a calculator and a piece of paper. The PDP's share of the 2002 vote does nothing to affirm the proposition that it is the principal voice of the Kashmir region. Indeed, the combined vote share of the PDP and the Congress(I) in Kashmir only narrowly exceeds that of the defeated National Conference (NC). In the north Kashmir district of Baramulla, over half of the PDP's votes were cast in a single constituency, Gulmarg. The PDF exeeded the NC's vote share in only three of the Valley's six districts, all in central and southern Kashmir. Two of those districts registered below average voter turnout, and five of the PDP's 16 MLAs were elected in constituencies where terrorist violence led to an exceptionally poor turnout. Indeed, three of them won by a margin of less than 1000 votes.

To say this is not to undermine the decisive rejection of the NC in the elections, but only to show that the battle for oppositional space has had a multi-dimensional outcome. Prior to the elections, the PDP had rejected efforts by the Congress(I) and smaller parties like the Communist Party of India (Marxist) to arrive at a seat-sharing arrangement. PDP tacticians believed that its special character as a sub-regional party would allow it to emerge as the main axis of the evident resentment against the NC Indeed, the party symbol, an inkpot, was chosen with care, for it was used by the centre-Right and anti-NC Muslim United Front in 1987. In the event, the decision cost the Opposition the opportunity to win a decisive majority in the Assembly. While the PDP did eat into the NC's electoral base, it principally eroded the electoral constituencies established by independents in the 1996 Assembly elections. Had it chosen to arrive at a seat-sharing deal with the Congress (I), the alliance would have gained a staggering number of 11 additional seats in the Kashmir Valley.

While the PDP's Kashmiri-chauvinist position has allowed it to gain the office of the Chief Minister, the victory is not without its costs for the party. It has, most important, given a new lease of life to the Rashtriya Swayamsewak Sangh-backed Jammu State Morcha, which has been demanding the creation of a separate State for the southern region. The Morcha succeeded in winning just one seat, which went not to an RSS activist but a long-time Congress(I) dissident who jumped ship after being denied the ticket. But on October 28, RSS activists were able to shut down much of Jammu in a protest strike. The Bharatiya Janata Party, which won only a single seat in the elections, has now started demanding that local body elections be held in the State: evidently it is hoping to cash in on regional anger. Similar regional aggression is evident in Kashmir. On November 1, for example, the Kashmir Bar Association threatened to boycott the courts, claiming that Muslims from the Valley were under-represented in the

Jammu and Kashmir High Court, and demanding that Kashmiri Muslim judges currently posted outside the State be brought back.

At least one potential flashpoint is already visible on the horizon. Jammu has for long been under-represented in the Assembly, because of constitutional provisions that had suspended the delimitation of constituencies until after the completion of the 2001 Census. In the last Assembly elections, approximately 78,000 registered voters in Jammu and Ladakh were represented by each of 37 MLAs; in Kashmir, each bloc of approximately 55,000 voters was represented by 46 MLAs. Now that a Commission has been charged with redrawing constituency boundaries to ensure equitable representation, a struggle seems to be inevitable. Sayeed's demands for a Kashmiri person as Chief Minister, said Bhim Singh a day before he accepted his leadership, "substantiated the claim of the people of Jammu that the future growth of their identity, culture and language is possible only when they are accorded statehood." Unless the new government handles Jammu's legitimate concerns with care, its historic contribution might just be the tearing apart of Jammu and Kashmir along ethnic-communal lines.

Few people in the new government, sadly, are likely to have time to address long-term problems. With the caucus of 12 independent MLAs on whose support the government depends, having decided to offer only issue-based support, survival itself will be time-consuming business. Then, the alliance will have to find acceptable ways of implementing its 31-point Common Minimum Programme (CMP). The CMP rests on three major pillars, all intended to bring what Mehbooba Mufti tirelessly refers to as a "healing touch". First, the CMP mandates the assimilation of the Special Operations Group (SOG), alleged to be responsible for human rights abuses, in the Jammu and Kashmir Police. Second, the alliance has said it will terminate the use of the Prevention ol Terrorism Act (POTA), and release alleged terrorists held for long periods of time facing trial for minor offences. Along with this, the quantum of compensation to the families of victims of terrorism is to be doubled, while the children of killed terrorists will receive state support for their education. Finally, the CMP calls for an unconditional dialogue with terrorist groups.

At least some of these promises mean very little. The SOG has always been part of the 60,000-strong Jammu and Kashmir Police, and constitutes less than 5 per cent of its overall strength. Its troops and officers arc drawn from the same ranks, wear the same uniforms, earn the same pay, and report to the same superiors. As such, its "assimilation" will mean little other than a re-branding of the product. The end to the use of POTA and the release of prisoners will also have marginal impact. An estimated 190 people are held under the Act, eight of them of Pakistani origin, including those released on bail. Figures on the precise numbers of people held on terrorism-related charges are unavailable, but data published in October 2001 suggested that the number of those who had not by then secured bail was just 366. Interestingly, all of 13 individuals have actually been convicted of terrorist crimes since 1989 — an index both of the efficiency of the criminal justice system, and of the kinds of redress available to victims of terrorism.

The PDP-led coalition's promise to initiate dialogue with terrorist groups is another case in point. Each Prime Minister since P.V. Narasimha Rao has offered to initiate such a dialogue. Atal Behari Vajpayee actually began negotiations with the Hizbul Mujahideen faction of Abdul Majid Dar during the Ramzan Ceasefire of 2000-2001. Why such dialogue went nowhere is a matter of record. Groups ranging from the mainstream Hizbul Mujahideen to the Lashkar-e-Toiba and the Jaish-e-Mohammad have made clear that they will not engage in a dialogue until India commits itself to final status negotiations with Pakistan. Pakistan's militaty establishment sees continued violence as an instrument to secure concessions from India, concessions of a scale no government in India can make. Sayeed may succeed, as others have in the past, in beginning a dialogue with secondary terrorist groups, but such initiatives have had little concrete impact. Nor has the PDF made clear just what it intends to negotiate, since India-Pakistan issues are outside its remit.

What is perhaps most disturbing about the CMP is that it appears to have no real vision of what political vision its leaders have for Jammu and Kashmir. As the CPI(M) recently pointed out, the document has no reference to greater federal autonomy. Nor is there evidence that the new government has any real conceptual framework to address issues of violence. Speaking in New Delhi after the PDP-Congress (I) alliance was formalised, Arjun Singh, a former Governor of Punjab, said the alliance drew on his experience in Punjab, where terrorism was solved by means of dealing with "each and every small thing". He perhaps forgets the record. Arjun Singh's own single contribution to Punjab was installing the Surjit Singh Barnala-led Ministry, whose indiscriminate release of jailed terrorists and winding-down of police operations laid the foundations for five more years of bloodshed. Six months on, Governor Siddharth Shankar Ray and Director-General of Police Julio Ribeiro were brought in and assigned the impossible task of fighting terrorism without the cooperation of the State government. When terrorism was finally stamped out, not one of the issues that Arjun Singh had privileged, from the status of Chandigarh to the sharing of river waters, had been resolved.

In May 1990, three young men walked into the home of Srinagar religious leader Mirwaiz Mohammad Farooq, and shot him in his study. The leader of the hit squad, Mohammad Abdullah Bangroo, was shot in an encounter less than a month later. The bothes of both of them rest today in a graveyard near the Idgah in downtown Srinagar, just a few dozen metres apart. Both victim and assassin are revered as martyrs; martyrs, moreover, for the very same cause. The PDP is now in power having marketed itself as a representative of the same cause. Now it needs to work out just what the cause might be.

## *Profile*

### Mufti Mohammad Sayeed

For most of Mufti Mohammad Sayeed's 43-year-long political career, his opponents were sure of two things. The man wanted, more than anything else, to be the Chief Minister of Jammu and Kashmir one day. And, second, he would never, ever hold that coveted post. "He had a suit tailored for his swearing in at a shop on Residency Road in Jammu," Farooq Abdullah acidly used to tell anyone who cared, to provoke him on the issue, "and it's been gathering dust there for decades".

Sayeed's suit is, so to speak, off the shelf today, while Farooq Abdullah's has had to be mothballed for the foreseable future, Mufti Mohammad Sayeed now heads the first non-National Conference government in Jammu and Kashmir in more than 27 years. He is doing so not as an agent of the Congress(I), which he served with loyalty for many decades, but as the leader of a regional formation that stands opposed to many of the ideological postures he took for much of his political life. A decade and a half ago Sayeed was an architect of the state terror, on opposing which he has now built his political fortunes; and four decades ago he began his political life in the party to whose decimation he devoted much of his political life.

Born in Baba Mohalla at Bijbehara in January 1936, Sayeed's early life was typical of the new bourgeoisie that emerged in Kashmir in the middle of the century. Having graduated from S.F. College in Srinagar, he went on to obtain a degree in law, and a post-graduate degree in Arab History from Aligarh Muslim University. Although he hoped to get government employment, he was persuaded by his friends to start a law practice in Anantnag, and to join politics. In the late 1950s he joined the circle around prominent lawyer and NC leader P.L. Handoo. He followed Handoo into the breakaway Democratic National Conference (DNC), led by G.M. Sadiq, along with D.P. Dhar, Syed Mir Qasim and G.L. Dogra. He was now appointed district convener of the new organisation, the first formal post he held.

When the DNC rejoined the NC, Sayeed went with the flow. It paid him rich dividends. He was elected to the Assembly from Bijbehara in 1962, and retained the seat in 1967. As a result, he was appointed a Deputy Minister by G.M. Sadiq. He switched sides to Syed Mir Qasim after a New Delhi-engineered palace coup, and in 1972 was rewarded with a Cabinet berth and also made the party's leader in the Legislative Council. Soon afterwards, however, things began to go badly wrong. Prime Minister Indira Gandhi made her peace with Sheikh Abdullah; Sayeed failed to do so. In 1975 he was made the leader of the Congress Legislature Parry and Pradesh Congress president - his appointed youth wing leader was Ghulam Nabi Azad. But Sayeed lost the elections from Bijbehara in 1977 and 1983, on both occasions to the NC

Sayeed's wilderness years, at least as far as State politics was concerned, had begun.

In 1986, Prime Minister Rajiv Gandhi rescued Sayeed from near-oblivion in the State, and appointed him Union Minister for Tourism. This relationship too soon soured. Incensed by the Rajiv-Farooq Accord of 1987, which led the NC and the Congress (I) to contest that yeat's Assembly elections jointly, Sayeed resigned from the government and the party. The act of rebellion enabled Sayeed to hitch his wagon to Vishwanath Pratap Singh's rising fortunes, but did little to strengthen his position within Jammu and Kashmir itself. He was appointed Union Home Minister in 1989, after having won the Lok Sabha elections of that year as the Jan Morcha candidate from Muzaffarnagar in Uttar Pradesh. Sayeed was now appointed Home Minister — a position without precedent for a first-time MP.

Sayeed's management of the second most important job in the Cabinet was an unmitigated disaster. On December 11,1989, five days after he was sworn in, the Jammu and Kashmir Liberation Front kidnapped one of his three daughters, Rubaiya Sayeed. While both the NC and Central intelligence officials were convinced that the JKLF would release her in the face of public outrage, the Home Minister ensured that the jailed terrorists for whose release the kidnapping had been committed were released. Most experts agree that the release set the tenor for an inchoate security response to an insurgency, which has by now claimed over 33,000 lives. Soon afterwards, Sayeed compounded the error. In February 1990, backed by the Bharatiya Janata Party, Sayeed secured the appointment of Jagmohan as Governor of Jammu and Kashmir, precipitating the resignation of Farooq Abdullah and laying the foundations for an ugly strangling of democracy.

Many experts believe that Sayeed's well-known mismanagement of the crisis in Jammu and Kashmir was just part of a larger inability to comprehend, and to engage with, the multiple problems of terrorism India was confronted with at the time. When he took office, former Punjab Director-General of Police K.P.S. Gill pointed out in a recent article in the *South Asian Intelligence Review,* Khalistan terrorism had been contained — to just four of 15 police districts of Punjab, all along the border with Pakistan. Sixty-five per cent of terrorist crime was confined to areas under just 13 of 207 police stations. Where 1989 had seen only 2,072 terrorism-related fatalities, 1990 saw 4,263, and 1991 saw 5,265. By the end of Sayeed's term in office, only four of the 15 police districts registered an average of less than 10 civilian casualties, and violence had spread to the entire State.

Gill believes that the problem was conceptual. Sayeed and the dispensation he represented, Gill argues in his article, "assumed that with a few sympathetic, sentimental gestures, the terrorist movement — at that time in its tenth year in Punjab — would simply 'wither away'." If that was indeed Sayeed's belief, it seems of a piece with his position now — something that ought to give anyone with some respect for history some cause for concern. But, since 1996, when Sayeed returned to political life in Jammu and Kashmir, it is also true that there has been an enormous discontinuity in his understanding of politics. Until 1996, he believed that the keys to power lay in New Delhi; today his vision only just extends to the six districts of the Kashmir Valley.

How has this transformation come about? Any full understanding must be left to biographers, but it is possible to venture a few guesses.

Sayeed's return to Kashmir politics after having rejoined the Congress in 1996 holds some clues. His youngest daughter, Mehbooba Mufti, won the Bijbehara Assembly seat, although his wife, Gulshan Ara, lost from Pahalgam. Sayeed himself won the Anantnag Lok Sabha seat in 1998, but soon resigned from both his position and the party to form the People's Democratic Party (PDF). The key to this break seems to be the belief that the Congress(I), with its pan-State and pan-national character, could not appropriate the vacant political space in Kashmir. The PDF seemed to understand the space as that occupied by the Muslim United Front in 1987, an alliance of the religious Right and centre-Right against the NC The issues that were aggressively articulated by the PDF, notably the release of jailed terrorists and alleged atrocities by security forces, could never have become exclusive leitmotifs of any Congress(I) campaign.

Mehbooba Mufti appears to have been central to this ideological formulation. The only one of his three daughters still to live in India, she undoubtedly wields considerable influence on her father's appraisal of the situation. She, many people believe, is the true heart of the PDF. Whether she will go on to inherit a real political legacy, or whether a dynasty will crumble before it could be born, will depend on just what Sayeed manages to achieve in the three years he has now been promised in office.

## The New Stalwarts

**Mufti Mohd Sayeed:** The senior most aspirant for the CM's job. The kidnapping of his daughter, Rubaiya, marked the formal start of militancy and his supporters say he is the man best placed to put an end to it. He started the PDF in 1999 as a regional alternative to the NC. He has waited long enough and will be reluctant to drop his claim.

**Mehbooba Mufti:** The PDP's most visible face during the campaign. The Mufti's daughter is not expected to become CM because of other senior contenders within the party, and also because Congress stalwarts like Mangat Ram Sharma — whom the party would want as deputy CM if Azad fails to get the top job — would probably not want to work under someone so young.

**Ghulam Nabi Azad:** The man who spearheaded the revival of the Congress in J&K, Azad is the party's logical choice for the post of CM. As someone from Doda, he would have acceptability in both Kashmir and Jammu. But is he keen? Or would he prefer national visibility in the event of a Congress government at the Centre in 2004? Even so, the smart money is on Azad as CM.

**Ghulam Mohiuddin Sofi:** The only one of the rebel — or proxy — candidates from Abdul Ghani Lone's People's Conference to win a seat (Handwara), Sofi has taken the clever step of establishing the Democratic People's Forum uniting several independent winners. As a potential kingmaker, he is expected to bargain hard in any government formation.

**Bhim Singh:** This maverick leader of the JK National Panthers Party surprised everyone by bagging four seats in the Jammu region. His support could prove crucial though it remains to be seen how he will extract his pound of flesh.

PART — II

# Face to Face
## (Interviews)

## Chapter 4

# Mufti Sayeed on His New Tasks

Mufti Mohammed Sayeed describes the beginning of his innings as Chief Minister of Jammu and Kashmir as a "turning point" in the history of the state. He sees an opportunity in the days to come to prove that good governance matters, and pays and is confident that his government will last out its full term. In an interview with the *Hindustan Times*, he dismisses talk that he is soft on militants and points out that much of what he has said on the issue was brought up earlier by the Prime Minister and government officials. Excerpts from the interview :

***How do you feel after being in the chief minister's chair for almost a week now?***

It is a big challenge and opportunity. I see it as a turning point in the history of Jammu and Kashmir. I want to make a difference with good governance and that is my primary aim.

***It is said that becoming the Chief Minister was your ultimate ambition. What do you have to say?***

It is not correct. It is baseless. I have never bothered about the chair. I have seen high office (as Union Home Minister). There were many occasions in the past when I could have become the chief minister. There were days of conflict between G.M. Sadiq and Mir Qasim. I was a minister in the Rajiv Gandhi Government. I was the chairman of the Janata Dal Parliamentary Board. These things have not bothered me.

Indira Gandhi once asked me why I opposed Sheikh Abdullah. I told her when I am in opposition, my job is to oppose and criticise. My job in the opposition is not to knock at doors and seek favours but to raise issues of the people. I stood my ground. Tell me, if there is any one who has stood his ground like me in Jammu and Kashmir. Becoming chief minister was not my dream.

*Then what exactly have you achieved?*

I have provided an alternative. I had no ill-will against Sheikh Abdullah. As far as Farooq Abdullah is concerned, I have met him. He is a pleasing personality But then, there are differences of policies and programmes.

*How are you going to facilitate the dialogue process?*

We have already taken measures to create an atmosphere for that. POTA is not going to be used. The role of the Special Operations Group of the state police is going to be changed. A multi-pronged strategy has to be adopted to fight militancy. We are going to take care of the victims of militancy If someone is a militant and is killed, what is the fault of his wife or children? We have to take care of their education and socio-economic problems.

*Will you ask for a unilateral ceasefire during Ramzan?*

Why should I?

*You were reported in the media as saying so.*

That was put out of context. What I said was that unilateral cease-fire has no meaning unless it is reciprocated and respected. It cannot be a one-way traffic.

***You said that the All Parties Hurriyat Conference is yet to prove its representative character.***

Yes, I said so because they did not prove it. They had an opportunity in the elections. They did not avail (of) it.

***Will you start talking to the Hurriyat leaders?***

Why should I? Let them talk to Government of India. I would be a facilitator. Let the Government also talk to the elected representatives and also other sections of people. We have already taken measures as I have listed those before.

***You are regarded as being soft on militants.***

That is the double talk of the BJP that is trying to run down our ally, the Congress. Didn't Prime Minister Atal Bihari Vajpayee say from the ramparts of Red Fort on Independence Day that we have committed mistakes in Kashmir in the past? Didn't Union Home Secretary travel to Srinagar to hold talks with Hizbul-Mujahideen in August 2000 after the Hizbul-Mujahideen announced cease-fire? Didn't Prime Minister announce a unilateral Ramzan cease-fire two years ago? Didn't he appoint K.C. Pant to hold talks with the people and separatists in Kashmir ? If I am saying the same thing, what is wrong with it?

There was a policy of sticks for 14 years and rarely carrots were offered. Now there will be a change and a consensus. My effort is to evolve a consensus not only in Jammu and Kashmir but also at the national level. Farooq Abdullah could have done that. But he didn't do that. Now I am going to do it.

***On the face of it, your words sound promising but the numbers are fragile.***

I can tell you, this is going to be the most stable government in Jammu and Kashmir. It is not the game of numbers. It is the verdict of the people of the state that matters and that gives stability to the government.

***There are fears that there will be a witch-hunt of your political rivals.***

Let me assure you that there will be no victimisation. There will be no witch-hunt. I am not goiny to dig into the past and start hounding people. Not at all. But we will not allow anyone to tamper with the system. Even if someone sitting on my right hand side is found guilty of doing anything wrong, he will face the consequences.

There is going to be authority with accountability.

***There are apprehensions that you would undertake a massive administrative and police reshuffle.***

Have I done that? There is the same set of people. We have to take work from them in a proper fashion. I have already said that there would be no witch-hunt or victimisation.

***Why is your Common Minimum Programme silent on autonomy?***

You cannot put the cart before the horse. Once the negotiations start, let's see what emerges. If autonomy is the only thing in the kitty, why should it be said that autonomy is there to be offered? Let there be talks first.

***You are saying that you bear no ill will towards the Abdullahs. How would you justify engineering the dismissal***

***of the Farooq Abdullah government in 1984 and the installation of the Ghulam Mohammad Shah government? Wasn't that an undemocratic act as part of your plans to become chief minister?***

On hindsight, I think it was the right thing to do. Farooq was roaming with Shabana Azmi on a motorbike, while governance was suffering. Those NC men who joined to form the G.M. Shah government, are described as traitors. But the fact of the matter is that they worked with sincerity and honesty. Look at Ghulam Hassan Mir (Housing Minister in the new, government). He won by 20,000 votes. Hakim Yasin won, Dillwar Mir won, so did Mehboob Beg. They were elected because they have worked. My mantra is that (good) governance pays.

***There are numerous challenges. How are you going to overcome those?***

My first and topmost priority is to provide a clean administration. There are many problems that can be resolved by good governance. My commitment is to give a transparent and accountable government. I know that people have many problems and we will address their problems one by one. You take it from me that results will soon be known to the people.

***How are you going to politically manage the coalition partners?***

(Through the) Common Minimum Programme we are going to implement it in letter and spirit. All coalition partners are in agreement and there is no deviation from the CMP.

Chapter 5

# Mehbooba Mufti on Her Role

The new face of hope in Kashmir could may not be the chief minister of the state. Clearly though, Mehbooba Mufti will certainly play a significant role in the new government. Expectations are high, but the 38-year-old PDF leaders ready for the challenge...

***Will the new equations — both at the state level and in terms of Centre-state relations — work?***

With a coalition government, it is not going to be an easy task for us. But whoever joins in to form a government will understand that this is an opportunity to make it work. If we succeed in delivering the goods without too many contradictions amongst ourselves, we will gain in the long term. But if we mess it up now, we won't get an opportunity in future. We must not forget people here have voted under great duress and have put their faith in us.

As for relations with the Centre, there are many state governments in the country right now which are not allies of the ruling coalition at the Centre. But they are functioning and Kashmir should be no different. In a democracy one has to accept the mandate of the people. We expect the Centre to give us enough space to work and be generous towards a state in an economic mess.

***Is this the beginning of the end of militancy?***

We want to create a situation where those who took up militancy, can return home with honour and dignity and get involved in the mainstream. The affected families have to be rehabilitated. Also, something should be done to make the security forces more accountable. The groups led by Ram Jethmalani, K.C. Pant and the rest should remain consistent in their positions. We expect Delhi to be very serious on these issues.

Local militants have everything at stake — their homes and families are all here. So they will view this opportunity very seriously Pakistan is a problem, but if we can sort out our local problem, they will have no option but to lay off. But it will take time.

***Is J&K closer to autonomy?***

Some kind of political package — call it autonomy or whatever else —will have to be worked out. It is important to talk to the right people, rather than the likes of Farooq Abdullah who are already with the state. Militant groups like Hizb-ul-Mujahideen, political leaders like Yasin Malik, Shabir Shah, and other Hurriyat leaders can help in sorting this out. Nobody .wants the state to disintegrate. This election could have a role to play in bringing peace to Kashmir.

***Will development now top the agenda?***

The most important agenda for us is to do away with the sense of insecurity that prevails in the state.

***What's the toughest job ahead?***

To live up to the expectations. People are expecting miracles. So the power they have given us comes with a lot of responsibility.

***You stopped short of going to be the CM?***

It was a trivial issue. What is important is to work out a common minimum programme for the government. The future will depend on that.

(Mehbooba Mufti is the dynamic leader of People's Democratic Party.)

Chapter 6

# The Father-daughter Duo on Post-Election Scenario

***On the reasons for the PDP's electoral success:***

*Mufti Mohammad Sayeed:* We were able to find the right candidates who could channel the anti-government sentiment in the State. People had understood that their biggest problem was the National Conference government, which had to be removed, after which other things could be talked about. That was the reason for the massive participation in the elections, despite incidents like the assassination of Mushtaq Lone. I must tell you, even the People's Conference people played a great role in building an atmosphere for democracy to flourish. Except in Srinagar, where the National Conference benefited due to low voter turnout, we did well.

*Mehbooba Mufti;* Our party is very young, and we managed to create an atmosphere in which people felt able to reject the National Conference and bring the Opposition to power. I think we deserve credit for that. We deserve power. I remember, at one time when the Congress (1) had some 24 or 25 MLAs, of whom just one was from Kashmir, it elected the Kashmiri MLA as its Legislature Party leader. Ghulam Nabi Azad is a Kashmiri, but has not presented himself as one. During his campaign he made himself a Jammu man. He fought the election on this issue; he made the fight for Chief Minister one between Jammu and Kashmir. And in Kashmir, the numbers game works in our favour, since we have more representatives in the region rb.au the Congress (I). There are certain things our party cannot agree to, and one of them is adding salt to the wounds of Kashmiris. Of course, some people are suggesting a non-PDF Kashmiri as Chief Minister, but we cannot have any Tom, Dick or Harry running the State.

***On the regional issues raised in the course of the fight for power:***

*MMS:* We do not have one-party rule any longer. In the new scenario, we will have to arrive at solutions through consensus among various political groups. Any one man will no longer decide the State's destiny. Jammu's interests will be looked after; so will those of Ladakh and Kashmir. No region will appear hegemonic. If you look at economic development, Jammu has done better than Kashmir in the last several years. The real problem has been a sense of participation, which will now be addressed. I think this is in the best interests of the country.

*MM:* Kashmir has been in turmoil for the past 12 or 13 years, and the Valley has borne the brunt. The problem, after all, is in Kashmir. In Jammu you do not have a problem about its relationship with the rest of the country. So instead of addressing the alienation of Kashmir, if we get a Chief Minister from Jammu, what kind of message will that send to them? It will further alienate the people of Kashmir. It will add salt to the wounds. The Congress (I) just got 15 of its 20 seats from Jammu, despite saying it would have a Chief Minister from there. So, it did not succeed in making this a big issue in Jammu either.

***On the PDP's priorities in office:***

*MMS:* You know we have taken a stand against the Prevention of Terrorism Act, against atrocities, against human rights violations, and for dialogue with militants. Even Sonia Gandhi agrees with us, for she recently spoke about just such a dialogue. But a dialogue may take a year to yield results, or even longer. We want a cessation of hostilities, as the Prime Minister had given an undertaking some time ago. Meanwhile we have to deal with issues such as corruption, economic development and governance.

*MM:* Our party says that Kashmir is bleeding, and that we are going to search for an honourable way out. All that the Special Operations Group and surrendered militants have achieved is to add to the misery of the people through atrocities, disappearances and custodial killings. Farooq Abdullah says I am pro-militant. I am pro-people.

Militants are a part of the people. If we want to get the people out of the clutches of violence, we have to address the problems of the Kashmiri militants. They have not taken up the gun for the fun of it. We have to solve their problems. Instead of talking about peace and good governance, the Congress (I) is fighting over who should be Chief Minisrer. Rather than betray our people, we will prefer to sit in the Opposition. We do not want to be seen as power-seekers at the cost of principles.

Chapter 7

# Ghulam Nabi Azad on His Party's Performance

***The Congress(I) has now had several rounds of negotiations with the PDP, and you have met Mufti Mohammad Sayeed on more than one occasion. Given that these meetings have achieved little, what gives you the hope that an alliance can still be realised:***

You need to place the current situation in the context of the tremendous optimism these elections have generated in Jammu and Kashmir. Before the elections, hardly anyone believed that the elections would in fact be free and fair. Now the results are out, and we have all had to concede that these elections have been the best ever held in Jammu and Kashmir, And that fact places a very special responsibility on all of us. The mandate of the people is for a government that is responsive to the aspirations of the people, and acceptable to all three regions of the State.

***The PDP seems to be insisting that it alone can represent the aspirations of the Kashmir region, and that its special needs demand that the Chief Minister belong to that region.***

You know, it's funny. My district, Doda, begins where Mufti Sahib's district, Anantnag, ends. Many people in my district speak Kashmiri; it is the bridge between Jammu and Kashmir. But the question is, who can provide an acceptable government that will last six years? The government will have to be strong, for it will have to face not only many local challenges in Jammu and Kashmir but also the onslaught inflicted on it by the hostile country across its western border. Now, the fact is that no political party has a majority. The options are simple. First, we can form a government along with the National Conference, without the support of any independents or smaller parties. We do not want to do that, because the mandate of the people is against the National Conference. The second is that we try to form a government along with the PDP, conceding all its demands. But even if we do so, we need the support of a large number of independents. The problem is that these independents are unwilling to back a Chief Minister from the PDP. The support of the Panther's Party and many independents is contingent on the Congress (I) leading the alliance. We simply cannot form a government without them.

***You have the third option, of course, of staking a claim to form the government without the PDP's support, and seeking to win over some elements from that party afterwards. Why did you not do so?***

We did not want to start out on weak foundations. We wanted an alliance that was as inclusive as possible, one that would be able to withstand the challenges any government will undoubtedly have to face over the next six years. Nor did we want to be accused of opportunism or encouraging defection or such things. Of course, the option of forming a government without the PDP is still open, but we do not want to take that particular path. We want to take everyone into confidence.

***Is the dispute just over who will be Chief Minister, or is it over the PDP's agenda as well?***

The PDP had discussions with our party leadership in New Delhi, also. We have had talks here, too. There is hardly any difference in our stands. The PDP opposes the Prevention of Terrorism Act, so do we. They want the Special Operations Group to be disbanded; we want to retain its good points and do away with the problems. They want unconditional dialogue with militants; we are happy with that, and would like furthermore to hold a dialogue with all sections of opinion. They want prisoners who have been held for a long time to be released; we are willing to support this, although individual cases must be studied and reviewed. There is very little difference, in fact, Mufti Sahib himself told us in Delhi that all this could be sorted out, once we agreed to a PDP Chief Minister.

[Ghulam Nabi Azad is the President of the State unit of Congress in J&K.]

Chapter 8

# Omar Abdullah on His Party's Defeat

*What next?*

I'm going to resign from the Council of Ministers though this does not mean our party is going to withdraw from the NDA coalition. I plan to concentrate on J&K and rebuild my party from scratch. How can I expect my MLAs to sit in the Opposition while I continue to enjoy the perks of power as a minister.

*Is it the end, for now?*

No way, I believe state elections are around the corner simply because whichever government comes to power, it is not going to last. For the present, I will continue to remain an MP and will represent my constituency to the best of my ability. We will be playing the role of a responsible opposition and it is not our job to make it easier for the opposition parties to form a government. We will be talking to everyone including the independents. Several members of the People's Democratic Party (PDF) came to visit Farooq Abdullah on Friday but that was in the nature of a courtesy call. I do not think the PDP is interested in entering into a coalition with us — after all they fought against us in the last elections.

***Have you done any introspection on why you lost?***

It is too early to list out the main factors. I have called a meeting of the NC working committee to analyse what went wrong. We need to do some introspection and will not hesitate to take corrective steps wherever required.

I would however like to stress that all the different political parties here ganged up against us by entering into one kind of pre-poll alliance or another. These parties may be masters at forming pre-poll alliances, now let us see what kind of a post-poll alliances they can come up with. This is not to say that the National Conference has become a pariah. Nor am I trying to say that we do not accept our defeat gracefully. The poll analysis shows that our vote percentage has gone down from 34 per cent to 30 per cent. Thirty per cent of the voters continue to give us their support. It was a 3-4 per cent swing that brought down our number of seats and I am convinced, that it is only a matter of time before we regain our vote bank once again, especially since no one party seems to be in a position to form the next government. Such a situation is not in the interests of the state.

[Omar Abdullah is the President of National Conference].

***There is considerable speculation that the National Conference is seeking to play a destabilising role, and is working to prevent major Opposition blocs from forming a government. Could you describe your current political strategy?***

We are not looking to destabilise anybody. We clearly do not have a mandate to form the government. But we are also not in a charitable organisation. My job is not to hand over government to Mufti Mohammad Sayeed or Ghulam Nabi Azad on a platter. My job is to make it as difficult for them as possible although, I must say, they are making it difficult enough for themselves as it is! Therefore, we are engaged in discussions with like-minded individuals and groups on the political possibilities before us, and will continue these discussions irrespective of what government is formed. Let us see where these talks lead.

***To what factors will you attribute the defeat, the scale of which has far exceeded what anyone had anticipated?***

I don't think it is possible to attribute the defeat to any single reason. First and foremost, one has to look at the way in which the opposition handled its campaign. National Conference workers were not allowed to campaign in many areas because of terrorist threats. Bombs went off on polling day, miraculously enough, only in areas that were National Conference strongholds. We were, you see, up against all sorts of odds. I'm not denying that there was public anger against us in some areas, of course, but these are all factors we will be analysing in the coming days and weeks.

***What specific failures of governance will this introspection focus on?***

Well, not just governance, but the whole gamut of issues before us will be discussed. We've thrown the floor open for everyone in the party to say what they want to.

***On your own defeat in Ganderbal, you have attributed that to party infighting and not to the government's performance as such.***

To a large extent, yes, infighting was responsible for what happened. We have two major factions there, both so determined to destroy each other that they brought the party down along with them. The fact is, we have done an enormous amount of developmental work in Ganderbal, which was completely overshadowed by the problems within the party. I've seen all these reports suggesting that I lost because the local people thought I'd just arrived from London, or wherever, but that's nonsense. After all, I fought a parliamentary election from Srinagar, and the largest numbers of my votes came from Ganderbal, and the adjoining Assembly constituency, Kangan.

***Now that you have resigned as Union Minister of State for External Affairs, how do you see your own political future?***

I have a lot to do here. I still have the job of representing my parliamentary constituency, Srinagar. I hope to spend a lot more time on this than I was able to do while discharging my responsibilities in New Delhi. I also have the job of rebuilding the party here, given that an election could be called any time.

***So you believe that a new government that will take charge will not last?***

I believe that we are going to be in election mode pretty much from Day One, if at all a government is formed! I just can't see how people without any ideological or political coherence are going to pull along. I have this dictum, call it Omar Abdullah's law of coalition politics if you will. And the law is this: there has to be an inverse relationship between the length of time it takes for a party to stake its claim to power and the length of time the coalition lasts! The amount of time these people have taken just to put together their alliance doesn't suggest that they're going to spend very much time together running the government.

***Where do you see your relationship with the National Democratic Alliance headed from here? After all, it didn't help you gain any real economic benefits, nor a meaningful dialogue on autonomy. And many people believe it cost you the elections.***

I think it is imperative that the autonomy dialogue with Arun Jaitley now continue, particularly since there is now only one member of the Assembly, the Bharatiya Janata Party MLA, who is actually opposed to greater autonomy for Jammu and Kashmir. As for the rest, I do not wish for any drastic change to be made in a hurry. Let us wait and see how the situation develops.

PART — III

# Post-Election Scenario

## Chapter 9

# A New Dawn

After more than a fortnight's intense discusssions, hectic parleys and hard bargaining the Congress and PDF agreed to form a coalition government in J&K, the first of its kind in the State, based on a common minimum programme (CMP). And it must be said to the credit of the Congress leadership in general, and party President Sonia Gandhi in particular, that by offering Mufti Mohammad Sayeed, the former Union Home Minister and seniormost among the functional politicians in the State, the Chief Minister's post at least for the first three years of the Assembly's six-year tenure the mandate of the people of the Valley has been respected. This indeed is a turning point in the chequered history of the State. But whether it will become the precursor of a new dawn especially for the people of the Valley who have gone through numerous trials and tribulations in the last one decade only time will tell. However, there is no gainsaying that with the formation of this coalition government —which is to take office on November 2 in Srinagar— hopes of peace, stability and prosperity returning to the Valley have soared among all sections of the populace, something none can possibly ignore or overlook.

In this context it is worthwhile taking a close look at the common minimum programme (CMP) agreed upon by the Congress-PDF alliance in J&K.

It sets as its goal the following:

To heal the physical, psychological and emotional wounds inflicted by 14 years of militancy, to restore the rule of law in

Jammu and Kashmir, to complete the revival of the political process, which was begun by the recently-concluded elections, and to request the Government of India to initiate and hold, sincerely and seriously, wide ranging consultations and dialogue, without conditions, with the members of the legislature and other segments of public opinion in all the three regions....to evolve a broad-based consensus on restoration of peace with honour in the State.

With that end in view the State Government shall review all cases of detenus being held without trial for long periods... all such laws that have been used in the past decade to.deprive people of their basic rights to life and liberty for long periods of time, without due legal process.

The document then says:

All cases of custodial killings and violations of human rights shall be investigated and persons responsible for them will be identified and punished appropriately. While pledging to "implement special schemes to rehabilitate former militants who have forsworn violence and rejoined the mainstream" it promises to ensure that the government reaches out to the children, widows and parents of the deceased militants and make endeavours to provide education to the militancy affected orphans. The CMP speaks of setting up .a commission for making recommendations for reform of the police administration to make it a more effective and humane instrument for investigation of crimes and enforcement of law and order. Thereafter it declares:

The Government will ensure that the personnel in the Special Operations Group (SOG) are assimilated/relocated. within the regular police establishment. What is more, it underlines the following: The coalition government considers that there are enough laws in existence to deal with militancy,therefore, it will not implement POTA in the State.

As regards the Kashmiri Pandits, it reaffirms that their "return to their homeland is an essential ingrethent of *Kashmiriat* and assures to "create an atmosphere conducive for their safe return" with the cooperation of all.

These are all confidence-building measures no doubt but they are something more as well. These are concrete steps towards shaping the outlines of a political resolution of the Kashmir problem.

The coalition government and the CMP together constitute a bold and daring endeavour to win back the hearts and minds of the alienated Kashmiris. The success of the democratic process—reflected in the holding of elections that brought about a change of government— must be consolidated through the effective functioning of the coalition government so that in due course Kashmir becomes a "beacon light to this benighted sub-continent" of ours, a fervent hope Gandhiji had nurtured way back in December 1947.

But these people are deliberately forgetting what the Bench stated thereafter. Since it had been clarified by the Commission that its August 16 order was taken without reference to Article 356, the Bench opined in that setting:

> The question of applicability of Article 356 on the infraction of Article 174 loses much of the substance and, therefore, application of Article 356 is not required to be gone into.

The Election Commission's observation had been guided by the understanding, shared by several legal brains of the country before the October 28 ruling of the Apex Court, that Article 174 (1) was applicable to a dissolved Assembly as well. With the SC Bench dismissing such an impression the issue of Article 356 became redundant. The Bench further clarified that in view of its opinion that Article 174 (1) was inapplicable to a dissolved legislature, "the question that the Election Commission is required to carry out the mandate of Article 174 (1) does not arise". This too goes in favour of the Commission and against the Centre's arguments.

However, in response to the contention (advanced by the Centre and others) that in the absence of any period provided either in the Constitution or the Representation of the People's Act (RPA) the Election Commission might not hold elections at all and that situation could herald the end of democracy, the Bench opined:

On the premature dissolution of an Assembly, the Election Commission is required to initiate immediate steps for holding elections for constituting the Assembly on the first occasion and, in any case, within six months from the date of premature dissolution of the Assembly. Here it must be pointed out that the Commission had at no point of time contemplated an inordinate delay in holding elections in Gujarat. And this became clear when within an hour of the Apex Court's reply to the Presidential reference the Election Commission announced December 12, 2002 as the date for holding the Gujarat Assembly polls. What needs to be comprehended in full measure is that unlike that the BJP politicians in the State or the Centre who were playing crass politics, the Election Commission did not engage in such an exercise. Though he did not explicitly say so, the fact that Chief Election Commissioner J.M. Lyngdoh, at the press conference held on October 28 to announce the date of the Gujarat elections, pointed to the Commission being compelled to go for a special revision of electoral rolls in 152 Assembly constituencies spread over 23 districts of Gujarat (since 2.24 lakh voters had not been located in the State as they had shifted, most probably due to economic reasons) was reason enough to convincingly establish that elections before

October 3 were absolutely impossible in the State. And yet, the EC ordered polls at the earliest opportunity.

Whichever way one looks at it, the entire premise of the Centre's attack on the EC has been demolished by the Supreme Court verdict. In effect the Apex Court's answers to the Presidential reference constitute a resounding triumph for democracy that the Central Government, in collusion with the Gujarat authorities, was seeking to undermine. As a matter of fact the SC Bench's stand is in confirmity with the Congress position as upheld in the course of arguments. As Congresss MP and Supreme Court advocate Kapil Sibal, who presented the party's case before the SC Bench, cogently explained, the BJP running the ruling coalition at the Centre and the Gujarat Government wanted to make a constitutional virtue of a political expethency, but that has failed due to the SC's clear-cut assertions.

Overall therefore this is a highly positive development whose implications could be far-reaching in the longterm.

## After the Elections

There were no bugles or fanfare as almost half-a-million Indian solthers began their march back to the barracks from the Pakistan border. The Union government's October 16 decision to pull back troops from the western frontier marks an end to arguably the most ill-conceived manoeuvre in Indian military history. Intended to signal India's willingness to go to war if Pakistan continued to aid cross-border terrorism, Operation Parakram ended as an ignominious retreat after having failed to secure even its minimum objectives. But the worst maybe yet to come, Pakistan has called India's cards, and discovered that its much-hyped hand contains no aces. Now, a new government in Jammu and Kashmir could face a significant escalation in cross-border violence: violence to which the security establishment has yet to consider how it might respond.

As late as August 3, Defence Minister George Fernandas had told solthers at Sharifabad, near Srinagar, that there was no question of a troop pullback until "the situation returns to normal". The subsequent collapse of Operation Parakram needs to be read in the context of the objectives that impelled it. Speaking in Washington in January 2002, less than a month after the attack on the Parliament building, Deputy Prime Minister and Home Minister L.K. Advani had spelled out a four-point agenda for de-escalation. Pakistan, he said, had to hand over 20 key terrorism suspects, 14 of them Indian nationals red-flagged by Interpol. It had, he continued, to issue a "categorical and unambiguous renunciation of terrorism", and close down training camps for terrorists, choke their finance lines and weapons supplies. And most important, Advani demanded the mailed fist behind the velvet glove of international intercession; as the sword arm of what bureaucrats in the Ministry of External Affairs refer to as coercive diplomacy. Data generated by the Ministry of External Affairs itself show how little effect the mailed fist in fact had. Pakistan's military ruler, President Pervez Musharraf, publicly promised to end infiltration into India but continued the country's long-standing policy of encouraging terrorism in Jammu and Kashmir. While the estimated levels of infiltration fell between January and September 2002, as compared to 2001, it was actually higher than the level recorded in March, April and May last year. More important, the level of infiltration remained adequate to replace the numbers of terrorists killed by Indian security personnel. Terrorists numbering 1,295, for example, were killed between January and September this year. A similar number of terrorists made their way across the Line of Control to maintain the numbers of cadre active in Jammu and Kashmir.

Indian military forward deployment, as a coercive gesture, also did little to deter terrorist attacks against the election process in Jammu and Kashmir. Eighty-four political worker-participants in the elections were killed between January and September this year, a figure that already exceeds the previous high of 75, through all of 1996. The data on violence directed at civilians show that the numbers killed and injured in terrorist violence by the end of September by far exceed the figures for any previous year since the first Bharatiya Janata Party-led National Democratic Alliance came to power. While these killings were not directly election-related, they do show a distinct upward trend from July, when it became clear that elections were to be held. As such, it seems fair to suggest that they were intended to provide military muscle to the terrorists' anti-election campaign. Despite the supposed success of Indian coercive diplomacy, then, Pakistan backed terrorist groups felt to act as they wished.

For military strategists, the collapse of Operation Parakram has underlined a particularly worrying fact. Put simply, India's conventional military superiority does not operate as a deterrent against Pakistan's sub-conventional offensive in Jammu and Kashmir. Secure in the knowledge that its nuclear capabilities will deter any Indian conventional response to low-intensity war in Jammu and Kashmir, Pakistan can escalate hostilities to levels that it might have considered inconceivable in the early 1990s. Since 1998-99, Pakistan has pumped in increasing numbers of well-trained and well-equipped terrorists recruited directly from that country, and to a lesser extent from Afghanistan, countries of West Asia and Central Asia, instead of depending on locally recruited cadre. In recent years, the data show, the numbers of foreign nationals crossing the LoC far exceed those of ethnic-Kashmiri recruits sent from the pools available in training camps in Pakistan. Indeed, if Indian intelligence estimates are accurate, the exfiltration of locally recruited cadre for training has dwindled to near-insignificant levels. According to estimates, almost half of all terrorists who are active in Jammu and Kashmir are of foreign origin.

Pakistan's offensive posture is also reflected in the recoveries of weapons made since 1997. Experts believe that these recoveries are a mirror image of the kinds of war materials that actually make their way across the LoC, If, for example, large consignments of rocket launchers are supplied to terrorists in Jammu and Kashmir, some of it will be recovered by Indian security personnel. Indian official data make it clear that since 1997 there has been a marked upward trend in the recoveries of heavy weapons, such as rocket-propelled grenade launchers and anti-tank mines. The amount of lethal Research Department Explosive (RDX) and electronic detonators discovered by Indian security personnel has also increased in the same period. The effects of this sustained upgrade have been sadly evident. Although the number of terrorists killed has risen each year since 1997, the figure masks a disturbing reality. In 1997, the ratio of terrorists killed to each Indian security force member killed stood at 10:17. Last year, that figure was 10:30. Put simply, more soldiers are laying down their lives to eliminate each terrorist than before.

All of this has alarming implications for the future of Jammu and Kashmir. When the National Conference took power after the 1996 Assembly elections, it was widely assumed that the government of Chief Minister Farooq Abdullah would be able to build on and consolidate the gains of an improved security situation. Years of offensive operations had succeeded, in the words of Texas University analyst Sumit Ganguly, in securing "order, if not law". For the first two years of the Abdullah government, the promises that underpinned the elections seemed to have been validated. Between 1997 and 1998, for example, the total numbers of terrorism-related violent incidents and attacks on security forces fell, along with the numbers of civilians killed and injured. Although the overall levels of violence remained appallingly high, it seemed that the coming of the new government had offered if not a window of opportunity, at least a small crack in the wall. Most people in the security administration believed that a responsive civilian administration would generate the kinds of developmental initiatives necessary to alienate terrorist groups from civil society.

Then came the Pokhran-II nuclear tests of May 1998, and the retaliatory tests at Chaga J. Prime Minister Atal Behari Vajpayee proclaimed South Asia's new bombs to be "weapons of peace", which made war an impossibility in the region. The proposition was soon mercilessly exposed by the Kargil war. While nuclear weapons had indeed made any full-scale conventional engagement between India and Pakistan near impossible, paradoxically it had opened the door for an escalation of sub-conventional conflict by Pakistan. While both India and Pakistan had for long been known to possess nuclear weapons, the demonstration of their capabilities worked to impose new thresholds on the use of India's conventional capabilities. India could no longer respond to heightened sub-conventional warfare by threatening to go to war. The effects were evident in Jammu and Kashmir. The year 1999 witnessed a sharp escalation in every index of terrorist violence — from the number of incidents of violence and security force casualties, to losses of civilian and combatant lives. Abdullah, over the next several years, was left carrying the can for New Delhi's nuclear follies: follies that he himself had cheerfully endorsed without concern for the consequences.

Estimates of the cost of Operation Parakram run between Rs.2000 crores and Rs.5000 crores, or anywhere up to Rs.3 crores a day. These figures do not include loss of life in the course of the operation owing to accidents in handling explosives, wear and tear caused to equipment brought out of safe storage or the still-to-be conducted return of material to peace-time conditions. It is hard not to conclude that the proceeds of the 4 per cent tax imposed to support Parakram in the last Union Budget could have been better used to upgrade counter-terrorism and surveillance capabilities. Portable surveillance radars recently purchased for Rs.350 crores from Israel, for example, could have been paid for with a fraction of the funds spent on Parakram. The El-Op manufactured radar, which can detect human movement at up to 4,000 metres, will be just a drop in the ocean. Troops engaged in counter-terrorist duties are still not routinely equipped with basic pieces of equipment like night vision devices. Even the supposedly elite Special Operations Group of the Jammu and Kashmir Police still depends on recycled Pakistani supplies made to terrorist groups, for night vision equipment, sniper rifles and rocket launchers. There is still no centralised database on terrorists, or a single worthwhile forensic laboratory in Jammu and Kashmir.

All this points to a deep malaise in the Indian security establishment: its failure to engage intellectually in any serious, long-term manner with Pakistan's sub-conventional offensive. Operation Parakram itself is a case in point. Despite repeated intelligence warnings that high-profile centres such as the Parliament building might be attacked, no initiative had been taken to plan responses to such incidents. Had Members of Parliament or Ministers been taken hostage on December 13, the security establishment would not have known how to respond. And, while the Indian Army had dozens of war-game scenarios for conflict with Pakistan, an apparently endless forward deployment was not one of them. At no stage were clear political objectives for the Operation conveyed to field formations. Indeed, Lieutenant-General Kapil Vij, the commanding officer of 2 Corps, a key strike formation, had to be removed from his command for pushing armour to war positions on the border — something he might be forgiven for believing was his brief.

The retreat was conducted with the same lack of clarity as the offensive or, rather, the offensive that wasn't. The National Security Advisory Board (NSAB) members who met on October 16 to discuss the pullback, had before them no study papers on the subject, nor detailed research data on the potential outcomes of the move. It took the NSAB barely two hours to recommend that troops be pulled back; the body was not summoned before Operation Parakram was initiated. The Cabinet Committee on Security (CCS) despatched the issue in all of 90 minutes, again without detailed consultations with top military officials or the internal security bureaucracy. While the Chief of the Army Staff, General S. Padmanabhan, was able to hold some discussions on the pullback with senior colleagues on October 17, highly placed sources told *Frontline* that his headquarters had not received any formal communique from the Cabinet until that evening. Critics of the decision — of whom there there not a few — were offered no formal opportunity to put across their points of view.

Few people in the NDA — or the security establishment, for that matter — seem to have taken the time to consider where India might go from here. Events in Pakistan have given the question particular urgency. The far-right Muttahida Majlis-e-Amal has already called for the release of top terrorist Masood Azhar — a sign of its intent. Terrorist groups operating from Pakistan will, for the first time, have access to overt political patronage, freeing them from any state control that existed over their activities.

The decision to pull back from the western border has received applause in the West, and given the fact that it was a move of little strategic value, there can be no purely military objection to the decision. Nonetheless, the problem that existed before December 13 remains. Should a major terrorist attack take place inside or outside Jammu and Kashmir, the NDA will have no real option other than begging the United States of America for redress. As the Prime Minister himself conceded, such appeals had been of limited utility on the ground. Speaking in London on October 13, he said: "The West finds its terrorism more serious, not ours. It has a double standard to measure terrorism".

He is right. Instead of bemoaning his fate, however, the Prime Minister will do well to apply his mind to just what he intends to do about India's problem of terrorism. Unless he and his colleagues start addressing the question, no number of elections will help address the murderous war in Jammu and Kashmir.

## Challenges Ahead

The results of the Jammu and Kashmir Assembly elections have cleared a lot of the haze from the national political horizon. While the Congress (I) is now seen as going its own way without crutches, and more confident than before, the Bharatiya Janata Party is groping in the dark for a new strategy. The good showing has emboldened the Congress (I) enough to declare that "there is no alternative for us but to go it alone in almost all States". The BJP, on the other hand, is still looking for reasons for its poor performance. Unconvincing explanations such as "we fared badly because there was confusion about our stand on the issue of trifurcation", or "we could not expose the misdeeds of the National Conference enough" are offered by the party — in an indication that it has fallen between the two stools of Hindutva and the compromises associated with coalition politics.

The contrast was striking at the headquarters of the two parties in New Delhi as the results started coming in. While there was jubilation at the Congress (I) office, a sense of foreboding hung over the BJP office.

The reasons are not far to seek. Jammu and Kashmir has become the symbol of India's fight against terrorism. The defeat of both the BJP and the NC proved that the people of the State had rejected the National Democratic Alliance (NDA) government's claim that it was effectively countering terrorism in the area. The fact that the people chose the Congress (I)'s candidates over the BJP's in the latter's stronghold of the Jammu region suggests that the Congress (I) is once again viewed as a party that can lead the State.

All India Congress Committee general secretary Oscar Fernandes said: "It is a mandate for peace and the fact that the Congress has got such massive support from the people shows they view us as the party that can bring peace and development." He said that the party had managed to show that it cared for the people. "Whenever there was a militant attack, or people got displaced because of such an attack, we sent relief for them. This was a gesture that the people appreciated, all the more because the government was certainly lacking in providing succour to these people."

According to Oscar Fernandes, the Congress (I) victory had a background that dated back to the day Sonia Gandhi took over as party president. Sonia Gandhi's strategy of reaching out to the suffering people irrespective of whether the party was in power in their State or not had been appreciated by them, he said. The Jammu and Kashmir election results, he said, proved this. "Except for Uttar Pradesh, Tamil Nadu, West Bengal and Bihar, we are strong everywhere. Even in these States, our performance will be better than last time." The Congress (I) is aware that its bargaining power *vis-a-vis* other non-BJP parties has increased. If the party can win over 25 per cent of the votes polled and bag 20 seats in Jammu and Kashmir, where it had just seven seats, it certainly has reason to be confident.

Havihg fallen between the two stools of Hindutva and coalition *dharma,* the BJP could neither speak out openly in support of the trifurcation demand of the Rashtriya Swayamsewak Sangh-backed Jammu State Morcha, nor criticise the NC strongly enough, though that party was held responsible for everything that went wrong in Jammu and other parts of the Kashmir Valley. Although the two parties contested against each other, they continued to be partners in the NDA government. As a result, the voter was left wondering about their credibility.

The party's debacle has triggered a debate over whether giving up its own core issues in favour of opportunistic politics has cost it dearly. "We have not given up the core issues such as the construction of the Ram temple, or the demand for the abrogation of Article 370. The only thing is that we cannot implement them unless there is a purely BJP government. Until such time, we would have to stick to the NDA agenda, said party general secretary Mukhtar Abbas Naqvi. He said that the BJP suffered because of "the injustice of the National Conference and its misrule" and not because the people had rejected it. Congress (I) workers believe that the raking up of the issue of Sonia Gandhi's foreign origin at this time is an indication that other political parties have accepted the fact that the Congress (I) will come back to power at the Centre. "They have no propaganda [planks] left..., so they are raising these petty issues," said Oscar Fernandes. He cited the instances of Sonia Gandhi being warmly welcomed wherever she went, whether it was in Gujarat, Jammu and Kashmir or Uttar Pradesh. Oscar Fernandes pointed out that in the last round of Assembly elections the Congress (I) had defeated either the BJP or other NDA constituents in almost all States. While the Congress (I)'s level of self-confidence has grown, taking it slightly ahead of the other non-BJP parties, in the NDA camp the BJP's allies are likely to stick closet to the BJP for their own political survival. The Congress (I) is, however, unruffled by the possible consolidation of pro-BJP forces. "Just wait and see. The simmering discontent in Gujarat against the BJP, though it may not be visible now, will show itself up at the time of elections," said Oscar Fernandes.

## Chapter 10

# A New Beginning

The elections in Jammu and Kashmir have very appropriately been hailed as the triumph of democracy. More than that, they also signify a triumph of the political sagacity and courage of the Kashmiris, and an emphatic assertion of their preference for a peaceful and negotiated settlement of the Kashmir issue within a democratic framework.

The election results threw up some surprises. At one level the fractured mandate is a clear rejection of the National Conference, which had a hegemony of sorts in Kashmir politics for decades, at another level it is also a relatively clear victory for the Congress and a new group of less than three years' standing, the People's Democratic Party (led by former Union Home Minister as also a former Congress leader Mufti Mohammad Sayeed). The two parties that together bagged 36 of the 87 seats in the House will now govern the State, sharing power between themselves and with the smaller groups and independents.

Numerically, elections for the 87 seats in J&K gave a hung assembly with the ruling National Conference emerging as the largest single party—though its tally reduced from 58 in 1996 to 28 seats, with party president Omar Abdullah being defeated in Ganderbal—his family's traditional constituency—at the hands of the People's Democratic Party candidate.

While the Congress based its claim on the convention that the largest group leads the coalition, PDF President Mufti Mohammed Sayeed insisted on leading the government because the wounded Valley gave them the mandate, to which all its 16 MLAs belong.

Ultimately, on October 26, after a fortnight-long war of nerves, the Chief Ministership issue was resolved and Congress agreed to have the PDF president, Mufti Mohammad Sayeed, as the Chief Minister of Jammu and Kashmir on a rotational basis of three years.

**Winners and Losers**

The reversal of the National Conference was on expected lines. The average Kashmiri was disillusioned with the Abdullahs and the poll outcome has only reflected that trend.

The loss of the National Conference cannot be attributed to the anti-incumbency factor alone. The NC was severely punished for its thoroughly opportunist alliance with the BJP with whom it has no ideological affinity, its monumental corruption, its betrayal of its own "autonomy" platform, its mal-governance, the former CM's tendency for long distance administration, and its unresponsiveness to the people's basic needs.

Also, the vote against the National Conference recognises the utter failure of the Central government, of which the NC was an adjunct, to combat terrorism within the State. The verdict has also been against NDA's policies of not doing enough to 'bring all elements, pro. and against the State's links with India, together, and to assure them that even when they have grievances against India, they would be heard and, wherever possible, redressed.

National Conference was routed in all the three regions. In the Valley, the PDF upstaged the NC, while in the Jammu region, the Congress emerged a decisive leader at the cost of the BJP, which did not win a single seat in its traditional stronghold. Congress won 15 constituencies in the Jammu region and made gains in the Valley, where its seats increased to five from a 1996 position of two seats.

The BJP's defeat is particularly important because it marks the rejection by Jammu region's predominantly Hindu voters of the regional and religious-chauvinist platform, as also of the trifurcation formula. It is heartening that Jammu's electorate voted against the BJP after the Akshardham incident in Gujarat. That event, the BJP had predicted, would turn the tide in its favour. This only goes to show that the people of Jammu and Kashmir, who know what it is to live under the shadow of violence, are far from gullible and are highly discriminating.

Among the other big losers were the *jehadis* who had said the elections were an affront to the people of Jammu and Kashmir who, they predicted, would boycott them *en masse*.

The next loser was the main separatist grouping, the 23-member All-Party Hurriyat Conference (APHC), and Shabir Shah's Democratic Freedom Party, who stayed away from the election process despite a great deal of pressure on them to participate, including from the international community. And the numbers of people who turned out to vote, despite their boycott call, have sent alarm bells ringing in this camp.

For the PDF, it is a remarkable achievement considering it does not count itself among the mainline parties; if anything, its pronouncements reveal a measure of sympathy for the separatists.

If that party could play the catalyst in bringing about a historic change through the ballot, much of the credit should go to Mehbooba Mufti, vice-president (and daughter of its president), who has emerged as an effective symbol for the aspirations of the Kashmiri youth.

## Common Minimum Programme

The Congress and PDF have formed a coalition, despite their ideological differences over solving the Kashmir problem. This could be a new beginning, if the two decide to complement each other's strengths. A combination of the Congress's mainstream moderation and the PDP's sensitivities towards the Kashmiri people might well be the answer to Kashmir's travails.

What bodes well for the future is that, in the course of electioneering, they had managed to have a tactical arrangement in a number of constituencies in the Valley, so as not to divide the anti-National Conference vote.

With their Common Minimum Programme (CMP), the parties have promised virtual disbandment of the controversial Special Operations Group (SOG), though not a total disbandment as the force will be re-trained and assimilated in other law enforcement agencies, and decided against implementing POTA in the State.

"The goal of the coalition government is to heal the physical, psychological and emotional wounds inflicted by fourteen years of militancy, to complete the revival of the political process which was begun by recently concluded elections", the CMP said.

The programme also promises to make efforts to ensure equitable share of resources available for development in the three regions of Jammu, Kashmir and Ladakh.

**Following are the other highlights of the CMP:**

- To protect people from violence and militancy, encourage those willing to return and cooperate with Centre to fight cross-border terrorism from Pakistan;

- Review all cases of detainees held without trial, release all detainees held on non-specific changes or not charged with serious crimes;
- Review operations of all laws which have been used in the past to deprive the people of basic rights to life and liberty;
- Probe all cases of custodial killings and human rights violation and strengthen the State Human Rights Commission;
- Formulate a comprehensive relief and rehabilitation package for those families affected by militant violence;
- Implement special schemes to rehabilitate former militants who have joined the mainstream;
- Reaffirms return of Kashmiri Pandits by creating a conducive atmosphere and approach the Centre for provision of adequate financial assistance for relief and rehabilitation of migrants from various disturbed areas of Jammu and Ladakh;
- To give top priority to rid the State administration of corruption and nepotism;
- Establish an institution or ehtisab for probing complaints received against Chief Minister or ministers or MLAs;
- A commission to recommend steps for reforming police administration;
- Several developmental initiatives also included for all-round development of the three regions.

## Democracy Won

There are three lessons we can draw from these elections. First, the people of J&K have rejected Pakistan's brand of terrorism. Second, they are now ready to accept Indian democracy, with all its drawbacks, and participate in the democratic process. Third, they have decided to throw in their lot with democratic India and not with a militarily controlled fundamentalist Pakistan.

Democracy produces a strange alchemy of astounding value and significance. In the case of India, in several hopeless situations when everything seemed to be falling apart, it has pulled us back from the precipice and opened the door to sanity. Democracy has proved to be indispensable for holding our society together. The ordinary voter, by embracing democracy, has, in the midst of the sound of the gunshots, proved that the power of the ballot is far stronger than the threat of the bullet. The voter has also demonstrated that the representative will of the people can only emerge by embracing the democratic process.

A vital arm of India's democratic process, the Election Commission, took several new initiatives this time around, by way of fine-tuning the mechanics and procedures, all aimed at reducing the scope for malpractices and facilitating free exercise of the franchise. It deployed handpicked high-level bureaucrats from outside the State — with a reputation for personal integrity — to function as observers. The voting was conducted using electronic voting machines in all the constituencies. And to ensure that all the Kashmiri migrants were able to vote, special polling booths were provided in transit camps or nearby locations in Jammu, Udhampur and Delhi. This was in addition to the postal ballot facility.

Faced with overwhelming odds — including a huge credibility gap arising from a long history of "stage-managed" polls — the commission under J.M. Lyngdoh, achieved the impossible, turning cynicism into hope for the ordinary Kashmiris.

Moreover, the significant presence of foreign and independent observers, diplomats and foreign media persons, ensured, contrary to New Delhi's earlier apprehensions, that the polls were not only free and fair but also seen to be so by the international community.

The threats and violence perpetrated by the militants did limit the participation but, at the same time, highlighted the fact that a good number of the electorate, was not cowed down by the fear of the gun. The reasonably good average voter turnout at around 44 per cent, should be considered "satisfactory", given heavy odds, in the face of escalating violence ordered by Pakistan so as to disrupt the election process. The voters, in most places, defied the poll boycott call of organisations such as the All-Parties Hurriyat Conference.

What is testimony to both wisdom and fortitude of the ordinary folks in standing up against terrorism, thus making the poll percentages more than respectable, is the fact that J&K witnessed a savage escalation of terrorist violence ever since the announcement of the elections. More than 800 people, including 270 civilians, 150 members of the security forces and 370 terrorists, were killed during the Assembly elections.

Despite the violence, the decent voter turnout in the four phases (47.25% in first phase, 40.6% in second, 42% in third and 52% in fourth) was indeed impressive.

Several factors contributed to popular enthusiasm for the polls. Most important was the decision by a group of separatists, candidates backed by the secessionist People's

Conference of Lone, (later it was forced by its umbrella group Hurriyat to expel these candidates for participating) to contest the polls. Their entry electrified not just their local constituencies, but had a huge impact on the mood in the Kashmir Valley.

It must also be recognized that the manner in which diplomats from the USA and the European Union backed the elections helped make the polls more inclusive. Western "persuasion" did have an influence on public opinion in the State, which began to take the elections more seriously than might have otherwise been the case. Tired of a decade of conflict that has wrecked their lives, most Kashmiris saw the post 9/11 situation — and especially the new international concern over violence in Kashmir — as an added window of opportunity for the peace they longed for.

Part of the reason for the high turnout, where it occurred, may be that this has been a more inclusive election than the one in 1996. Fifteen of the 105 candidates in north Kashmir were, for example, one-time terrorists, or individuals with terrorist links.

The degree of anti-National Conference feeling also motivated the voters. Voting was the highest wherever there was a serious contest against the incumbent NC candidate. Many defied the poll boycott call with the argument that *azadi* from the NC was more important and must precede *azadi* from India.

There was even an "election fever" in rural and border areas of Kashmir, where the turnout was 55 per cent.

In fact, a distinctive urban-rural divide characterises voter participation, with. the cities and towns tending to be more apathetic or wary for various reasons.

## Did India Win?

To interpret the verdict as a victory for India against Pakistan is rather too simplistic and is not supported by the facts. The percentage of persons who voted and of those who abstained is no measure of pro-India and pro-*azadi* sentiments in the State. Those who voted also include supporters of *azadi.* But, they are convinced that the role of the gun for its achievement is over. It is this section to which the PDF appealed for support with the promise of a dialogue with militants for a solution of the Kashmir problem. The expelled members of the People's Conference also contested the election on the slogan of *azadi.*

Thus, it would be a mistake to regard the verdict as an endorsement of New Delhi's Kashmir policy or a vote for a categorical "integration" of Jammu and Kashmir with the Indian "mainstream". More than anything else, the Kashmiris showed a strong urge for a return to more peaceful, less violent, normal life, and for the restitution of human rights and the rule of law.

However, there is a quantum jump in the march of democracy in the State and to count all those who did not vote as supporters of *azadi* is incorrect, as many did not vote because of fear. The Hurriyat's call to voters to boycott the elections made an impact only where it was expected to, in Srinagar and the bigger towns in the Valley. The *hartal* calls on election day were uniformly successful, with commercial establishments downing shutters, but this did not stop many people turning out to vote. The fact is that people came out to vote despite a very real threat of militant violence, and with far fewer allegations of coercion. This has put the APHC in a piquant situation. But the Hurriyat has tried to put a positive formulation on things saying that the places where the boycott was successful reflect its 'constituency'. The fact of the matter is the Hurriyat, as a totality, has no 'constituency'. Only three components of the APHC can claim to have popular support—Syed Ali Shah Geelani's Jammat-e-Islami, the late Abdul Gani Lone's People's Conference, and Mirwaiz Umar Farooq's Awami Action Committee.

Also, there are several people who genuinely believe that the best interests of the Kashmir lie in the continuation of its relations with India.

## Diplomatic Gains and Challenges

Clearly, the immediate benefit from the success is on the diplomatic front. Prime Minister Atal Bihari Vajpayee's bold gamble to facilitate a free and fair poll is bound to considerably strengthen India's case on Kashmir amongst the international community. The election results have dealt a resounding snub to those in the world who had doubted this country's ability to give the people of J&K a free political choice.

Indeed, the electoral outcome has made a mockery of Pakistan President General Pervez Musharraf's charge that the Kashmir polls would be a rigged charade, and also provides a hard rebuttal of Pakistani allegations about Indian "colonial rule" in Kashmir. As a matter of fact, the triumph of democracy in Kashmir has only served to highlight the pathetic electoral farce the Pakistan dictator himself has conducted with his two main political rivals banished into exile. It just goes to show that while in India the abandonment of the democratic process is an aberration, in Pakistan it is *vice versa*. Kashmiris in India rejected militancy, but the victory of the Muttehida Majlis-e-Amal (MMA) legitimises militancy in Pakistan.

Far from sharing Pakistan's view that the J&K poll was a farce, international community has recognised its significance and dubbed them as "free and fair". They regard it as a positive step but as part of a process to settle the Kashmir issue.

Now, there would be increased pressure from the international community on India and Pakistan to enter into a bilateral dialogue. Some analysts opine that it is a helpless situation insofar as India-Pakistan dialogue is concerned. The Americans cannot put too much pressure on Pakistan because Musharraf will point at the *mullahs* who have gained in the Pakistan elections. The anti-US feelings in Pakistan appear to be on the rise and the *mullahs* will now demand that the Americans should be out of Pakistan. Vajpayee too would simply say that he has done his bit by holding free and fair elections. Unless cross-border terrorism ends, he cannot move forward.

New Delhi should, therefore, be prepared for renewed exhortation from the world capitals for the dialogue resumption. But has it a coherent strategy?

## Roadmap for Peace

Opportunities such as the one thrown up by the J&K elections come but rarely in the life of a nation. Never has there been such favourable circumstances, national and international, to evolve a solution to the problem which has dogged the sub-continent for over five decades.

The challenge is for the new State government, in cooperation with the Centre, to translate the hope provided by the elections into a sustained climate of peace and stability.

To heal the wounds, to remove the deep-rooted and pervasive sense of alienation bridge divides, all the political forces in the State must open a dialogue with all, dissidents, and "militants", including the Hurriyat, and exiled *Pandits*, so long as they abjure the language of the gun. The Hurriyat's obvious willingness to be intermediaries between the new State government and the militant groups is something that can be usefully utilised.

Good and humane governance, an amnesty to those not charged with heinous crime, security of the citizens, development and multi-level discussions on State autonomy and regional devolution should be on the agenda of "the talks".

The National Conference, apart from PDF-Congress coalition, should also play a very important role in talks because, despite its corrupt administration, it provided a safety valve to Centre, particularly in the Valley, where virtually all other serious political configurations and parties clamoured for secession. Besides, once in the Opposition, it is bound to be more sharply focussed on its demand for autonomy, because this is the only way it can recapture lost ground in the State.

The Centre, whose approach so far has been singularly vague and ambivalent, must enunciate a clearly defined policy towards Kashmir, in respect of its internal as well as external dimensions.

When the option is between the secession and autonomy, the latter certainly appear to be the better choice. In an autonomous Kashmir, the Kashmiris would themselves eradicate the terrorism, avoid separatism and shun violence.

Autonomy would fulfil the aspirations of Kashmiri people to a great extent and would certainly reduce the inclination of some elements towards Pakistan.

The State of J&K already enjoys a special status under the Indian Constitution. Under such a situation, to consider the demand of autonomy may not be a sin, but only the extension of the existing provisions.

Thus, what survives is autonomy option on which meaningful talks must be held. Thus, the challenge for the Congress-PDF coalition will be to arrest a possible fragmentation of the State by shifting the debate on *azadi* from territorial to political parameters.

Apart from a purposive approach to evolve a political formula responsive to the aspirations of the people of the State, India's policy in Kashmir must also contain a measured mix of military decisiveness and politico-strategic flexibility in reviving the dialogue with Pakistan.

If we do not move out of the straitjacket of rejectionism about a dialogue with Pakistan, we will be isolated in the international community.

Equally important is the fact that there is a definite likelihood of not just continuing but increased terrorist violence sponsored from Pakistan.

This has to be countered within J&K, and, where necessary, India should not hesitate from taking pre-emptive action across the LoC. Such preventive action should be carefully calibrated to avoid full-scale conflict with Pakistan which is neither necessary nor desirable.

## Socio-economic Development

So busy have we been in claiming J&K as an inalienable part of the country that we have done little about ending the alienation of its people, an aspect that Pakistan has exploited to the hilt.

One, it needs to be appreciated that mis-governance and non-performance have aggravated the problems of unemployment and alienation in the State. This calls for fresh efforts to handle socio-economic problems.

Two, the Kashmiris often blame the Centre for foisting Chief Ministers and Governors on the State. Such practices are counterproductive and hence should be discarded.

It is a pity that even after the latest free, fair and transparent Assembly polls, the principal political characters in the State have to bank on the central Congress leadership for deciding the Chief Ministerial issue. The matter could have been left to the people's representatives.

Three, although the Centre has been more than generous with plan allocations and funds for development, there is still alienation among the people. This is because of the failure of successive administrations to provide a credible government, where funds have in reality not reached the common people. The Centre should evolve proper mechanism for disbursing the funds, so they are not misappropriated.

The new rulers must provide the people a clean administration, bereft of corruption and nepotism. Peace can only be brought about if the day-do-day problems of the people of Kashmir are addressed. Kashmir will not attract investment, nor will trade and commerce flourish till there is an acceptable resolution of the complex problems of the Kashmiri psyche.

Chapter 11

# Azad's Miracle

Once, the election was over, Mohammad Yousaf Taing, a senior National Conference (NC) leader and author of a seminal biography of Sheikh Mohammad Abdullah, echoed the widespread belief that furious voters had put a debased dynasty to the sword. Much media commentary took up Taing's theme, and blamed the NC's defeat. In the latest Assembly elections on everything from Farooq Abdullah's incompetence to Omar Abdullah's inexperience, and, in time-honoured Blame-the-Bahu tradition, even the supposed arrogance and interference of daughter-in-law Payal Abdullah. But the truth, as usual, is considerably more complex. 'The National Conference Ark might indeed be leaking, but those on board have more than an even chance of plugging the cracks with resin provided by its fractious opponents, and sailing on.'

Months after the most politically rich election ever in Jammu and Kashmir, efforts to create a new government have ended in deadlock. At the core of this political impasse is the stubborn refusal of the People's Democratic Party (PDP) to accept Congress (I) leader Ghulam Nabi Azad as the next Chief Minister. Interestingly, the PDP's insistence on the top job appears to have been something of an afterthought. Speaking to media even as the results came out on October 10, party chief and former Union Home Minister Mufti Mohammad Sayeed said that the question of who would become Chief Minister was "a small issue", to be decided "by the game of numbers". It was only two days later that his daughter, Mehbooba Mufti, insisted that the PDP could not allow a Congress (I) candidate to become Chief Minister, despite that party's numerical legislative superiority. Mehbooba Mufti argued that only an ethnic-Kashmiri Chief Minister would be able to address what the PDP believes is the State's core problem — the alienation of the ordinary Kashmiri from the Indian state. None of the PDP's stated arguments against Azad appear to be anything other than trivial. Mediators, for example, pointed out that Azad, whose family moved to Doda two generations ago from Kokernag, was from a Kashmiri-speaking region and an ethnic-Kashmiri. Mehbooba Mufti rejected this argument on the ground that Azad had projected himself as a representative of Jammu during the election campaign. But even if one admits the argument that nobody from Jammu is fit to be Chief Minister of the entire State, there is no persuasive explanation for why the PDF was unwilling to accept any of the Congress I's five Kashmir-valley MLAs, to former MP Saifuddin Soz, as Chief Minister instead. Speaking to the media, Mehbooba Mufti said that "any Tom, Dick or Harry" could not become Chief Minister, but Sayeed himself has no experience of ruling a State. Nor was his tenure as Union Home Minister at the start of the violent insurgency in Jammu and Kashmir a particularly luminous one. Indeed, the PDP's claims that representatives of the Valley must rule are excellent arguments for the NC to take power, since that party commands more seats in the region than either of its opponents.

The PDP's recalcitrance may, instead, be rooted in its conviction that fresh elections are not far off. The party's three key demands — unconditional dialogue with ethnic-Kashmiri terrorists, the release of terrorists held in jails, and the disbanding of the Jammu & and Kashmir Police's Special Operations Group — are all acceptable in principle to the

Congress (I). "The problem for the PDP is that all three demands will take considerable time to realise. Worse, given the experience of the Union government's dialogue with the Hizbul Mujahi-deen in 2000-2001, such dialogue may come to nothing. Should the PDP achieve little, its credibility with its constituency, much of it drawn from the ranks of the Jamaat-e-Islami, will be severely eroded. Under the circumstances, the party leadership sees it to be in its best interest to sit in the Opposition until elections come again. In this project, the PDP has the support of the Bharatiya Janata Party, which wishes to block the emergence of another Congress (I)-led State government at any cost. Indeed, the fact that the PDP's hardline posture emerged after an October 11 meeting between Sayeed and Home Minister L.K. Advani led at least some people in the Congress(I) to draw the obvious inference.

It is probable that the Congress-PDP impasse that blocked the process of government formation will be resolved in the not-too-distant future, albeit with a sub-optimal outcome. The Congress (I) commands the tentative support of 14 independent MLAs, as well as of four MLAs from the Panthers' Party", two from the Communist Parry of India (Marxist) and one from the Bahujan Samaj Party', The numbers put the party within striking distance of forming a government, should it manage to gain the support of PDP dissidents.

But this tactical impasse is merely a smaller part of a far larger deadlock in Jammu and Kashmir's political life. In essence, the neat division of political space between the NC and secessionist formations like the All Hurriyat Conference has collapsed, exposing a rich pattern of fissures along both regional and ideological lines. If the NC before the elections was ambiguous in its position on terrorist groups, for example, the carnage inflicted on its ranks through the campaign has made fence-sitting near impossible. And in this collapse lies enormous possibilities of political regeneration and transformation.

Consider, for example, the independents and the smaller parties that hold the balance of power in the now-suspended Assembly. Some, like the Panthers' Party, have power bases exclusively in Jammu, and see no benefit in supporting Sayeed. MLAs from Jammu, who beat back communal calls for the division of the State, understand that giving in to the PDP's chauvinist position will give renewed life to the now-decimated Hindu Right. Others, like the Communist Party of India (Marxist), have been at the receiving end of PDP campaigning led by Jamaat-e-Islami cadre and backed by Hizbul-Mujahideen guns. "We want a broad-based coalition against the National Conference," said Mohammad Yakub, the CPI (M) candidate from Devsar, "but we cannot forget that that the PDP cadre made calling us heathen and unbelievers a centrepiece of their campaign. Mehbooba Mufti even said at a public rally that we had forgotten how to read the kalima (funeral oration)." Others like G.M. Sofi, the MLA backed by the secessionist People's Conference, have obvious reasons to reject the PDP's claims to represent Kashmiri Opposition sentiment exclusively. "I repeatedly told Sayeed that even if the Congress supported him, the independents were unwilling to do so," says CPI(M) state chief and Kulgam MLA Mohammad Yousuf Tarigami, who held meetings with the PDP leadership on October 16, "but he just wouldn't budge from his stand."

Within the Congress (I), anti-Sayeed sentiment runs along two distinct tracks. Before October 12, the Congress (I)'s central leadership had been relatively open to the PDP's demands, hoping that some compromise could be arrived at. At his meeting with Congress (I) president Sonia Gandhi that evening, Sayeed focussed little on the party's programme, insisting only that he be made Chief Minister. When party MLAs were confronted with that prospect, many of them reacted with fun. Congress(I) secretary Shatrujir Singh Gaikwad, sources told the media that he even warned Sonia Gandhi of the prospect of a party revolt should the central leadership order them to accept PDF leadership of the alliance. Even the party's Kashmir Valley MLAs protested furiously. "We withdrew six of our candidates to help the PDF," said Dooru MLA Ghulam Ahmad Mir, "otherwise they would be nowhere. We did so even though the PDF did not reciprocate our gesture. Our sacrifice is being repaid with ingratitude." In the event, Tarigami and Sofi were asked to mediate with the PDP, but to little effect. A face-to-face meeting between Azad and Sayeed on October 17 also achieved nothing. After a series of discussions in New Delhi on October 19, former Union Finance Minister Manmohan Singh was pressed into service in Srinagar. He, too, had little initial success since Sayeed shot down suggestions that the PDP and the Congress (I) rotate the Chief Minister's post between them.

Given how far both the PDP and Congress (I) have committed themselves, it seems unlikely that a happy resolution can be arrived at. Should the Manmohan Singh initiative also fail, a split in the PDP would be the sole device through which the impasse can be resolved. Congress strategists have been engaged in a dialogue with Tangmarg MLA Ghulam Hassan Mir, whose efforts to stitch together a seat-sharing deal had been shot down by Sayeed and Mehbooba Mufti. Mir, sources say, may be willing to ally his party with the Congress should it be invited to form a government, along with Shopian MLA Ghulam Hassan Khan and MLA Ghaffar Ahmad Sofi. Two other PDP MLAs, senior party leader Muzaffar Beigh and A.R. Veeri, also oppose the Sayeed-Mehbooba Mufti rejectionist line on a Congress (I) Chief Minister. "The bottom-line in the party," says a senior

PDP leader, "is on how to understand the mandate. Have we seen a pro-PDP vote or an anti-National Conference vote? Will the PDP benefit from staying out of office, or will it then loose ground to whoever takes power?" Since the PDP is registered as a political party but is not as yet legally recognised as such, the provisions of the anti-defection Act do not apply to its MLAs.

Governor Girish Chandra Saxena, however, seems determined not to allow the kind of deal-making a Congress (I) government would be premised on. "The Governor," says one of his legal advisers, "believes that giving an invitation to a party to form the government, in the knowledge that such an invitation would invite defections from another group, would be unjustifiable. If defections were acceptable, he might as well invite the NC, since it is the largest single bloc."

Whatever the constitutional merits of such a line of reasoning, Saxena has so far acted by the book as he understands it. When independent MLAs signalled that they might seek to win over PDP dissidents, Saxena made it clear that he would invite a non-PDP, Congress(I)-led coalition unless it actually had the numbers. Then, on October 17, when Farooq Abdullah insisted that he would no longer stay in office since the term of the Assembly had expired, the Governor promptly imposed Central rule. For the moment, he has given no clear indication of what his future course of action might be. The fact that Saxena had not appointed advisers seemed to suggest that he saw the arrangement as a passing one.

Perhaps the only thing the new government will have going for it is that none but the father-daughter duo who control the PDP see any real interest in precipitating fresh elections. The campaign saw almost a hundred cadre and candidates from all major parties eliminated in terrorist attacks, along with several times that number of civilians killed in enterprises to render free elections impossible.

The BJP-led National Democratic Alliance in New Delhi, for its part, has an obvious interest in blocking the formation of a Congress-led dispensation, but has no interest in forcing fresh elections either. "Frankly," says a senior Intelligence Bureau official in Srinagar, "none of us have the energy to go through the whole exercise again." That means independents and members of smaller parties are likely to keep some government, any government, in power, long enough to recoup their energies. And it is precisely on this fact that the NC is staking its political future. Farooq Abdullah's decision not to continue as interim Chief Minister was intended to precipitate President's Rule, a signal to independents that his party was ready to do business with them if the Congress (I) and PDP failed to resolve the deadlock.

Media focus on the Congress (I)-PDP feud has deflected attention from the fact that neither is, on its own, commanding players in post-election Jammu and Kashmir. Although its electoral defeat is a historic event, the NC remains the largest single party in Jammu and Kashmir, both in terms of seats won and its vote-share. Even in the Kashmir Valley, the focal point of its defeat, the party gained more seats and votes than its two principal rivals. Indeed, its vote-share was only marginally lower than the sum of the PDP's and the Congress(I)'s put together. Yet, the dramatic growth of the PDP's base in Kashmir, coupled with that of the Congress and independents in both this region and Jammu, did enough to dash the party's hopes of coming to power with the aid of a few independents. Now, the NC hopes that the inability of its opponents to put together an even reasonably stable government will give the party a shot at power in the not-too-distant future with the help of the very independents who ruined its prospects. "We don't want to be seen as being power hungry," says a senior party leader, "and will not stake claim to form a government. But we might back independents and small parties should any future government fall apart."

Beyond the deadlock, then, lies the political future of Jammu and Kashmir. For decades, politics in the State had been constructed in two dimensions — with the NC pitted against an undifferentiated Opposition, hostile and servile in turn to an all-powerful Centre. That framework, and not the Abdullah dynasty, is what has truly been put to rest in these elections. It has been fashionable to blame the NC these past years for all of the State's problems, forgetting that the major contenders for power today have at one stage or the othct helped shape its unhappy destiny. The Congress (I), led by that other great dynasty which still guides its course today, was responsible for the gross subversion of democracy which was to give legitimacy to secessionist forces. And it was Sayeed, as Union Home Minister, who laid the foundations for the past 14 years of terror. The nuanced alliances now being born represent an effort to remake this history. Whatever government is formed in coming weeks, the processes that led to its birth are certain to transfigure Jammu and Kashmir in ways which will long outlast its term in office.

## The Congress Experiment

It has been a difficult choice for Sonia Gandhi to let go of the Chief Minister's post, but in the long run it may well be worth the wait for the party.

Making a virtue out of necessity. This is what the Congress(I) has done in Jammu and Kashmir. Senior party leaders are hailing its abject surrender to the People's Democratic Party, despite the fact that it is the larger of the two parties in terms of legislative strength and deserved to hold the Chief Minister's post, as a "sacrifice in the larger "interest of the nation". The Congress(I)'s unique three-year rotational arrangement with the PDP to lead the government was one born out of sheer political compulsions: otherwise the party would have had to face the prospect of yet another National Conference-led government. But the party's crisis managers in the Congress(I) are trying to make this politically expethent move appear to be a supreme example of moralistic politics that only the Congress (I) was capable of following. Seeking to give the situation of helplessness and moralistic sheen, its general secretary Oscar Fernandes said:

"We could have formed the government on our own. We had the numbers. But we wanted to carry everyone along. We wanted to have the PDP with us because there was some indirect understanding between us on the anti-NC plank. We had deliberately not contested in 10 constituencies in the Kashmir Valley in order to facilitate the victor of PDP candidates."

"Magnanimity of the big brother towards a younger sibling" is how he described the Congress (I)'s agreement with the PDP. It is being generally seen as an instance of succumbing to blackmail by the PDP, but the Congress(I) is trying to give a moralistic hue to its defeat at the hands of the PDP — but only after days of rough political bargaining. The fact that the Congrcss(I) simply could not form the government without the PDP's support, especially after it became clear that there was no sign of the PDP splitting as the Congress(I) leaders had hoped until the last moment, is being sugar-coated.

"We wanted to send out a signal that we treat even smaller partners as equals. Oscar Fernandes said: "Although we could have formed the government without the PDF, Congress president Sonia Gandhi wanted to show that the party could even sacrifice the Chief Minister's post to accommodate the other point of view in the larger national interest." He was trying to explain the party's grand climb-down after a massive stand-off with Mufti Mohammad Sayeed.

Meanwhile, fire-fighting measures are on as the party struggles to explain to its cadres at the grassroot level its decision to foresake its claim to the Chief Minister's post. "Our basic intention was to respect the people's mandate. The people had mandated against the misrule and injustice of the National Conference government and it was our foremost duty to ensure that the National Conference did not come back to power," party spokesman S. Jaipal Reddy tried to explain.

"In order to respect the people's mandate, sacrificing the Chief Minister's post in the larger national interest was only a small contribution," he said. The decision to give up its claim to the chief ministership should not have come as a surprise because "the Congress president's ultimate aim was to ensure such a solution so as not to fritter away the people's mandate," explained Ambika Soni, political adviser to Sonia Gandhi. Congress(l) leaders also take pride in the fact that a tough political problem was resolved with grace and there was no bickering , except for some initial murmurs of discontent within the party. "Responding to a query, the Congress president had said that she will solve the Jammu and Kashmir problem with grace, and that's exactly what she has done," Oscar Fernandes said. This is notwithstanding the fact that State party president Ghulam Nabi Azad, the man chiefly credited with the party's spectacular performance in the Assembly elections and a chief ministerial aspirant, reported "sick" the day after the announcement was made that Mufti would be the Chief Minister. Azad refused to meet the press, and subsequently left for Jammu.

Not withstanding the political compulsions involved, the rotational system is a novel experiment for the Congress (I). "No doubt it is a novel and bold idea. It goes miles to prove the statesmanship of the Congress president," said Motilal Vora, senior Congress(I) leader.

Across the political spectrum there is unanimity that the Congress(I)'s move is indeed a departure from the party's past resolve against entering into coalition arrangements. It had declared that it would try to form governments on its own wherever it could since coalitions have failed to deliver.

The case of Uttar Pradesh provides supporting testimony to Congress (I)'s go it alone approach. A firm commitment by the party to support a government led by Samajwadi Party president Mulayam Singh Yadav could have ensured the installation of a non-Bharatiya Janata Party government there in the earlier instance, but the Congress (I) went backstage when the S.P. was waiting for its crucial response, with the result that a Bahujan Samaj Party-BJP coalition government came into being in Lucknow. But even now as Mulayam Singh continues to hope for support from the Congress (I), which will enable him to unseat the Mayawati-led government, the Congress has preferred to remain non-committal. Considering this track record, the Congress (I)'s experiment in Jammu and Kashmir is indeed different. Maybe it is an indication of the shape of things to come when the party is able to make a bid for power at the Centre. In such an eventuality, it would expect a return of favours extended in the past. "We want to give out the signal that we treat our junior partners with equal respect, that we treat them as equals,"Oscar Fernandes said. This is a politically rich statement with wide ramifications.

With this halo of martyrdom and confidence of moral victory, Congress leaders hope to make political capital out of the Kashmir experiment in the times to come. "With this move we have shown that we are the only truly national alternative to the National Democratic Alliance government. We have proved that we believe in carrying all sections of people along," said Vora.

One thing, however, goes without saying. The Congress (I)'s decision to accommodate the PDP has evoked a general sigh of relief in the State and an unmistakable feeling of euphoria. There is hope in the air that things will change for the better in this trouble-torn region. "Inshah allah, better days seem to be lying ahead. We are looking forward to those good old days when film shooting can once again become the order of the day in our beautiful valley," said a senior State official.

Indeed, a look at the common minimum programme (CMP) arrived at by the two parties, shows that their hope is not misplaced, provided the promises are fulfilled. For example, the CMP has given top priority to "restore the rule of law" in order to complete the political process, which was initiated by the holding of elections, and persuade the Centre to hold unconditional talks with the members of legislatures and "other segments of public opinion in all the three regions of the State, to evolve a broad consensus on restoration of peace with honour in the State." It goes without saying that "peace with honour" is the crying need in the State. Only after peace is restored can the process of healing the psychological, emotional and physical wounds of the past 14 years of militancy begin.

Rightly enough, the CMP lists as its second priority, "ensuring safety of lives and properties, restoring dignity and honour of all persons" along with full cooperation with the Government of India to contain and combat cross-border terrorism originating from Pakistan. If the coalition government manages to achieve just these two objectives, the rest of the 31 promises in the eight-page CMP become natural corollaries because containing corruption, stopping misuse and overuse of coercive laws, protection of human rights and providing relief and rehabilitation, can only be thought of once there is peace, security and safety. Other points regarding development, creation of job opportunities, special assistance to women who have suffered the most due to militancy, a transparent and fair administration with the right checks and balances, all spell hope, but can only follow if the first two are achieved. The biggest immediate relief to the people of the State, however, will come if the promise of the reorientation of the much-maligned Special Operations Group and the decision not to implement the provisions of the Prevention of Terrorism Act in the State are realised. The SOG, the CMP promises, will be amalgamated with the State police and given a human face, an idea that has been welcomed . Similarly, there was unanimity that enough laws existed to tackle terrorism and that POTA was not required for that purpose. The promise of its non-implementation has been welcomed.

There is optimism in the Congress (I) too that the rotational arrangement, unlike a quasi-similar arrangement that was in place in Uttar Pradesh, would become a success and set a new political trend. As they say, well begun is half done. If the CMP is anything to go by, then good days are ahead for the people of Jammu and Kashmir. Although the Congress (I) may have suffered a setback in losing the chief ministerial post, it has earned people's goodwill, not only in the State but all over India. This could pay rich dividends for the party in the long term.

## No Escape

The All Parties Hurriyat Conference {APHC) leader Syed Ali Shah Geelani should be out of the Ranchi jail. And then, his real problems would begin.

Geelani's dilemma is emblematic of the problems confronting secessionist forces within and outside the APHC today. The State government's decision not to use the Prevention of Terrorism Act means that money-laundering charges against him are unlikely to be pursued. His colleague in the APHC, the Jammu Kashmir Liberation Front's (JKLF) Yasin Malik, is also likely to head back to Srinagar. Both will owe their freedom to Chief Minister Mufti Mohammad Sayeed. Should they accept his regime, however, they will be preparing the ground for the euthanisation of their own political careers.

Sayeed's campaign tapped much of the political space that the APHC has for long had command of. In many areas the People's Democratic Party (PDP) used cadre drawn from the ranks of APHC constituents like the Jamaat-e-Islami. Many ground-level PDP workers make no secret of the fact that they see the formation of this government as one small step in a larger struggle for "liberation from India". All of this should make the APHC happy. Its problem, however, is that the rise of the PDP leaves it with no real agenda. It has, therefore, extended a cautious welcome to the major elements of the PDP-Congress(I) alliance's Common Minimum Programme, and at once insisted that the formation of a government will not address what they describe as the "real problem" of Jammu and Kashmir.

Nonetheless, the APHC is aware that doing nothing is a recipe for irrelevance. On what it ought to be doing, however, the formation is less clear. APHC chairperson Abdul Gani Bhat spent his time in New Delhi even as the Congress(I)-PDP dialogue was on, seeking a dialogue with the Pakistan High Commission on the post-election situation. As only the Deputy High Commissioner was available, no discussions could take place. Mirwaiz Umar Farooq, for his part, threw his weight behind the Ram Jethmalani-led Kashmir Committee's plans to hold a dialogue with "certain elements" in Pakistan after a Prime Minister took office in that country. Farooq argued that such a dialogue would be a step towards the realisation of the APHC's long-standing demand for a dialogue with Kashmiri leaders on the other side of the Line of Control.

But not all those within the APHC stand to gain from hitching their horses to the Kashmir Committee. The Kashmir Committee announced its plans on October 28, after holding discussions with Bhat. Five days earlier, however, the JKLF rejected the idea. The Kashmir Committee, a spokesperson said, had no right to speak for the people of Jammu and Kashmir. In 1998, he pointed out, the organisation had even attacked the then-Pakistan Foreign Secretary Samshad Haider for arrogating that right to himself in the course of India-Pakistan talks. Underlying this point of principle is a pragmatic political concern. Malik and Geelani, since they have been in jail, have had no role in the Committee. Neither is keen to see a platform that is perceived as being close to Bhat and Farooq take the initiative in a dialogue that would exclude them.

Yasin Malik, meanwhile, has other problems to deal with. On October 31, JKLF cadre led by a dissident, Iqbal Gandroo, expelled him, and his second-in-command Javed Mir, from the organisation. Gandroo, who now claims to be the head of the JKLF, has allied himself with breakaway elements of the APHC, led by Nisar Ahmad Sabzwari. Speaking to journalists on November 1, Sabzwari said he represented upwards of 12 political and armed organisations including top formations such as the Jaish-e-Mohammad, the Lashkar-e-Toiba and al-Jihad. His dialogue partners in these groups, Sabzwari claimed, were ethnic-Kashmiri cadre who now wished to chart their own political destiny. The new "parallel Hurriyat", he said, would take Sayeed's words at face value, and was willing to start negotiations with the new government. "The time for the gun is now over," he said, "and we must achieve liberation through dialogue."

No one is certain how credible the group's claims are, but the fact is that there has been a good amount of subterranean movement within terrorist groups. While organisations like the Lashkar, the Jaish and al-Umar were quick to condemn the PDF as a puppet government, the Hizbul Mujahideen took time to do so. Some observers believe that was because many of its local commanders have been supporting the PDF, hoping to have a say in any fuiure dialogue with New Delhi.

Abdul Rashid Fir, the Hizb's central division commander who operates under the alias Shardar Fir, is believed, correctly or otherwise, to have had close contact with senior PDF figures in the course of their election campaign. Fir is thought to have acted on behalf of Amir Khan, who is now a member of the Hizb's Muzaffarabad-based Central Command Council.

Whatever the truth about the Hizbul Mujahideen's relationship with the PDP might be — on record both formations deny that anything of the land exists — it has provoked a minor rebellion among hardline figures in the terrorist group. On October 21, its Lolab area commander, who operates under the name Muneeb-ul-Islam, left the organisation to join the more directly Pakistan-controlled Jamaat-ul-Mujahideen. Muneeb-ul-Islam complained that the Jamaat-e-Islami's Amir (supreme leader) Ghulam Hassan Rhat did not consider the armed struggle to be a *jehad*. He added that although Hizbul Mujahideen leader Mohammad Yousuf Shah considered it to be a jehad he did nothing to punish deserters or meet "the Mujahideen's war needs." The fact that the Lolab terrorist made public his dissent suggests he had at least tacit support from Pakistan's intelligence establishment.

Mufti Mohammad Sayeed is sitting pretty for the moment. By taking a soft line on secessionist organisations, he can consolidate his hold over his constituency, and keep lines of communication open to armed groups as well. As long as the APHC sticks to its rejection of the mainstream democratic process, it does not threaten the PDF in any manner. The real problem will emerge if the organisarion is ever engaged in a dialogue with New Delhi — or if any of its elements chose to join in electoral contest. Today's unquiet allies could well then be transformed into bitter enemies.

PART — IV

# Acid Test

## Chapter 12

# ISS Study Team Report

The Institute of Social Sciences (ISS) conducted a study of the four-phase Assembly elections in the State of Jammu and Kashmir (September 16, 24 and October 1, 8, 2002).

While the detailed analyses of the poll process and the voting behaviour are awaited, the study team has come up with certain conclusions. The 47-member study team comprised social scientists, journalists, civil rights activists and concerned citizens besides the ISS faculty members and researchers. The study covers all the 14 districts. Our team visited 65 of the 87 constituencies and oversaw the voting in about 450 polling stations. The 47 individual reports and the group reports by various teams have been analysed to come to the following conclusions.

## Why the J&K Elections Study?

The Institute aims to study contemporary social, political and economic issues, with an interdisciplinary perspective. It is engaged in study and research on socially relevant issues, participatory governance and grassroots democracy. We make our research findings and recommendations available to government bothes, policy-makers, social scientists and other national and international agencies so as to sharpen and widen their options for action. The Institute monitors public policy and engages itself in consistent advocacy. Since its inception in 1985, the Institute has sought to bring to the centre-stage the issues to participatory local government, people-centric development, women's political empowerment and democratic decentralisation.

Since participatory democracy and governance, particularly at the local level, constitute the core of our research and advocacy, the ISS took up this election study in Jammu and Kashmir. For one, the Institute has undertaken several election stuthes in the past. In fact, two of our first election stuthes were titled 'Voting Behaviour in Punjab Elections 1985' and 'Voting Behaviour in Assam Elections 1985'. For another, the Institute has undertaken a number of research projects on Jammu and Kashmir. While several of our projects and publications have focussed on the Panchayati Raj system'and decentralised governance, we have just completed a volume, *State Development Report on and Kashmir* 2002, commissioned by the Planning Commission. The State of Jammu and Kashmir is deficient in data on human resource development. Our study has sought to fill that gap. In the next six months, the ISS has definite plans to organise conventions of Panchyati Raj representatives in Jammu, Srinagar and Leh.

There is another reason for undertaking the present study. The 2002 Assembly elections in the State of Jammu and Kashmir are seen as landmark elections. Elections have been held under the shadow of the gun. The outcome of the poll is likely to have a bearing, on the Central and State governments, separatist groups like Hurriyat, as also on the global war against terrorism. Prolonged periods of violence and their tragic aftermath have tended to cloud the reality existing on the ground. A study such as this can provide useful information, which is vital for peace and normalcy in the State.

## Methodology

Since the elections were staggered over nearly a month in four phases, with wide gaps between the phases, the Institute decided to send four teams to study and observe the elections. The mandate was to cover the maximum number of constituencies.

The team members reached the respective areas two days ahead of the day of polling and spent two days after the poll, in the constituencies. This was intended to familiarise them with the polling stations, constituency profiles, voting trends, issues involved and the situation on the ground besides observing the conduct of the poll. They were in touch with representatives of political parties and candidates, election officials, civil rights groups, community leaders, and Army and police officials as well as ordinary citizens.

On the last day, the campaigning was often on its feverish pitch. Our team observed a few election meetings and campaign rallies, which gave them an idea about the mood of the electorate, security arrangements and, the preparedness of the State machinery to deal with any contingency. The Institute had written to the Election Commission about the visit of our study team and the EC had sent letters to the State election authorities to facilitate the visit of our team members to the respective constituencies. The Institute team had little difficulty in getting access to the polling stations and the members could talk freely to election officials, candidates, their agents, police and security officials, and voters. They encountered no hostility from any quartet. On the contrary, people were quite forthcoming. Extensive briefings and debriefings were organised at the Institute where all the team members and Institute faculty participated.

## What Did the Team Observe?

The Institute team followed the following parameters to study the conduct of the poll:

- Level and intensity of violence/clashes before, during and after the polls.
- Use/misuse of three Ms—Money, Muscle and Machinery—to influence the outcome.
- Level of intimidation of voters/candidates by security forces, militant groups or representatives/supporters of rival political organisations.
- Percentages of voters' turnout and coercion to vote.
- Impersonation/tampering of votes, security lapses.
- Role of security forces vis-a-vis voters.
- Voters' age groups.
- Turnout of women.
- Functioning of the Election officials/EC.

*The following are the findings of the ISS Study Team:*

## Elections Fair but Not Necessarily Free

The elections in Jammu and Kashmir, which were held in four phases, were fair. But they were not necessarily free, particularly for those who have seen and lived with violence for the last 12 years. After all, the State is far from normal. It is in this context that today Kashmir of the Sufis is a figment of imagination. For the people of Kashmir life has been and is a fight against terror. It did not change during the elections; in fact, it only worsened.

The militants had threatened to disrupt the polls forcing the government to deploy the largest-ever security forces to help in the conduct of the polls. The militants did not remain content with their threats. They organised a series of attacks against political parties contesting the polls, security forces and the ordinary voters using all kinds of weapons and incendiary materials. On the penultimate day of the second phase of the polling a total of 45 violent incidents were reported, triggered by the militants. They even succeeded in killing a Minister of the J&K Government. Even on the eve of the third phase of the elections Jammu and Southern Kashmir districts witnessed greater incidents of violence. In all, 830 people were killed in the State since the commencement of the poll process. It is against this backdrop that we describe the elections as being not free for the people.

## Low Polling

There is no disputing that many constituencies in the Valley recorded low polling. In Srinagar, there were some booths which recorded zero per cent voting. In most other booths in the city, the voting percentage was in single digits. This only proves the fairness of the election process. No attempt was made to jack up the polling percentage. It is a testimony of the impartiality of the election officials, who did not want the election process to be vitiated in any manner.

## Azadi, the War Cry

It may be stated here that the All-Parties Hurriyat Conference enjoys support in the Valley. Its call for a boycott of the poll and had considerable influence on the voters. But most of its supporters would not admit this in public. Instead, they would express their lack of faith in the election process. They would say that elections were not going to solve Kashmir's problems. For instance, in Anantnag, they gave several reasons for not voting: "Elections can never be free in Kashmir. No development has taken place in our area, so why should we vote? We want *azadi*, not election."

The majority of the Kashmiri people are in favour of *azadi*, but they are not very clear about the nature of the *azadi* they desire. To some, *azadi* is a cry for good politics and good governance, to others it is freedom from both India and Pakistan. The ideal solution of the Kashmiri people, they maintain, is *azadi*. However, when pressed, they broadly hint at maximum autonomy for Kashmir as a way out. They further point to the unfair means adopted in the past elections to buttress their point that elections could not be free and fair. But these opinions were expressed before and not after the polling. Those who boycotted the polls could be divided into those (a) who were intimidated into doing so; (b) those who were convinced that voting was useless; and (c) those who believed that *azadi* is the only option for Kashmir.

It will be wrong to say that all those who took part in the elections are against *azadi* and those who abstained from them are for *azadi*. The definition of *azadi* also varied from place to place and voter to voter, as mentioned above.

## Coercion by Security Forces

Coercion by the security forces is a complaint, members of the study team who visited the Valley frequently heard. In several places people complained that they were forced to vote by the security forces. In Sopore town our team reported that they landed in a big demonstration of people in the New Colony, face-to face with the gun-totting BSF, with armoured cars standing in position. People told them that at 3.00 pm on the voting day (September 16) the BSF had announced from the Mosque that only one hour was left and people should go to vote. It was reported to the team that when people did not vote, the security forces went door-to-door asking them to come out. "Some women showed us scratches on their shoulder, some men beating signs, one bleeding from teeth," said the report. Since nobody saw the security forces beating the people we have to leave these statements, as conveyed to us, entirely to the credibility of those who gave them.

At Kulangam in Kupwara district, we were told that the Army had announced that everyone would have to vote or face the consequences.

At one place in Desvar constituency in Anantnag district, our team met two groups of people. Both complained about coercive voting. While one group said they were voting due to coercion by the security forces, the other said that despite coercion, they would not vote.

It is difficult to rule out coercion entirely. There is the possibility of some overzealous security officials taking upon themselves the duty of reminding the voters about the need to take part in the polls or even herding them to the polling booths. These were isolated events and cannot be generalised. But in the overall situation in the State, such incidents could not have had much of an impact on the election process. In any case, coercion will be marginal to the outcome of the election.

However, in few other areas, the team was told that they had only heard about such incidents having occurred in nearby areas. The possibility that in some cases complaints of such nature may have been orchestrated for political purposes cannot be ruled out.

It is significant that even those who complained about coercion by the security forces were not frightened to speak freely and candidly in front of the security forces. Yet, the expression on their faces was not of fear. They appeared to be jubilant and enthusiastic about voting. It appeared that the voters were keen to vote but were afraid of the militants. To protect themselves from the militants, they needed to say that the security forces had forced them to vote. At Lingayat in the same district many people claimed they were "Voting under threat" but they came from far-flung areas just to vote. Since the voters in some areas were really afraid of the militants, it was convenient for them to use "coercion" by the security forces as a ruse to exercise their franchise. This way they could both vote and yet steer clear of the militants.

A significant point that needs to be taken note of is that even those who complained about the security forces coercing the voters to go to the polling booths did not make any complaint that the voters were forced to-vote for any particular candidate or party. In other words, once inside the polling booths, the voters were free to exercise their franchise in any manner they liked. Coercion, wherever it existed, ended outside the polling booth and not inside it.

Complaints were heard that some security officials used the public address system in mosques, etc, to exhort voters to exercise their democratic right. But there was no complaint of such announcements favouring any candidate or political party.

## Fear All-pervasive

Fear was all-pervasive. Nobody knew what would happen the next moment. In some areas, the militants had, through writings on the walls and posters, warned the voters against taking part in the elections. Under persistent questioning, a shopkeeper in Anantnag revealed that his decision to boycott was final and it had been prompted by the militants threats. He said posters of militant groups like the Al-Badr were seen in the town prohibiting people from voting.

## Nearer to the City, Farther from Polling Booth

But the large turnout of voters in some rural areas which have been identified as the hub of militancy disprove the point that it was fear alone that kept the voters at home on the polling day. In Srinagar, which was the most well protected area, the polling percentage was the lowest. This only proves the point that they did not vote out of their own volition. In fact, the impression that the team gained was that the farther the voter was from the city-centre, the likelier he was to vote. (Nearer to the city, farther from the polling booth like nearer to the church, farther from God.)

## Women Constables

In areas where heavy polling took place like, for instance, Badgam, the absence of adequate number of women constables created problems. There was only one woman constable per polling booth and they were unable to cope with the rush of women. Since Photo Identity Card was not a must for women voters and many of them came in *burqa,* cases of impersonation by women voters was rampant. Girls, some of them in their early teens, were found voting. In rural areas, women police were not present. The presence of women constables enthused women voters in taking part in the elections. Overall, there appeared to be a gender divide in voter turnout. Women's participation was a little higher where there was a woman candidate like Mehbooba Mufti or a strong CPM candidate in Kulgam like Yusuf Tarigami. It bears repeating that of all the 727 candidates, only 18 were women. And that a 71 year-old party like the National Conference has still not reserved seats for women.

## EVMs — a Mixed Bag

Electronic Voting Machines (EVMs) added novelty to the elections this time. Though some people expressed apprehensions that the EVMs might facilitate rigging, the voters were generally happy with the system. They found it quite convenient. Though the EVMs marginalise rigging and speed up the actual act of voting, some voters were simply baffled by the burtons in front of them. For this reason some voters asked for assistance from the polling staff and at other times the latter offered their help needlessly. Obviously, this is an area that requires attention. The voters had not received advance training on how to cast their votes. This resulted in longer queues in many booths and harassment to the voters. It also raised questions about the secrecy of the voting. In Bundialgam, a teacher told us that voters were being told to press the first button to start the machine. In doing so they automatically voted for the NC candidate whose name appeared first. In fact, it is the polling officer who presses the button to activate the EVM.

## Courage of the Voters

In many areas voters showed remarkable courage in defying the threat of the militants and taking part in the elections. Particularly admirable was the courage shown by the women voters, who turned out in large numbers in many constituencies. After all, the women of Kashmir are the worst victims of violence. It is they who have to look after the families when the breadwinner is killed by the militants or the security forces.

## No Communal Polarisation

A significant feature of the elections this time was the absence of communal appeal. The communal polarisation, typical of the J&K Assembly elections, witnessed in the past two decades—the predominantly Hindu Jammu region voting for the BJP and the predominantly Muslim Valley voting for the National Conference—seemed to have broken down in this election. Instead, the issues that concerned them were the growing rate of unemployment, lack of adequate infrastructure like roads and hospitals, restrictions imposed by security forces and absence of good governance rather than religious or caste slogans.

In the Jammu region, a matter of grave concern for the electorate was the so-called discrimination of the region by the State and Central governments. Except the National Conference, nearly all the parties complained of the "subjugation" of the Jammu region by Srinagar. Their usual arguments were: despite a large population and a larger electorate, Jammu had fewer seats (37) in the State Assembly than the Kashmir Valley (46 seats); only a small fraction of the Jammu people were employed in State Government services that were completely dominated by people from the Valley and only a small fraction of the total development funds meant for the State came to Jammu. In fact, some of them went to the extent of saying that if Srinagar was the colony of Delhi, then Jammu was the colony of Srinagar. Demands for separate Statehood for the Jammu region and trifurcation of the State were hotly debated in the polls. Campaigning in the Jammu .region was very similar to campaigning in the rest of the country. In any case, centralised rigging had never taken place in the region in the past.

## Good Candidates Matter

The presence of "good candidates" in the fray drew larger number of voters to the polling booths in the Valley. The Kangan constituency is a classic case of this phenomenon. The voters seemed quite happy with the performance of the National Conference candidate who was the Health Minister in the Farooq Abdullah Ministry. They were keen to vote for him, although they said they did not like his party at all. In Badgam where a Shia noble was a candidate, Shias in large numbers queued up from early in the morning to vote for their candidate.

## Presence of Observers a Helping Factor

The presence of observers/ diplomats/ ISS/ Press helped in the smooth conduct of the polls. They kept the polling officials more vigilant. The voters also saw their presence as a reassuring factor. In fact, in many booths they flocked around such teams to complain about police excesses or unfair means being employed by some candidates. The visiting teams had free access to the polling booths and they could see for themselves how the voting process, was going on. In retrospect, the government should have welcomed anybody and everybody to visit J&K to watch the elections. Such a stand would have only added lustre to the democratic process in the State.

## Deficiencies in Arrangements

There appeared to be some deficiencies in the conduct of the elections. These did not amount to rigging but to inadequacies and inconveniences that could put off voters. Lack of adequate infrastructure in the polling booths was a major complaint the polling officials made. There were many booths where there were no chairs for the polling officer and others assisting him.

The voters' Photo Identity Card was a problem area. Voters had many complaints about the card. Even if a person had a Photo Identity Card, it did not mean that he could exercise his vote. His name should be on the electoral roll as well. Many voters did not find their names in the voters' list. The voters' list had many drawbacks, which the Election Commission could not rectify in time. The electoral rolls had not been revised since 1989. But no detailed analysis of the impact of this could be made so quickly. However, it was pointed out that the electoral rolls used in the parliamentary elections in 1999 were used in these elections as well. A question was raised about the '"*gair hasti*" name being present in these parliamentary rolls, which are usually absent in the Assembly election rolls; this created problems for the voters.

In the ballot-paper system, the voters had the option of invalidating their votes. But the voters cannot invalidate their votes when they vote using an EVM. Some voters felt that the right not to vote is also a democratic right and the voters should not be deprived of this right in the name of EVM.

In some constituencies, there was need for more booths and electronic voting machines. The Election Commission could have thought of ways to do away with the system of applying the indelible ink on the voter's finger. Many voters did not vote as the mark would make them easy targets for militants. On the other hand, we have come across several people who proudly showed the ink mark to tell us that they had indeed voted. If anything, this shows that it is difficult to portray the situation in Jammu and Kashmir in pure black and white terms. There are many grey areas. This is true about J&K Elections, 2002 too. But this does not, however, detract from the fact that the polls were fair, the polling arrangements were elaborate and strong.

## Election Commission, the Victor

The Election Commission enjoyed a good image in the State. Even those who complained about rigging in the past elections mainly complained about the Central and State leaders than the Commission. The reputation of the Chief Election Commissioner, J. M. Lyngdoh, for honesty and integrity also helped in the process. The voters saw the Commission as an impartial entity. Particularly significant was the step taken by the Election Commission to confine the much-maligned Special Operations Group and the Special Task Force to the barracks.

Chapter 13

# Comments by Pak Press

## New Ground Reality

The elections in Indian-held Kashmir (IHK) have put paid to the Abdullah family. Thank God. While New Delhi claims 46 per cent turnout in the elections, independent observers, including India-based civil rights groups, have put the figure at under 40 per cent. But it is the message that Kashmiris have sent out to India and the world that is more important. They don't want the BJP's Kashmiri puppets to represent them — a snub to the Bhartiya Janata Party that supports the Abdullahs' National Conference. So a captive electorate has sent a clear signal of the ground realities. But does an increase in the fortunes of Sonia Gandhi's Congress mean the Kashmiri electorate has agreed to stay within India or become the rubber stamp of another New Delhi-centered party, as some analysts are wont to believe? We think not. Given the absence of the All Parties Hurriyat Conference and the average voter turnout, the choice was between the NC-BJP combine and the likely Peoples Democratic Party-Congress coalition. To that extent, the results are a no-confidence vote in the previous dispensation without necessarily a yes vote for the acceptance of the current status of the state itself....

*The Daily Times*

## The only way forward

The results of the recently concluded state polls in Jammu and Kashmir represent a serious setback for New Delhi.

Marred by violence and widespread accusations of rigging and voter intimidation, the elections brought to the fore the newly formed People's Democratic Party (PDF) which looks set to govern with the help of Congress and independents. The ruling National Conference and the BJP, meanwhile, were virtually ousted from the political arena. Significantly, National Conference president Omar Abdullah failed to win his seat despite being a federal minister and son of the incumbent chief minister, Farooq Abdullah... Unlike the hawkish National Conference and the BJP, the Congress and the PDP have urged peace talks with Pakistan to defuse the crisis. While New Delhi recently offered to talk to Kashmiri leaders about granting greater autonomy to the state, the umbrella All Parties Hurriyat Conference believes autonomy proposal is a mere ruse to prolong Indian occupation

***The Dawn***

## Shadow Play

The defeat of the National Conference (NC) in the Indian held Kashmir "elections" and the success of the Indian Congress, a few local parties and independents is no more than replacing one set of puppets by another. It will have no impact on the territory, as it will continue to be directly ruled by Delhi. However, a "government" was necessary to suggest that a democratic system was in operation like in other Indian states. It was a neat trick that totally misled the Americans who greatly praised the outcome of the polls. Even Pakistan was pressured by the US leaders to extend support to the "elections" without success.... A point that India has come to realise is that it cannot continue to follow its tough line of crushing the freedom struggle by force and needs to look for other means....

***The News***

PART — V

# Current Scene

## Chapter 14

# Terrorists on Prowl

The escalation of terrorist violence in J&K almost coinciding with the installation of a new government headed by President Pervez Musharraf's yes-man Mir Zafarullah Khan Jamali in Pakstan is a matter of grave concern. This has been heightened by the attacks on the famous Raghunath and Shiv temples in Jammu on November 24, obviously with the objective of sparking a communal conflict—the ulterior motive of the Pak authorities ever keen to destabilise and, if possible, dismember India. No doubt the Pakistani hand behind the spurt in such activities is too transparent to be ignored. And yet, as the Vice-President of the People's Democratic Party, Mehbooba Mufti, has explained in her recent conversation with BBC World's *Hardtalk* host Tim Sebastian :

"If you have a problem at home the neighbour is definitely going to take advantage of that but if you are able to keep your home intact, if you are able to address your problems at your home, the neighbour doesn't have much of a role to play there...

... If we don't have any combustible material inside, the other person—the neighbour—cannot ignite it. But until we don't address the internal problem, the role of Pakistan will go on increasing."

That is the crux of the matter. The internal problem of Kashmir must be addressed. The alienation of the people must be removed. Just when the Mufti Mohammad Sayeed Government has embarked upon that very task, the Pakistan-backed Lashkar-e-Taiba militants, marginalised in the wake of the popular goodwill towards the ruling Congress-PDP alliance, have struck with a vengeance. And playing crass politics the BJP-led NDA Government at the Centre has also sought to weaken and derail the Mufti Ministry's peace efforts by raising all kinds of questions regarding the specific steps taken by the current administration to provide the healing touch in Kashmir—particularly the release of several militants which was carried out in good faith, and after consultation with the Central intelligence agencies, by Mufti Sayeed.

It is a complex process. While the terrorists have to be tackled with a stern hand this should not lead to renewed popular alienation as a consequence of the security forces' high-handed measures affecting the public at large. In fact there is no option for the authorities, both at the State level and the Centre, to bring about an early end to that sense of alienation among the public. That is precisely what the Mufti Sayeed Government is doing. And at this stage it is most unfortunate, as Mehbooba has alleged, "certain parties" in the NDA "are trying to make Kashmir a battlefield to win the Gujarat elections". Hence the Deputy PM's public criticism of the J&K Chief Minister of being soft towards the terrorists.

It is necessary for the Government of India to understand the imperatives of bringing back peace and normalcy in the trouble-torn State. Politics should not be allowed to get priority over the national task of waging a joint struggle against terrorism through military as well as political means while straining every nerve to win back the hearts and minds of the Kashmiri populace.

## Assault on Jammu Temples

The Fidayeen Militant attacks on two places of worship recently in Jammu — the famed Raghunath temple, which had suffered a similar assault earlier this year, and another shrine nearby — condemnable as they are in the strongest of terms, for their barbarism and heinousness, are clearly a part of the foreign-backed subversive elements' sinister design to damage the credibility of the new Mufti Mohammed Sayeed-headed coalition Government in Jammu and Kashmir. In fact, their 'campaign' in the form of escalated violence had started a few days earlier — to be precise, on the day after the first sitting of the new Assembly — when suspected Lashkar-e-Taiba cadres broke into a CRPF camp in Srinagar, and there has been no let up since then. What marks out the latest Jammu episodes from the other major attacks — and therefore makes them all the more reprehensible — is that their chosen targets are temples and the devotees visiting them, not security personnel or other symbols of governmental authority. But then, picking on places of worship, which by their very nature qualify as 'soft targets', has been a preferred strategy particularly of the jehadi terrorist groups in recent times because of its potential to trigger a communal backlash and thereby serve their diabolical ends, and this trend would seem to have been reinforced by the sort of aggressive majoritarian thrust (typified by the Muslims-targeted post-Godhra pogrom in Gujarat) that contributed to the vitiation of the communal milieu in general.

Disturbing as the recent spurt in militant activity certainly is, it is imperative that the Government should spare no effort in heightening the vigil and beefing up the security system, both its operational and intelligence gathering components. In this, the State administration undoubtedly needs unstinting cooperation and critical support from the Centre in every respect. On the wider political and administrative planes, the Mufti Mohammad Sayeed regime has, in a manner truly reflective of its sensitivity to the innate feelings of Kashmiris, come up with some commendable initiatives in the few weeks it has been in office. For instance, the release of political prisoners who had been in prolonged detention for no valid reason, the decision to 'assimilate' the discredited Special Operations Group into the regular police force and the move to rehabilitate the families of the victims of militancy, not to speak of the Bill seeking to set up an institutional mechanism to ensure the "accountability" of public functionaries from the Chief Minister downwards. Add to these, the new Government's democratic legitimacy acquired through an universally acclaimed and transparent electoral process and also its commitment to strive for an inclusive 'dialogue' aimed at finding a political solution to the Kashmir imbroglio, the 'compulsions' of the terrorist elements to frustrate its purposeful endeavour and undermine its credibility should be apparent.

At the operational level, the coalition regime has taken a conscious decision not to invoke the inherently oppressive POTA and it is perfectly in keeping with the Government's declared core policy line of healing the "physical, psychological and emotional wounds inflicted (on the people of Jammu and Kashmir) by 14 years of militancy". However, the ruling political establishment's detractors, especially the BJP and its ally (and erstwhile ruling party of the State), the National Conference, have always been highly critical of such a course, contending that not using POTA and setting free the detained secessionist leaders and militants will together constitute an open invitation to heightened insurgency. Given this context, these political parties may well be tempted to see the spurt in militant attacks as a vindication of their position and adopt an 'I-told-you-so' attitude — this is indeed discernible in the way some of the leaders have reacted to the Raghunath temple episode. But any formulation that seeks, in the name of facing the challenge of militancy more effectively, to reverse the Mufti Mohammad Sayeed

Government's wholesome initiatives on the human rights front will be short-sighted, the ultimate objective of ending the pervasive alienation of the Kashmiris is getting lost. Above all, it will also amount to playing into the hands of the subversive elements.

## Escalation of Terrorism

The sudden escalation of terrorist violence in J&K recently especially the assault on the historic Raghunath temple in Jammu, is a bloody reminder that the merchants of death are determined to ply their trade to win the communal-political goal of detaching the Kashmir Valley from India. There is no question that the state and civil society must summon every resource to defeat the terrorist challenge. These are the first terror strikes since the people of Kashmir surprised the world by casting their ballots for peace in a blood-soaked election. The people's verdict, and their aspiration for a normal life, clearly have no meaning for the murderous foreign gangs and their mentors and political abettors.

This is a clear lesson for the Mufti Mohammad Sayeed government as well as the Centre. All-concerned need to understand that the terrorists have gone into top gear precisely because they are afraid that the steps being taken by the state government are proving to be reasonably popular in predominantly Muslim Kashmir. In the event, hitting at temples, blowing up a bus-load of passengers in the Hindu-dominated Jammu area, and targeting CRPF personnel and their families, constitute a bid by the Pakistan-inspired mercenaries to exacerbate communal tension in the hope of re-establishing ideological sway in the Valley. Their message to Kashmiri Muslims is that their lives are not safe, no matter who is in power.

Terrorist designs can only be defeated if the state and the Centre treat the fight against this menace, as well as for peace and dignity in the bruised state, as a common cause. Unfortunately, we have only seen a lot of finger-pointing. The observation of Union Minister of State for Home I.D. Swami that the "healing touch" of the state government has started showing its adverse effects, was uncalled for. It suggests that .the Centre is against the peace-oriented programme of the state government. The BJP and its allies need to appreciate that laws like POTA did not stop terrorist attacks during the earlier National Conference regime in J&K. The chief minister, too, needs to consult the Centre on refurbishing the internal security mechanism in the state if his government's common minimum programme is to attract greater all-round support.

## Trail of Terror

Since 1957, eight state assembly elections were held in Jammu and Kashmir with power being shared between the National Conference and Congress.

In the **1953-1975** period, Sheikh Abdullah was in and and out of prison and his political platform was the Plebiscite Front headed by his friend Mirza Afzal Beg.

**1975:** Beg-Parthasarthy accord led to the political rehabilitation of Sheikh Abdullah after nearly two decades.

**1977:** Widely regarded as J&K's first free and fair poll under Janata regime. Largest voter turnout. Sheikh Abdullah swept to power.

**1983:** NC won 46 seats, Cong 26. CM Farooq Abdullah dismissed the following year and GM Shah sworn in. State came under President's Rule in March 1986.

**1987:** The election that is said to have catalysed the insurgency. A Farooq-Rajiv Gandhi alliance preceded an allegedly rigged poll. 'Losers' included Syed Salahuddin, and many constituents of present-day Hurriyat.

**1990:** Hizbul Mujahideen came into being. Amidst rising insurgency, Farooq resigned, Central rule imposed.

**1993-1995:** The birth of *jehadi* forces like Lashkar-e-Taiba and Harkat-ul-Ansar.

**1996:** Insurgency contained somewhat and elections held in which NC won 57 seats, Farooq returned as CM.

**1996-2002:** After a short lull, *jehadi* groups got more brazen. IA plane hijacked from Kathmandu, leading to the release of Masood Azhar who started the Jaish-e-Mohammed. Kargil war in 1999, followed by suicide attacks on Red Fort, 2001 attacks on Kashmir assembly, and National Parliament, 2002 attacks on temples in Jammu.

## Chapter 15

# Countering Terrorism

No one knows just what implications the rise of Mufti Mohammad Sayeed might have for the future of counter-terrorist operations in Jammu and Kashmir. The Army, for one, does not want to take any chances. A confidential paper prepared by Northern Command headquarters in Udhampur has called for drastic changes in the structure of command. If the ideas are implemented, the Army would have direct command of not only of counter-terrorist operations, but also influence key processes of civilian governance in the State.

In April, sources told the media, that Army Headquarters in New Delhi circulated a document called "J&K Strategy for Resolution of Internal Conflict". The Northern Army Commander, Lieutenant-General R.K. Nanavaty, was charged with fleshing out the document, and providing a structure in which the Army would acquire what it describes as a "lead role" in the management of the low-intensity war in Jammu and Kashmir. Gen. Nanavaty's recommendations have been circulated among the Central bureaucracy and Intelligence community, and Sayeed himself is to be briefed on the issue in the coming weeks.

Gen. Nanavaty has recommended that overall control of all counter-terrorist operations in Jammu and Kashmir be handed over to a new Action Group in the Ministry of Home Affairs. Within Jammu and Kashmir, command would rest with the State Security Council, chaired by the Chief Minister. All its constituents would have representation in three subordinate bodies, the State Internal Development Office, chaired by the Chief Secretary; the Public Information Office, chaired by an officer on special duty; and the State Internal Review Committee, chaired by the Intelligence Bureau. Actual control of operations would lie with a Regional Operations and Intelligence Coordination Committee, chaired by the commanders of each Corps in Jammu and Kashmir, which would have an intelligence sub-comrnittee chaired by the Corps-level officers.

Annexure 4 of Gen. Nanavaty's paper gives the Army "primacy... for the conduct of counter terrorist operations in (the) State." It calls for "all central SF (security forces) specifically allotted to the State for counter terrorist operations" to be placed "at the disposal of Northern Command." "PMF (Paramilitary Forces) and CPO (Central Police Organisation) — sector, unit and sub-unit down to company level (or equivalent)", the document continues, will be "at the disposal of Army formation HQ and/or unit as applicable. " Northern Command would have overall responsibility to "deploy, employ and task all such forces." The paper asks planners to, "wherever feasible, ensure co-location of military, civilian and police HQ and coordination of boundaries."

Northern Command has clear ideas on the kinds of civilian initiative needed to hold the ground. It suggests that the Army be given direct control of developmental work and administration of special border areas, starting with Kanzalwan, Tangdhar, Uri, Poonch and Rajouri. It calls for "strict control" of Gujjar and Bakkarwal settlements in the "non-traditional areas" like the Hindu-dominated areas of Jammu — a long-standing demand of 16 Corps. It asks that migrant communities, which provide shelter to terrorists at altitude, be denied access to Ladakh. Finally, the paper calls for a one-time payment of Rs. 5 lakhs compensation to surrendered terrorists, to be released after a five-year "good behaviour" lock-in period.

The objectives of the set-up would be much the same as they were for the old. Gen. Nanavaty's paper calls for "effective military domination of the Line of Control and (the) IB (International Border)", which would "deny any encroachment, intrusion, infiltration and/or exfiltration." To this end, it demands the suppression of "all terrorist groups opposed to a peaceful resolution of conflict." This would be done by sharpening the divide between foreign and ethnic-Kashmiri terrorists, neutralising the terrorist leadership, eroding the groups' support base and over- ground infrastructure, and building public support through "people-friendly operations".

On just how all this is to be achieved, however, the Northern Command is vague. Paragraph 22 refers to the need for fare and direction-finding gear, night vision devices, surveillance radar and even non-lethal weapons. The rest of its strategy seems to depend on variables well outside the Army's control. The economic measures suggested to bring pressure on Pakistan include revoking the Most Favoured Nation-status that India has granted it, suspending the Indus Waters Treaty, and forcing "competitive defence spending". Not a great deal of thought seems to have gone into these proposals. It will be decades before India could, for example, build dams on the Indus that would give meaning to suspending its treaty. Nor is the volume of Pakistan's exports to India adequate to ensure that their loss would impose significant costs on that country. Instead, the paper focusses on external instruments to bring about the desired results. Paragraph 3 calls for India to work to "increase international (US: brackets as in the original) pressure to force Pakistan to stop proxy war and support for terrorism in J&K." It asks that India strengthen its "strategic partnership with the US with particular reference to (the) global war against terrorism." India's diplomatic establishment has been trying to achieve exactly this, with no evident success. The reason is well known. The US sees Pakistan as a key partner in securing its objectives in West Asia and Central Asia. It is simply not willing to sacrifice that more crucial objective because of Pakistan's well-documented role in encouraging terrorism in Jammu and Kashmir. The Army's proposals, then, rest on the a priori assumption that handing over control of operations would in itself improve efficiency. There is little introspection on why it has not been able to contain infiltration from Pakistan to any significant degree, or what institutional and structural reforms are needed to improve depth-area efficiency. The fact is that rigidly hierarchical command structures of the kinds that Central police organisations and the paramilitary forces are as mired in as the Army, are fundamentally unsuited to counter-terrorist work. This has been a long-standing problem in Jammu and Kashmir, and although most officials in private acknowledge that the problem exists, no initiative has been taken to address it. The best results have come where the multiple forces operative have achieved functional relationships at the grassroots level, a process that cannot be duplicated by the mindless application of new command system.

Nonetheless, the Gen. Nanavaty proposals have pointed to issues confronting the management of internal security. Many of the officers now commanding counter-terrorist operations have already cut their teeth in Punjab, and none is keen to experience the tragic wake of 1988 again. Then, the security establishment was forced to work outside the control of the ruling Shiromani Akali Dal government of Surjit Singh Barnala, which was a near-impossible task. The problem applies not only in the Army, but even the State police. No Director-General of Police since 1996, for example, has been free or post officers he believes are efficient even at relatively junior levels, and political interference has been rampant. The 15 Corps Commander, Lt. Gen. V.J. Patankar, made clear at a recent press conference his disquiet over the decision to wind down the Special Operations Group - another sign of political disregard for the concerns of security professionals.

Just how far the new proposals will go, of course, remains to be seen. Past efforts by the Army to take overall control of Central forces, and to have a say in administration, were scuppered by the bureaucracy. A problem has now been stated front-ally: and it is up to the politicians to find workable answers.

## Plight of the Pandits

Official mismanagement and lack of proper leadership deprive the displaced Kashmiri Pandit community in Delhi of a role in the recent election process in their home State. For most displaced Kashmiris, the recent Assembly elections in Jammu and Kashmir held little meaning. Their virtual non-participation in the process can be attributed to two factors. One, the shoddy administrative management when it comes to the affairs of displaced people in the country. Two, the extremist positions taken by Kashmiri Pandit groups, most of which speak the language of the extreme Right.

Administrative mismanagement was evident on August 27 when the Election Commission published an advertisement in national newspapers asking all unregistered Kashmiri migrants living in Jammu, Delhi and Udhampur to get their names included in the voters' list. The last date for the inclusion of names in the voters' list for elections that were to take place in Srinagar and Badgam was the day the advertisement was published.

The result, as one Kashmiri Pandit organisation, Kashmir Samiti, claimed, was the exclusion from the election process of up to 50,000 Kashmiris living in Delhi. The numerical correctness of the claim put forward by the Samiti remains doubtful. The organisation's president Sunil Shakdher said that the figure was only an estimate.

The majority of Kashmiri Pandits in Delhi could not get themselves enrolled on the dates designated for them. One such person, Rakesh Razdan, said: "There are 40 people in my family whose names do not figure in the electoral rolls. We come under the Habbakadal constituency. 1 read the newspaper advertisement on the morning of August 27 and rushed to Kashmir House around afternoon. After a long wait I got a registration form but I found that the registration involved formalities like getting the signatures of two gazetted officers. I had two hours to complete these. It was an impossible task, so I came back home. I did not vote."

Manoj Kumar, who unsuccessfully tried to get 18 families as also himself registered, said: "I received a phone call from the Sub Divisional Magistrate a few days before the last date. He said that a survey would be taken up of Kashmiri people in Delhi who were unregistered. We identified the unregistered voters around the area I live. But the time was too limited. I did go to J&K House but could not get anything done."

The Election Commission, however, defended its action. The Secretary to the Resident Commissioner in Delhi, M.H. Malik, said: "Before the last date, we visited Kashmiri camps to explain to the people the process of inclusion of their names in the electoral rolls. A system is in place." Malik admitted that the advertisement in the print media came late but said that prior to that the government had been advertising on radio and television.

The Election Commission also has its limitations. For one, it finds access to the displaced people difficult. While some of the displaced people live together in camps or settlements, the majority are dispersed across India.

In Delhi, only 237 families live in the 14 camps. Together they account for some 40,000 people. According to the E.C., in all there are one lakh displaced Kashmiri people in Delhi. Said Malik: "We reached out to the people in the camps and gave them application forms. For the rest, we used the mass media. Most of them do not seem to be interested in the election process."

Before elections most Pandit organisations did not assist the E.C. in its administrative functions. Worse, they adopted a confrontationist attitude, thereby making it difficult for the state to help them. What complicated the situation was that the Pandits are not a cohesive lot. There are several Kashmiri Pandit organisations and they speak in many voices. Each claims to represent the real Kashmiris. Some of these groups even held meetings with top state functionaries to express their dissatisfaction with the electoral process. On September 1, members of the Kashmir Samiti met President A.P.J. Abdul Kalam, complained that the "elections were a meaningless exercise" and demanded two constituencies in exile.

On September 2, another organisation, called Panun Kashmir, known for its rightist leanings, met the President to say that the Pandits would boycott the elections as elections would not address their problems. Panun Kashmir leaders charged the E.C. with "hoodwinking" the country on the issue of the Jammu and Kashmir elections. Its leaders apprised Kalam about their "neglect" by successive governments. They told the President of the need for the displaced community to make a "permanent return to the Valley". Both these organisations lambasted the E.C. for its decision on Gujarat.

They charged that the E.C. had shown double standards in the discharge of its duties, for it had postponed elections in Gujarat because 16,000 people were displaced whereas it held polls in Jammu and Kashmir despite an entire community of over 3.5 lakh Kashmiri Pandits remaining displaced. The argument, however, fails to take the broader aspects that were taken into account by the E.C. before declaring elections in the States.

Now, the Kashmiri Pandit organisations have unabashedly hitched on to the Shiv Sena bandwagon. They remain grateful to Sena chief Bal Thackeray for helping the community out. While in power, the Shiv Sena had instituted quotas for Kashmiri Pandits in colleges in Maharashtra. Kashmiri Pandit organisations in Delhi are particularly sore about the Bharatiya Janata Party not doing anything to revive the registration process for migrant identity cards.

The Centre had stopped registering displaced Kashmiris who reached Delhi after October 1992 in order to discourage further migrations from Kashmir. In March 2002, Kashmiri Pandit organisations approached the National Democratic Alliance (NDA) government confident that the right-wing government would get them their migration cards. The Kashmir Samiti had approached the government with a request for reopening registration procedures for Kashmiris who migrated after 1991. It wanted the migration cards to be issued to the displaced so that they could apply for admission in educational institutions and gain access to employment and cash assistance schemes. Their demand was not met. A letter written by Home Minister L.K. Advani to Defence Minister George Fernandes on March 28 stated that there is "no *prima facie* reason for reopening registration in Delhi for the Kashmiri migrants".

The Kashmiri Pandits continue to lambast the Muslim 'other'. "The candidates who stood in Kashmir were only bothered about the Muslim population of the constituency," said Avtar Krishan Kaul, President of another Kashmiri Pandit organisation called J&K Migrants' Camp. Kaul, who runs a photocopying shop in Delhi, misses no opportunity to blame Kashmiri Muslims for his displaced status. It is this mindset which feeds on the bitterness of the displaced and makes them see planned strategies by Muslims to wipe out Pandits. It stops them from taking help from the right channels and participating in democratic exercises. Amidst all this, the more important issue of identifying the genuine problems of the displaced community has been relegated to the background.

## India's Palestinians

'Palestinians' has collectively become a byword for persons hounded out of their homes and surviving as refugees in their own country. From the time of the implemention of the Balfour Declaration in 1948 and establishment of Israel as a Jewish homeland on what was earlier Palestine, the Palestinians have had varied images. Sometimes they were marked down as terrorists who staged daring hijacking of Western and Israeli civilian aircraft or killed and maimed Israelis whenever an opportunity arose. The skyjacking of a Libyan aircraft that ended in the spectacular Entebbe rescue operation and the massacre of Israeli sportspersons at the Munich Olympiad stand out in that connection. Despite their desperate efforts, the Palestinians have remained victims of eviction from homes and denial of repatriation. Deprivation has become their middle name.

Backed by the resources and organisation of international Jewry, there had been organised immigration into what was Palestine of Jews from the former Soviet Union and Eastern Europe—as also the victims of the 1930s Nazi persecution dispersed in different countries. Sizeable numbers of them were smuggled in violation of the administration. In the process, the Palestinians were uprooted and driven out, offsetting any satisfaction that the Jews had found a home.

It was in 1989-90 when Mufti Mohammad Sayeed was the Union Home Minister and his nominee Jagmohan was the Governor of Jammu and Kashmir that the Pandits from the Valley were hounded out of their homes. First targeted for attacks and killings, men, women and children had to flee what had been their home for centuries. It was said the essence of *Kashmiriyat* or the Kashmiri way of life was that Muslims and Hindus would live in harmony. It was Sufi-based eclectic Islam distinct from what obtained in the rest of India and Pakistan. In pursuance of the repudiation of *Kashmiriyat* there were heinous crimes attributed to the Hizbul Mujahideen. They included the assassination of Mirwaiz Maulvi Mohammed Farooq (1992), the burning down of the Muslim shrine of Charar-e-Sharif (1995) and the slaughter of 23 Kashmiri Pandits, including nine women and four children (1998). The security forces, particularly the much-maligned Border Security Force (BSF), were conveniently blamed for them. The cruellest irony was Maulvi Farooq, the present Mirwaiz, supping with the assassins of his father. He had been the President of the 'secular' All-Parties Hurriyat Conference, which included the Jamaat-i-Islami also.

The former Mirwaiz and his uncle Mirwaiz Yusuf were bitter enemies of Sheikh Mohammed Abdullah. Mirwaiz Yusuf was the leader of the Muslim Conference pitted against the National Conference. He had fled to Pakistan after the accession of Jammu and Kashmir to India. Presumably the atrocities against the Pandits were meant to test the depth of Maulvi Farooq's commitment to Pakistan; to see how far he would go in repudiating *Kashmiriyat*. Equally probable was the claim that they were the work of Pakistani and other mercenaries to widen the wedge between the Kashmir Liberation Front, agitating for autonomy, and the pro-Pakistan insurgents. Soon after, there were clashes between locals and foreigners within the Hizbul which led to the formation of Al-Badr.

In this context, it is necessary to distinguish between Pandits, who had collaborated with the Dogra rulers against the National Conference, and the present-day "the nowhere people"—the apt expression for 'internally displaced persons' in a recent publication edited by Siby Tharakhan and published in Bangalore.

The Pandits of the Dogra period had a vested interest in keeping intact the autocratic rule of the Maharaja because they had the lion's share of benefits from the regime. Ramachandra Kak, the last Pandit Dewan of the Maharaja—replaced by Gopalaswami Ayyangar as the Dogra dynasty came to an end-personified that attitude. Nikhil Chakravartty , in a series of articles published in *Mainstream* in September 1967, had given a graphic account of religion-based discrimination practised by the Dogra ruler. Plum posts in the administration and a disproportionate share of educational opportunities went to the Pandits at the cost of the majority Muslims. Incidentally, Makhanlal Fotedar was one of the leaders of a black flag demonstration staged against Nehru's visit to the State in 1946.

Later, Fotedar was Indira Gandhi's pointsman in her dealings with Jammu and Kashmir and played a key role in the dismissal of the Farooq Government by her in 1984. He was also close to Rajiv Gandhi, even if as an errand man. B.K. Nehru vividly describes in his memoirs Fotedar's role in souring the Centre's relations with Jammu and Kashmir. Mufti Mohammad Sayeed as the chief of the State Congress Committee was a collaborator in the anti-Farooq manoeuvre.

There is no agreement on the number of Pandits housed in refugee camps in Jammu and Delhi. The Pandits put it at as high as over 300,000 while the Kashmir Government would say they were about 200,000 . Whatever their number, they represent the suffering humanity whose plight was no fault of theirs. When Saifuddin Soz was a Minister in the United Front Government I asked when the Pandits would be able to go back to their homes. He was then in the National Conference. He promised that they would be rehabilitated in the Valley and compensated. It did not happen under the Farooq Government.

During a visit to north Kashmir in 1995, I saw the properties abandoned by the Pandits taken over by Muslims. It was the same story in Kupwara, Baramulla and also Srinagar city. The new owners were not willing to vacate the houses. Nor was the situation conducive to the Pandits living in peace and security if they returned. The terrorists had dealt a deathblow to Kashmiriyat.

The Pandits boycotted to a man the recent Assembly elections. Fewer votes were cast in the special polling booths set up for them in Udhampur, Jammu and Delhi. Analysts ignored the development even while they dilated on the poor turnout in parts of the Valley on account of the Hurriyat's poll-boycott call. The Pandits' protest was not under the fear of gun or on the basis of a formal boycott campaign. It was spontaneous and universal.

The common minimum programme of the People's Democratic Party (PDF) and the Congress, to be formed, has promised to ensure the return of the Pandits to their homes. It is also to establish a Minorities Commission for them—laudable moves. But one keeps one's fingers crossed until there is action on the ground.

Chapter 16

# By Way of Negotiations

Pakistan having disavowed the Simla agreement, has all along been harping on the UN resolutions for a solution to the Kashmir issue. Kuldip Nayar elaborates that the UN resolutions on Kashmir gives only two options -- joining either Pakistan or India; there is no third provision.[1] He asserts that in fact, it will be difficult for Pakistan to comply even with the UN resolutions because it will have to vacate the territories under its control before the people's wishes in the State are ascertained. There are two more riders to the resolutions: One, the entire State must come under India's control and two, normalcy must prevail before a plebiscite is held.[2] Pakistan may not be ready to vacate Gilgit, Baltistan and Azad Kashmir", and transfer them to India, till the normalcy prevails for a free plebiscite. The various UN resolutions that were carried through the machinations of certain powers who did not want to see non-aligned India as strong, independent country but wished to fish in the troubled relations between India and Pakistan. However, the resolution of August 13, 1948, which required Pakistan to withdraw its both regular and irregular forces from the territory of the whole J&K State was not only ignored and violated by the successive Pakistan Governments but they also further strengthened their military bases and strength in Pakistan occupied Kashmir. To demand plebiscite or self-determination after having violated this part of the 13th August 1948 Resolution is to say the least, illegal, unjustified, grave provocation to India of violation of the principles of the UN Charter.[3] Jammu and Kashmir is the integral part of India and the need for conducting any plebiscite in any part of India did not arise. Plebiscite in Kashmir is an old demand of Pakistan. Indian Government is justified in unequivocally rejecting Pakistan's proposal, linking future bilateral talks to holding of plebiscite in Kashmir. India cautioned Islamabad that it would not spare any effort to oppose moves against its territorial integrity.[4]

It was India, who referred the Kashmir question to the Security Council of United Nations, on January 1, 1948 under Article 35 of the UN Charter, though Jawaharlal Nehru had initially strongly opposed Mountbatten's idea of referring the Kashmir dispute to United Nations, and had agreed with reluctance.[5] Pakistan denied Indian charges of helping raiders and lodged a scries of counter-charges covering the whole range of Indo-Pakistan relations and requested the Security Council to consider the whole matter and not only Kashmir issue.[6] J.N. Dixit once remarked that "Pakistan had not studied the UN resolutions properly." That Pakistan is not really serious and honest about implementing fully the UN resolutions, it is only interested in internationalising the issue. Pakistan's relentless effort to globalise the issue and cloud the real import of the dispute. The writing on the wall is that if the fires of hatred and confrontation, now burning uncontrollably, are not extinguished, they can engulf the entire subcontinent before long.[7]

Islamabad may or may not have been emboldened to threaten the internationalisation of Kashmir issue because of President Clinton's letter dated December 27, 1993, to the Kashmir Action Council, offering to work with it and others "to help bring peace in Kashmir", but the fact remains that Pakistan has gone over the exercise many a time before Kuldip Nayar quips that Pakistan eyes have been too long fixed on international opinion, not Indian, which ultimately matters in finding a solution.[8] Pakistan may just not take the risk of withdrawing all its forces and other personnel from the occupied territory. Nor it may get back the territory ceded to China, Kashmir, China and Tibet problems, all are interconnected, interrelated and solution to these problems are to be found simultaneously.

Ultimately, both the sides—India and Pakistan have to sit across the table of course, without indulging in threats. Pakistan's Foreign Minister Asef Ahmad Ali recently has said that there will be a nuclear war between India and Pakistan if Kashmir problem is not solved. Kuldip Nayar clarifies that Pakistan's Foreign Minister does not realise that if a nuclear bomb is thrown on Delhi, the destruction of Lahore, Karachi and rest of the Pakistan will not be far behind. No such nuclear device has been invented which if detonated, leaves a neighbouring country unaffected.[9] B.N. Kohli is justified when he concludes that; Pakistan game plan seems to be to carry on with its "low-in-cost but rich in dividends", propaganda. The proxy war through its trained militants, whose subversive and terrorist activities have disrupted life in the valley. It has also helped Pakistan in internationalising the Kashmir issue by misrepresenting the Indian security forces actions to curb terrorist activities as atrocities on, and violation of human rights of the people in Kashmir.[10] India has thus no option but to beat Pakistan squarely in its proxy war also, even if this involves giving the infiltrators a hot chase in Pakistan-held areas and blasting their training camps.[11] The Punjab Provincial Assembly Speaker, Mohammad Hanif Ramay, during Commonwealth Seminar at Delhi, said, "we have been talking and talking. But if we go on talking without meaning, we will have another war."[12] Armed conflicts reflecting the passions of man, create a vicious circle. The lesson of history is that, instead of settling any problem finally, war creates more problems and generates greater tensions and results in another war. It creates a chain reaction and an unending process continues. Dr. Albert Einstein, late in his life was asked what weapons may be used in World War III. He said, "I do not know. But I assure you that World War IV will be fought with stones."[13] The analysis of the causes of war will show and establish without an iota of doubt that wars settle nothing at all. The three Indo-Pakistan wars fought since 1947, may convince any prudent man of average ability that wars rather create and not solve the problems—notably Kashmir. Rather it created economic problems in the Indian sub-continent. The next war if it is waged, will be nuclear war, which will mean global destruction. There is no going away from talks, however long and exasperating. The solution has to be found patiently. It is patience and perseverance which is likely to overcome even the mountains, emphasised Mahatma Gandhi. The two countries should never snap the dialogue.

T.N. Kaul is justified in saying that: "Ultimately, the problems of India, whether in Kashmir or elsewhere, must and shall be solved by Indians in India in an Indian way and not by anyone else, anywhere else, in any other way. We must depend on ourselves and not expect others to pull us out of our difficulties or allow them to interfere in our domestic affairs." According to him, this is the lesson, we must draw from our experience in the past in and outside the UNO.[14] According to Jagjit Singh, a defence expert the dispute regarding Kashmir since 1948, however, has been that Pakistan has not vacated parts of India under its occupation, though the Pakistan had agreed to vacate such occupied territory, while accepting the UN Resolution of August 13, 1948, which mandates Pakistan to vacate the Jammu and Kashmir in its entirety for India to retain its military and political presence in the State, and ensure normalcy, Pakistan's aggressions across the cease-fire line in 1965 and 1971 rendered the UN Resolutions meaningless and Shimla Agreement finally modified it.[15]

India has taken an initiative in bringing normalcy and peace in the region, by communicating six proposals to Pakistan, to resolve bilateral problems following a signal from Islamabad that it had not slammed the door on the process of negotiations. These proposals include steps to resolve the Siachen problem, demarcation of the boundary in the Sir Creek area and Tulbul navigation project controversy. The proposals also envisage additional confidence-building measures on the nuclear issue and stabilising the situation along the line of control in Jammu and Kashmir without prejudice to each other's claim.[16] The problem relating to the Siachen, Tulbul project and the demarcation of the boundary in the Sir Creek area, the two countries had reached near agreement in 1991-92. New Delhi's proposal to resolve the Siachen provides for disengagement and redeployment of the troops in the area without prejudice to the known position of either side. India appears to be prepared to pull back to east of the Saltoo Ridge area and expects Pakistan to withdraw to the west of Gryong area.[17] India and Pakistan had already exchanged instruments of ratification on non-attack of each other's nuclear facilities and installations. It has now proposed a "no first use" of nuclear capabilities against each other side.[18] Recently Delhi worked on a set of steps which, if implemented, could change the climate of hostility in the sub-continent. The proposals ranged from another look at the Siachen problem, the demarcation of the maritime boundary in the Sir Creek area and an assessment of the Tulbul project to the transformation of the line of control (LoC) in Jammu and Kashmir into a line of peace and an assurance of "no first use of nuclear arms against each other." By rejecting the proposals relating to Siachen, the Tulbul barrage project and the maritime boundary, and also for ensuring peace between the two countries by entering into a "no first use" nuclear pledge or extending the agreement not to attack each other's nuclear facilities to cover population centres and economic targets. Pakistan seems to have put up inseparable barriers.[19]

The reasonableness of these confidence-building measures seems to have been lost on Pakistan which has preferred to harp on a plebiscite in Jammu and Kashmir. The Spirit of 'globalisation' has failed to percolate down to the ruling circle in Pakistan.[20] The belligerant posture adopted by Pakistan on the concrete proposals made by India to lessen tension in the region and create an atmosphere in which all bilateral issues can be purposefully discussed and ultimately resolved, therefore, has come as a shock to right thinking people—particularly in our part of the globe.[21] However, the popular opinion in both Pakistan and India was vehemcntly opposed to any concessions on Kashmir. Pakistan was still committed to the demand for a plebiscite. India still maintained that there no longer existed a Kashmir problem at all. India and Pakistani statesmen and diplomats were seen back to their habitual exchange of accusations and condemnations.[22]

The army of Pakistan had long been accustomed to declare that it could, given the chance, it was said, was the equal of three Indian soldiers. How much of this kind of statement was propaganda and how much was actually believed by men in positions of responsibility, it is difficult to say.[23] However, recent history has belied such a declaration, and Indian soldier has sufficiently established its know how and power during the 1947, 1965 and 1971 wars waged by Pakistan against India. *The Times of India*, in a lead article "Stalemate in Kashmir" writes: as long as Pakistan continues to believe in the efficacy of armed insurgency and continues to send trained personnel and weapons and explosives across the Line of Control, it is unlikely to accept any proposal to "stabilise" the line. After all, in the past few years, Islamabad has consistently breached the line by sending across armed militants and thereby violated Article IX, Section 2, of the Simla Agreement.[24]

Gandhiji was not for division of Kashmir and as such the question of stabilising Actual Line of Control would not arise. The question arises, as to how the Azad Kashmir is brought back to the mainstream. Gandhiji viewed: "There was now talk about the viviscation of Kashmir. It was fantastic. It was more than enough that India had been divided into two. One would have thought it impossible for man to divide a country, which God had made one. Yet it had happened and both the Congress and League had decided upon it, though for different reasons. But that could not mean that the process of dividing should be further extended.[25] Congress and Muslim League divided the country, the people of two countries are likely to do the historic job of unifying the two, as the people are not divided.

The virtual rejection by Islamabad of the very idea of keeping up a serious dialogue with India after the recent talks between the two Foreign Secretaries is not accidental. Benazir Bhutto has already said much to convince Pakistan's military elite that both of them are on the same wavelength. The Pakistani leaders are obsessed with enhancing Pakistan's military might. Ms Bhutto's belligerence on Kashmir and her bid to deflate the notion of a dialogue with India have amply served this purpose.[26] What seems to be going on in Pakistan is militarisation under civilian aegis. Pakistan's political system is essentially a military dominated, notwithstanding some democratic trappings.

It would be wise for both India and Pakistan to announce the resumption of their interrupted dialogue. Shimla agreement on bilateral Relations between the Government of India and Pakistan, entered on July 2, 1972 and signed by Zulfikar Bhutto and Indira Gandhi, mandates the respective Heads of both the Governments met again and discussed at a mutually convenient time in the future including the questions of..... a final settlement of Jammu and Kashmir and the resumption of diplomatic relations. The saner element in Indian sub-continent are for continuing dialouge between India and Pakistan. Inder Malhotra asserts: It's time both India and Pakistan realise that by keeping their talks going, neither side is going to have a favour to the other. As the relations between the two are so bad, there is overwhelming reason to keeping talking rather than start fighting.[27]

Former President, Dr. Shankar Dayal Sharma, once indicated in his speech : "Let the Indians and Pakistanis pray during the holy month of Ramzan as desired by Pakistan and then resume their dialogue. India and Pakistan can live in a climate of peace and co-operation." Both India and Pakistan should focus on employing practical ways and pragmatic approach, to resolve specific problems, such as demilitarising the Siachen glacier. Since India and Pakistan are both potential nuclear powers, it is all the more important that they settle their differences through negotiations. The dialogue must continue on.

India's dialogue should also continue with China because that can give an opportunity to take back 37,555 sq.km. of Kashmir's territory under China's illegal occupation and one-third of Kashmir under Pakistan occupation. Kashmir issue needs to be resolved peacefully through a meaningful dialogue. It needs to be remembered that a few months after 1962 Chinese invasion, Pakistan signed an agreement virtually gifting several hundred square kilometres of "Azad Kashmir" to the Chinese, which India is to have back. In nations life opportunities do come and a vigilant nation must keep itself on the heels to avail the opportunity, Kashmir in its totality including the areas in occupation of Pakistan and China needs to be addressed on a priority basis. There is no point in skying away from the issue. But a temporary truce may be possible only if India insists on Pakistan giving up violence against India.

## NOTES AND REFERENCES

1. Kuldip Nayar, "Globalisation of Kashmir", *The Tribune*, January 19, 1994 p. 6.
2. Ibid.
3. T.N. Kaul, "Without home and hearth", *The Tribune*-Sunday Reading January 23, 1994 p. 1.
4. *The Tribune*, January 20, 1994, p. 1.
5. H.V.. Hodson, *The Great Divide*, (1970) p. 465.
6. The Security Council Official Records, (1948) pp. 1, 2. Also see Gulab Mishra, *Indo-Pakistan Relations*, (1987) p. 96.
7. Ibid.
8. Ibid.
9. Kuldip Nayar, "Globalisation of Kashmir", *The Tribune*, January 19, 1994 p. 6.
10. B.N. Kohli, "Pakistan's game-plan". *The Tribune*, January 18, 1994, p. 8.
11. Ibid.
12. "Pakistan Warns of another War", *Indian Express*, January 18, 1994, p. 5.
13. Sampooran Singh, *India and the Nuclear Bomb* (1971) p. 170. Kashmir Imbroglio : Diagnosis and Remedy
14. T.N, Kaul, "Without home and hearth", *The Tribune*-Sunday Reading, January 23, 1994 p. 1.
15. Jagjit Singh, "Options on Kashmir", *Indian Express*, December 11, 1993.
16. "India Sends Pak Six Proposals", *The Tribune*, January 25, 1994 p. 1.
17. Ibid., pp. 1 and 16.
18. Ibid., p.1
19. *The Times of India*, January 30, 1994, p. 10.

20. "Pakistan-Backward March", *The Tribune*, January 28, 1994, p. 10.
21. Ibid.
22. Alastair Lamb, *The Kashmir Problem : A Historical Survey*, p. 135.
23. Ibid.
24. "Stalemate in Kashmir", *The Times of India*, January 30, 1994, p. 10.
25. D.G. Tendulkar, Mahatma, Vol. VIII, (1990) p. 211.
26. "Her War Like Posture", *Indian Express*, January 31, 1994, p. 6.
27. Inder Malhotra, "Time for Talks", *Sunday*, December 12-18, 1993 p. 19.

PART — VI

# The Real Issues

## Chapter 17

# Secularism at Stake

The Himalayas are not only the mightiest but the most fascinating mountain ranges in the world. According to the ancient Indian Scriptures, these mountain ranges are so sacred that as the dew is dried up by the morning sun, so are the sins of mankind at the sight of the Himalayas and "the one who thinks of the Himalaya is better than the one who performs all worship at Kashi." Lord Krishna in *Bhagvad Gita* says: "Among mountains, I am the Himalaya." Nature has shaped the Indian sub-continent into a compact physical mass of region with rich resource base. The region is surrounded by the Himalayas in the North, Hindmahasagar—the Indian Ocean, in the South, Bangladesh and Bay of Bengal in the East and NWFP in the West. It is a compact unit. The region has been mostly defended by its natural boundaries. One of the unifying factors of India has been the physical and geographical continuity of the land, stretching from the Himalayas to the Indian Ocean and from Brahmaputra to Sindhu with the valleys of their tributaries.[1]

The people of India and Pakistan, who have the same origin and belong to the same stock, were separated by the partition of the country. Many Hindus were no doubt forcibly converted and many accepted Islam as they wanted to be on the right side of the power.[2] Some of the Hindus, as in East Bengal, may have accepted Islam voluntarily. But it would be in bad taste to comment on the circumstances to which their ancestors changed faith.[3] But despite change of religion, they belong to the same Indian stock. The change of religion would not change the culture.

J.V Gupta, says that: India being accepted as an ancient country, the culture and heritage of Rama and Krishna cannot be denied by those who had been living in this country since ages. A few of them became Muslims or Christians due to historic reasons but that did not change their culture.[4] The most salient feature of Indian history is the unity in diversity, where different diversities coexist. The strength of India lies in its diversities and diversities are the strength of Indianness. It is the strength of Indian culture, a common heritage of India that strengthens Indianness and unites the people.[5] However, after more than five decades since the partition of the country an emergence of the Pakistan as a fait-accompli, a psychology among the majority community—Hindus, appears to have been generated that wherever in India, the Muslim is in majority, the non-Muslim, particularly Hindu, is treated as alien and is being constantly squeezed and is a refugee in his own country. Baljit Rai elaborates : There is a realisation that Lebanon in 1947 was a Muslim minority (and Christian majority) country. But today, in just forty years the Muslims are in majority in Lebanon and the Christians in minority. This has consequently resulted in a civil war between the two communities for the last fifteen years. "The apprehension is that it may be the future scenario in India."[6] In Kashmir, terrorism reigns and appears to control the administration. Terrorism has no respect for the sanctity of human life. The terrorist's ethos is that of the criminal—kill, maim and destroy. And the bonds of religion, family history, culture; shared traditions of mutual help, courtesy and hospitality that characterised the sub-continent have been torn callously by propounding a criminal philosophy of separation. And the land of laughter and plenty is today coloured by the blood of innocents sacrificed at the altar of terrorism.

## One Nation, One People

It cannot be brushed aside and ignored that the separatist movement and ethnic cleansing of Hindus in Muslim majority

Indian State of Kashmir, the unhampered infiltration of Muslims into India from Bangladesh, Pakistan, Afghanistan, Iran and some other West Asian States, developments in Afganistan, the rising *crescendo* of Islamic fundamentalism, coupled with the Indian State's unwillingness to counter such dangerous developments have also been instrumental in the resurgence of Hindu nationalism.[7] It cannot be lost sight of that even before the advent of Islam, India was a nation. A nation has perpetual existence and a Hindu Nation has existed for ages. It is time for a realization that Indian sub-continent does not consist of two nations, two people, but one people and one nation.

From the Himalayas in North to Hind Mahasagar in South, Bangladesh in East and NWFP in the West situated a culturally compact unit and the region was once defended by the Himalayas. But it is no longer true: after the forcible occupation of Indian territory by the Chinese army and creation of Pakistan. India now stands divided into three—India, Pakistan and Bangladesh. This division of India has shattered the unity of India. The Himalaya mountains which extend for about two thousand miles, from Afghanistan to Myanmar, serve as a great divide between Central Asia and South Asia. Geographically, India has been one and indivisible. Communications and close cultural affinity linked the people of the different States. The States more often unitedly flourished within the natural boundaries, and the physical features of India constituted a source of strength in terms of geographical unity, but its unity has been disturbed by unnatural partition. Only unification is likely to solve Kashmir and other problems faced by the people. The Himalayan ranges remain a source of attraction and inspiration to the people of Tibet and India.

Since independence and Kashmir's accession with India, millions of Kashmiris have been rendered homeless by the

Muslim fundamentalist and terrorist activities. These people are refugee in their own country. A N. Dar emphasised in 1994 that India's political antenna should remain tuned to the spread of Islamic fundamentalism. This can spell in the years to come greatest danger to India's national interests. The tidings comming out of most of the Muslim world are such that India cannot be complacent. Fundamentalism is gaining ground and showing its fangs in much of the Muslim world,[8] and the kind of troubles India is likely to face in the near future. To the extent the fundamentalism goes on spreading, India can expect innovating of pressure to that extent, both internationally and within Kashmir. The organisation of Islamic conference, going by its past stance, will be only too glad to follow the Pakistani lead in maligning India. If fundamentalism gains strength, India should expect more volunteers from fundamentalism States crossing over to Kashmir.[9]

Kashmir represents the unity, territorial integrity and the sovereignty of the whole of secular India. T.N. Kaul asserts that no government in India can stay in power, if it allows the unity and integrity of India, whether in Kashmir or anywhere else in India, to be violated. There is a national consensus on the Kashmir question and it is the duty of the people of India and all the political parties, to close ranks and stand united in upholding fundamental human rights of all the people, specially the minorities, be they Sikhs, Christians, Pandits and Muslims in every part of India.[10] The people of India must stand together united in the battle against religious fanaticism and fundamentalism. The problem of Kashmir is not merely a question of real estate or a piece of territory but the survival of India's cultural synthesis and the right of human beings to live in their homes with dignity, security and harmony among themselves and with others. T.N. Kaul is justified when he says that:

"Kashmir is a symbol and testing ground of the policy of democracy, humanism and secularism which was propagated by Mahatma Gandhi, Pandit Nehru, Sardar Patel, Maulana Azad and other leaders who inspired Indians during their struggle for freedom."[11]

Islamabad has been complicating the lives of not only Kashmiris but also of 120 million Muslims of India by giving moral and material support to militancy in Kashmir Valley, Pakistan has by now developed a vested interest in keeping the Indian Muslims "Constantly unsettled and in turmoil", by whipping up frenzy on Kashmir issue.[12] C.K. Jaffer Sharief recently said it was ironical that Pakistan which came into being ostensibly to protect the interests of Muslims in the sub-continent had developed a vested interest in keeping the Indian Muslims constantly unsettled and in turmoil, so that secularism in India fails because success of Indian secularism undermines the very concept of Pakistan.[13]

To understand the Kashmir syndrome in Pakistan politics, we will have to go back to the rise of the Muslim League in India in thirties and forties. At that time, even before Jinnah emerged on the scene, there was the fear of Hindu domination combined with the nostalgia of Muslim rule. Playing music before mosques was the first form of agitation. Then, as the freedom movement gathered strength, one after the other came the demands for separate electrorates, reservation in services, Jinnah's 14 points and finally, the Pakistan resolution. Each time there was a demand, it was followed by a riot and an appeal to the British district officers to intervene and save Muslims. When the idea of Pakistan was not accepted in northern States of India, the Muslim League sent out its goons to drive the Hindus out of Lahore, Multan and Rawalpindi to appropriate their property. Then Dera Ismail Khan, Hazara and Bannu were set on fire.[14] The expectation that if demand of a separate Home for Muslims - the demand for Pakistan is conceded and the two out of one nation are constituted, the two nations will live in peace.

The two new States—India and Pakistan—joined the comity of nations on August 15, 1947. There were many who confidently looked forward to a bright future for them.[15] There are, perhaps, no two countries in the world with as much common as India and Pakistan. Many factors like historical, geographical, linguistic, cultural and economic had contributed to much hope of happy Indo-Pakistan relations. The hope still persists, in spite of an uneasy peace between India and Pakistan. There had also been major clashes in 1947-48, September 1965 and December 1971. The history of Indo-Pakistani relations may be termed as history of conflicts.[16]

The noted world historian Prof. Arnold Toynbee, in a lead article unequivocally stated that the creation of Pakistan is the first successful step of the Muslims in the 20th Century to realise their twelve-hundred year-old dream of complete subjugation of India. Their direct aggression, wetted by their first success, then turned against Kashmir. There too they met with success, though partial. One third of Kashmir continues to be in their clutches even to this day.

India achieved independence under Indian Independence Act, 1947. The country was divided, partitioned, rather vivisected on the basis of two-nation theory—on religious basis. However, Muslim Majority NWFP was Congress ruled province and Punjab was ruled by Unionist Government, supported by Congress. The people of Baluchistan had no right to franchise. The people who were for partition belonged to hinterland. After partition such people appear to have reconciled to the secular India and have stayed back. During the exchange of population i.e., Hindus to India and Muslims to Pakistan—most of the Muslims stayed back in India and their population as of today is about 120 million in India.

Hindus who left Pakistan for India were primarily not received as Hindus but as Pakistani refugees. Similarly, the Muslims from India to Pakistan were, basically and primarily not received as Muslims but as Indian refugees, though the country was partitioned on the basis of two nation theory—Hindus and Muslims. Thus outcome of partition, so far as, two communities are concerned is unnatural. The people living in Indian sub-continent are one people of one nation and by no stretch of imagination can be said to be two people. The people living here are those who are Hindus and those who were Hindus. T.K. Thomas is justified in saying that before their conversion, the Indian Muslims and Christians were Hindus.[17] Lawrence is also of the view that, Musalmans of the valley may have retained for sometime after their conversion to Islam, some of the Hindu customs of endogamy within the caste and exogamy outside the gotra but there is no trace of these customs now and the tribal names or Krams are names and nothing more.[18] A Pakistani national who served in a responsible capacities frankly confessed recently to a visiting Indian dignatory that: "there are only two categories of people in Indian sub-continent, "those who were Hindus and these who are Hindus". Sawant, J. in Indira Sawhney's case while discussing caste system, emphasised that, "Almost all followers of non-Hindu religions except those of Zoroastrianism, are converts from Hindu religion and in the new religion they carried with them their castes as well.[19] T.K. Oommen explains; that the religious collectivities of India may be grouped into three, based on the sources of their origin: (a) those who prefer religious faiths which originated in the region—Hinduism, Jainism, Buddhism and Sikhism; (b) those who migrated to India due to persecution and oppression in their respective homelands—the Jews, the Bahas, the Zoroastrians; and (c) those who converted to religions of alien origin like Christianity and Islam, which were perceived to be religions of the colonisers and conquerors. However, the

Muslims are perceived as a threat by the Hindus in India, although an overwhelming majority of Muslims are converts from local castes and tribes.[20] Dr. T.K. Oommen, J. in Indira Sahni's case supra, explains what fetters Hindus and Muslims is not the religion but their badges of poverty, disease, misery, ignorance and humiliation.[21] To Mahatma Gandhi the "Two Nations" theory was an untruth. Thus to the very year of Jinnah's success in breaking India into two nations, Mahatma continued his desperate fight against the untruth.[22] Mahatma is no longer alone in this struggle against untruth. Josh Malihabadi, in a published report, said: "According to me, Pakistan has proved harmful for both Hindus and Muslims. It has shattered the composite culture evolved over a thousand years. The civilisation of decency and tolerance has suffered a setback. The two-nation theory is absolutely untenable for humanity, transcends national barriers religion cannot be the basis of nationhood. With the change of religion one will not suddenly cease to be a Pathan or an Indian or a Pakistani. Similarly, an Englishman will not become an Iranian if he embraces Islam. Religion has no co-relationship with nationality. It is preposterous to carve out a country on the basis of religion.[23] The people of United India, for centuries have shared historical memories and felt and behaved as one nation. John Stewart Mill who had gone deep into the question as to what constitutes a nation, said that it is not a language which would define a nation, because there is one nation which speaks two or three languages, like Switzerland. Then, it is not religion which defines a nation, because many nations have got a number of religions. So, finally he came to the conclusion that it is a group of people who have shared historical memories and feel as a nation.[24] The concept of India or whatever term one may use, is a foreign term and we did not call ourselves by that term—there is an integrated entity. Sethu Himachalam from Baluchistan to Burma, can be called the India civilisation. There is a civilisationally integrated society, which the rest of the world took note of, which we believe in, and all felt that we belong to that entity, that is, many millennia old. Therefore, while one can talk about various kinds of diversities in India but no reasonable person of ordinary prudence may be able to come to the conclusion that India is a multiplicity of nationalities.[25]

Right from time immemorial Bharat, that is India, has been envisioned and has existed as one single nation not withstanding the fact that different rulers, indigenous or foreign, held sway over principalities of varying domain at different stages of our history. The Vedas speak of one single entity stretching from Himalayas in the North to Kanyakumari in the South; from Sindhu in the East to Bengal in the West. Other extant literary and historical record of the times—Hindu, Muslim and Anglo Indian—all speak in the same vein, Kashmir finding prominent mention, amongst the areas comprising the Indian Nation as such. As recently as in nineteenth century it formed an integral part of Maharaja Ranjit Singh's Sikh Empire. Socially, culturally, politically and historically, therefore Kashmir has remained and still continues to be a vital organ of the territories of Indian Nation.

India is a multidimensional country inhabited by peoples professing different religions. Legally or in practice, however, no discrimination is made or tolerated on the sole ground of religion. The concept of Two Nation Theory that unfortunately gave birth to the partition of the country is antithesis to the concept of secularism, the main creed of India's Constitution. In secularism the people of Jammu and Kashmir have affirmed their faith and belief through their representation on more than one occasion and at appropriate Constitutional forum. For the simple reason that the State is a Muslim majority area, Pakistan has no locus standi to claim the territory as part of that country. The truism that Jammu and Kashmir is irrevocably integral part of India is thus beyond any doubt, no matter what Pakistan or his allies or countries playing politics might say.

Kashmir is home not only of Hindus and Muslims—Sunnis and Shias but also to Buddhists and Christians who have lived in harmony and amity. They arc being driven out of the valley in what is one of the ugliest form of ethnic cleansing.[26] It must be remembered that if Kashmir valley is allowed to go out of India, it will be the end of India's secular democracy and cultural harmony and synthesis. It will also make the position of millions of Muslims in India untenable and could lead to an unprecedented communal holocaust in the whole sub-continent, including Pakistan where ethnic, linguistic and even religious divisions are present. T.N. Kaul, justifiably says that: Pakistan may call itself an 'Islamic' State but cannot force India to become a 'Hindu' State. We must preserve our secular democracy synthesis and harmony and our more than 7000 year old conviction in Vasudhaive Kutumbakam.[27]

However, secularism is at stake in Kashmir, rather Kashmir is the acid test for secular India. Terrorism in Kashmir seeks to destroy India's sense of nationhood, unity, democracy and secularism. The unity of the people which is the key objective of the constitution is not to be destroyed by religious fanaticism and orthodoxy of certain powerful factions of the country. The Indian constitution as such, seeks to maintain complete religious neutrality and refuses superiority of race, colour, creed, religion or region. It seeks to establish equality, toleration and social justice, in all spheres of life, by doing away with casteism and communalism. Thus, secularism in India is not a particular creed, but a way of life which does not recognise superiority but equality and harmony. The freedom of religion is not incompatible with good citizenship and loyalty to the State, and all progressive societies must respect the religious beliefs of their minorities[28] and vice-versa.

The constitution of India guarantees perfect impartiality towards all religious communities in the State and grants to profess whatever religion one seeks to follow. What it seeks to eschew is religious or communal fanaticism which destroys unity and cohesion of the national life.[29] The word "Secular" was intentionally inserted by the constitution (42nd Amendment) Act, 1976.[30] Secularism is a "system of social ethics based upon a doctrine that ethical standards and conduct should be determined exclusively with reference to the present life and social well being without reference to religion."[31] But in general paralance secularism means separation between State and religion i.e., the temporal power should keep its hands off from religious world.[32] "Secularism" means a State which does not recognise any religion is a State religion. It treats all religions equally. The concept of secularism is implicit in the Constitution, "Liberty.... belief, faith and worship". Articles 25 to 28 of the Constitution guarantee to every person the freedom of conscience and the right to profess, propagate and practise religion.[33]

Secularism is actually, the affirmation of the principle that all the Indian citizens are equal whatever their religion. It is the affirmation of the principle that affirmative action should be taken in favour of disadvantaged. Secularism also means a strict adherence to the principle of separating religion from politics.[34] India is secular because of the people, its culture and the ethos of this country are secular.

## An Attitude of Mind

Secularism is an attitude of mind. It can be cultivated through education and concerted efforts by progressive elements. Then and then alone we can attain what Swami Vivekananda called a "Hindu brain in Islamic body."[35] Indian secularism establishes a harmony in religious freedom and power of the State to exercise control over this freedom. Even in pre-independence period the British, seemingly kept the State and religion separate from each other and religious beliefs and social customs and traditions of different sects and communities were recognised by the Courts unless they were found opposed to the principle of equity and good conscience.[36] As conceived by our Constitution makers secularism means, Sarve- Pantha- Sarva-Bhava, i.e.. equal respect for all religions. Secularism as embedded in the Indian Constitution has three important ingredients, namely—rejection of theocracy; equality of all the citizens irrespective of their faith; and full freedom of faith and worship.[37] L.K. Advani says: "We also believe that India is secular because it is predominantly Hindu. Theocracy is alien to our history and tradition."[38] His Holiness the Dalai Lama expresses Himself candidly on secularism in India that: India's resolution to respect all faiths by adopting a secular constitution was born out of its ancient philosophy of non-violence and long standing heritage of cultural diversity.[39] Secularism is India's manifest destiny.

However, secularism is not ingrained in the hearts and minds of the millions and millions of the people of India; whereas religion is. A fake superimposition of a non-workable, non-popular or a pseudo concept of secularism won't work in this country or in any other, if indeed it could, then why was the partition of the country and the people allowed in 1947? On the other hand, if it be laudable goal to make people rise above the narrow confines of religions, the effort should be made to the present Pakistan as well, because nothing could demonstrate the validity of the principle better than a United India in which Hindus and Muslims could live under the umbrella-concept of secularism. Anything less would not be able to clinch the issue.[40] Having allowed the country to be vivisected on the "Muslim and Hindu nations" theory, the leader cannot pull woolover the eyes of the remaining population here by saying we ought to eschew religion from politics.

Secularism is antithetical to Islamic tenets, which not only tell you the way to heaven but also how to found and run one on earth: the Islamic State. It is just about impossible for a Muslim to realise an Islamic State within a secular set-up.[41] After partition of the country, its leaders made India secular. Secularism was not a choice, it was a necessity, if India were to succeed. Gandhi Nehru knew this, for it was the basis of their strategy for unified nationalist movement.[42] Secularism, first and last implies a philosophical or psychological revolution, a revolution in the minds of men as individuals. This revolution means a fundamental change in the outlook of men, in their outlook on life, society, history, in fact, on everything that concerns man and life here, in this world.[43] Secularism as understood today was nothing but political expediency.[44]

Most of the Kashmiri politicians were adept in speaking with two voices. They could be secular as well as communal, democratic as well as dictatorial, secessionist as well as pro-Pakistan. The underlying motivation was not principles but power—power for the person and for the coterie around. If the Central leaders allowed the Kashmiri leaders to rule the State in whatever manner they liked, whether or not it was in the interest of the country as a whole or even in the interest of the State, they swore by principles of democracy, socialism and secularism and accession to India was declared as final, if, on the other hand, any question was raised in regard to the exercise of authority, or any personal ambition was checked, accession became temporary and issues of autonomy, or identity and of the personality of Kashmir were raised, and communal feelings aroused.[45]

The concept of secularism was debased and despiritualised by the power-crazy and compromising mind of Indian power wielders. Justice, equity and truth were sucked out of it. The concept was reduced to a mantra—the repeated recitation of which was believed to propitiate the goddess of power. Commitment was not to the cause but the expediency.[46] People in the country at large are being regularly explained about the secular foundations of our polity and about the virtues of secularism in a multi-religious society set on the path of development and modernisation in a modern democracy, preoccupation with worldly or secular issues on the socio-economic plane involving active participation of the people can be more effective in combating religious fundamentalism.[47]

According to Justice Beg, Indian secularism is a midway between individual freedom to follow any religion to practice and to propagate religion freely and the right of the State to regulate such activities which are not integral part of religion. "Our Constitution-makers certainly intended to set up a Secular Democratic Republic, the binding spirit of which is summed up by the objectives set forth in the Preamble of the Constitution."[48] From a reading of the Preamble to the Constitution and Arts. 25 to 30, it is clear that the object behind constituting India into a secular State is not to prevent the practice of religion, but to provide liberty, freedom, equality and fraternity between persons belonging to different religions. It is not the object of the Constitution to turn the country into an irreligious place. Secularism is at once an ideal and an inspiration, a goal as well as a striving force, a product as well as a process. It is made of aggregation rather than segregation, or synthesis rather than separatism, of pluralism rather than dominance.[49]

The fate of Kashmir is intricately linked with that of the 200 million Muslims of India. When Pakistan was created, it did not think about the fate of Indian Muslims or the tragedies that' might befall them. It just took at chunk of India thinking it has got a homeland. In the ultimate analysis India and Pakistan would have to live together and work together for the progress and welfare of the people. The money being wasted on fighting could be used for development and combating poverty, illiteracy, disease, unemployment and for improving the quality of life. Dr. Abdullah viewed Kashmir as a bridge of friendship between India and Pakistan and not a battle ground between the two neighbours.[50]

The people need to be educated on Secularism, it is a conviction and not a expediency. The Secular nature of India is one of the basic structures of the Constitution.[51]

The preamble of the Constitution is an integral part of the Constitution. Democratic form of Government, federal structure, unity and integrity of the nation, secularism, socialism, social justice and judicial review are basic features of the Constitution.[52] Praful Bidwai, airs his views on the recent judgment of the Apex Court in S.R. Bommai's case that separation of religion from politics—is part of the basic structure of the Constitution.[53] M. Rama Jois, in a recent published article, "Secularism as dharma: Supreme Court has reaffirmed. Hindu Wisdom", explains: It is indisputable that "secularism" has been the basic feature of our civilisation and culture from time immemorial.[54] R.L. Nigam elaborated :

Secularism has a history of its own, spanning centuries in the course of which it acquired its contemporary universal meaning and definition. It cannot, therefore, mean one thing here and quite another elsewhere. It is not open to any one or any country to give it a meaning fundamentally different from position of secularism acquired through an evolutionary process.[55]

A Secular India was promised by the national leadership when it called upon all Indians to fight for freedom, most notably in the Karachi resolution of 1931; and our Constitution has sought to give shape to such a secular polity. It must be defended.[56]

The 42nd amendment has inserted three new words in the preamble, including Secular. Belligerence on the part of India or Pakistan will ultimately bleed both, and the resources needed for survival of the people of the sub-continent will be diverted to the military industry of the developed countries. India and Pakistan should help create a climate in which even complex issues can be sorted out. The Kashmir problem some say, possibly cannot be solved as long as India and Pakistan pose as adversaries. But in a climate of confidence even a "lost case" can be won. Both India and Pakistan must learn from their history that neighbourly problems can hardly be resolved by forces across the seven seas.[57] The solution to Kashmir Problem may never be found on narrow religious sectarian and racial grounds.

Secularism in the realm of philosophy is a system of utilitarian ethics, seeking to maximise human happiness or welfare quite independently of what may either be religious or the occult.[58] If all human activity in this world could be labelled "Secular" on the ground that it pertains to "this world" as against the "other world", all religious thought and activity could be described as "Secular", as it takes place in this world. But the term is not used so broadly. It is convenient label to distinguish all that is done in this world without seeking the intervention or favour or propitiating a super human of Divine power or being from that which is done professedly to please or to carry out the will of the Divinity.[59]

We must try to make up with the people of Kashmir. Those who have been misled by Pakistani propaganda have now known that India cannot be pushed around too long.

Many there realise that Pakistan's strategy is to fight India to the last Kashmiri. Such Kashmiris should be befriended and brought closer. The long-suffering Kashmiri Pandits and migrant Muslims should be enabled to So back to start a process that will bring stability to the scene. The estranged Kashmiris, who have taken to the gun but have found that Pakistan on which they relied so heavily was a paper tiger when it came to the crunch, should not be left to lick their wounds by themselves but welcomes back to the fold as peace loving secular Indians.[60]

Freedom of thought and conscience, freedom of worship and religion, and freedom of speech and expression bred a certain catholicity of outlook and temperament in ancient India and it has protected the Indian society from the excesses of fanaticism and exclusiveness. For centuries, it gave Indian society a remarkable power and frequent opportunities of assimilation and absorption. Kabir and Guru Nanak brazed new trails of thought and illuminated the ethical, spiritual, rational paths of Indian secularism, thus providing fruitful and harmonious oneness of synthesis rising above the pettiness of parochialism of sectarian establishment.[61]

Secularism is under serious threat in the continent. A secular Indian sub-continent is a best guarantee of political stability in the region and economic growth is the best ally of secularism.

The only symptom of our sovereignty in the Kashmir valley is the presence of our armed forces. If there are any elements loyal to India they have either migrated or become totally invisible. Indian statemanship will have to rise to the highest to terminate the feeling of alienation that doubtless exists. The Muslim leadership of India will have a very effective role to play. Without mincing words it should be clear that their attitude and advice to the Muslims of Kashmir will be a test of their sincere commitment to Secularism.[62]

Pakistan has realised that it cannot dislodge India from the valley except by a full scale war. There is a risk that the next war will be a nuclear war. India's military capability including nuclear capability is vastly superior to that of Pakistan. This should be a sufficient deterrent. But frustration often leads to desperation which in turn can produce the most appaling miscalculations. India may well emerge victorious. In all probability it will.[63]

Secularism is the oxygen without which India cannot survive. The secular interests of all the communities in the continent deserve to be harmonised, to evolve a sense of common nationhood and to annul the artificial partition which resulted in dividing the people and there in also lies the answer to Kashmir Problem.

## NOTES AND REFERENCES

1. M.G. Chitkara, *Indo-Pak Amity*, (1994).
2. M.R. Malkani, "Looking at the future", *The Hindustan Times*, Sunday, March 17,1993,p.4.
3. Ibid.
4. J.V. Gupta, "Demolition, Explosion of Hindu Sentiments," *The Tribune*, February 1993,p.12.
5. Ramji Lal, "Communal Scenario in India and its way out", published in Communal Problem in India. A Symposium, (1988) p. 1. Edited by Dr. Ramji Lal.
6. Baljit Rai, *Muslim Fundamentalism in the Indian Sub-Continent*, (1991) p. xi.
7. Amar Zutshi, "Rise of Hindu, Nationalism", *Indian Express*, March 2, 1993, p. 6.
8. A.N. Dar, "Islamic fundamentalism in 1994", *The Tribune*. January 17, 1994, p. 8.
9. Ibid.

10. T.N. Kaul, "Without Home and Hearth", *The Tribune*, Sunday Reading, January 23, 1994, p. 1.
11. Ibid.
12. C.K. Jaffer Sharief, "Pak unsettling Indian Muslims", *The Tribune*, February 1,1994,p.5.
13. Ibid.
14. K.F. Rustam Ji. "Towards Confederation?." *The Tribune*, January 13, 1993 p. 8.
15. Jyoti Bhushan Dasgupta, *Indo-Pakistan Relations* (1958) pp. 45-47. Also see, Gulab Mishra, *Indo-Pakistan Relations* (1987) p. 1.
16. Sisir Gupta, *India's relations with Pakistan* (1958) p. 1, Alse see, Gulab Mishra, *Indo-Pakistan Relations*, (1987) p. 1.
17. T.K. Thomas, "Identity Question", *The Times of India*, February 25, 1993, p. 10.
18. *Keys to Kashmir*, Lalla Publications, (1953) pp. 32-33.
19. Sawant, J. in re : Indira Sawhney and others vs. Union of India and others, JT 1992 (6) SC 273 and 454, para 478.
20. T.K. Oommen, "Meaning of The other : Perceptions in Indian Society". *The Times of India*, January 19, 1994, p. 8.
21. Sawant, J. In re: Indira Sawhney and others vs Union of India and others. JT 1992 (6) SC 368-369.
22. Manmathnath Dass, *Partition and Independence of India*, (1982) p. 31.
23. Rajendra Sareen, "Stern action against Josh demanded," *The Tribune*, December 31, 1974.
24. K. Subrahamanyam, *Problems of Living in Nuclear Age*, (1985) p. 17.
25. Ibid. p. 18.
26. Mrs. Neelam Subharwal, "Pak should stop telling lies", *The Times of India*, February 26,1994,p.10.

27. T.N. Kaul, "Without home and hearth" *The Tribune.* Sunday Reading, January 23,1994,p.1.
28. Ayyar, J. in re: Kerala Education Bill, AIR 1958 S.C. 956.
29. P.C. Pati, "Secularism in India" *AIR 1994 Journal Section* 33, at p. 34.
30. Durga Das Basu, *Constitutional Law of India,* 6th ed. (1991) p.2.
31. *Webster's New International Dictionary.*
32. P.C. Pati, "Secularism in India" *AIR 1994 Journal Section 33.*
33. J.N. Pandey, *Constitutional Law of India,* (1986) p. 33.
34. Mani Shanker Aiyer, *The Times of India,* November 18, 1992 p.18.
35. K.B. Dalike, "True Secularist", *The Times of India,* November 12, 1992, p. 6.
36. P.C. Pati, "Secularism in India" *AIR 1994 Journal Section 33.*
37. L.K. Advani, *Indian Express,* December 27, 1992, p. 9.
38. Ibid.
39. The Dalai Lama, "India's deepening crisis: Imperatives of Harmonious co-Existence", *The Times of India,* December 10, 1992, p. 6.
40. R.L.M. Patil, "Secularism: The Fall of a False God", *The Indian Express,* December 20, 1992, p. 5.
41. C.P. Surendran, "Swan Song", *The Illustrated Weekly,* December 12-18, 1992, p. 16.
42. Gautam Adhikari, "Understanding India", *The Times of India,* December 23, 1992,p.8.
43. R.L. Nigam, "Defining Secularism: Neither a negative concept nor anti-religion", *Indian Express,* January 23, 1993, p. 6.
44. U.R. Lalit. "Secularism must be redefined", *The Tribune,* January 25, 1993, (9-16).

45. Jagmohan, *My Frozen Turbulence in Kashmir*, (1991) p. 134.
46. Jagmohan, "Crisis of the Polity", *Indian Express*, January 5, 1993, p. 6.
47. C.H. Hanumantha Rao, "Religious Fundamentalism", *Indian Express*, January 28,1993,p.6.
48. Beg J. in Ziauddin Bukhari Vs Mehra, Civil Appeal No. 134 of 1973, decided on 25.4.1975 Also see P.O. Pati, "Secularism in India", *AIR 1994 Journal Section 33.*
49. Athiest Society of India Vs. Govt. of A.P. AIR 1992 and Para 319 para 27.
50. Dr. Farooq Abdullah in "Farooq for LOC as International Border" by Subhash Kirpekar from Geneva, *The Times of India*, March 5, 1994, p. 10.
51. Keshavananda Bharati Vs State of...., AIR, 1973 SC 1461, Also see S.R. Bommai and others Vs. Union of India and others, *J.T. 1994* (2) SC 215.
52. S.R. Bommai and others Vs. Union of India and others, *JT 1994* (2) SC 215.
53. Praful Bidwai "Verdict For Secular Democracy", *The Tribune*, March 21, 1994,p.8.
54. M. Rama Jois, "Secularism as Dharma: Supreme Court has affirmed Hindu Wisdom", *Indian Express*, April 1, 1994, p. 6.
55. R.L. Nagam, "Defining Secularism: Neither a negative concept nor anti-religion", *Indian Express*, January 23, 1994, p. 6.
56. Irfan Habib, "The case for reason: Arguing with Communalism", *Indian Express*, January 5, 1993, p. 7.
57. O.P. Shah, "Kashmir which way to go", *The Tribune*, September 1, 1992, p. 8.
58. Ziyauddin Burhanuddin in Bukhari Vs. Brijmohan Ram Dass Mehra, (1976) 2 SCC 17 at 32.
59. Ibid.

60. A.N. Dar, "What after Geneva", *The Tribune*, March 17, 1994, p. 8.
61. Dr. L.M. Singhvi, *Freedom of Trial*, Also see Athiest Society of India Vs. Govt. of AP, AIR 1992 AP-312 at 319, para 26.
62. Ram Jethmalani, "Post-Geneva agenda", *Indian Express*, March 19, 1994, p. 6.
63. Ibid.

Chapter 18

# Roots of the Problem

In a painful development, on 14 August, 1947, Pakistan—a Muslim State emerged from partition of British India, in pursuance to the idea of a separate State for Muslims of the sub-continent. The idea was the part of the theory that Muslims, by virtue of their religion-Islam and cultural distinction, constituted a separate nation. Poet-Philosopher Barrister, Dr. Muhammad Iqbal—a Saproo Kashmiri Pandit convert, articulated the concept of Pakistan in its basic form in 1931, when he proposed a separate State comprising Muslim majority areas in north-western India. The All-India Muslim League under the leadership of Muhammad Ali Jinnah adopted the concept in 1940.

The partition of British India into independent India and Pakistan was an extremely complicated process for which the British had made absolutely no preparation. The Kashmir dispute was a direct consequence of the inefficiency with which the process of partition in the Indian sub-continent was prepared and executed. It was a bit of unfinished business arising from partition.[1] Until it was settled, partition could not be said to be complete. Partition, in the form that it finally took in the sub-continent, was an idea which the British brought themselves to accept with some reluctance. Many servants of the British Raj, now in retirement, will still bemoan the tragedy which brought about the destruction of the united sub-continent, that masterwork of the British imperial genius.[2] The Kashmir conflict between India and Pakistan has often been expressed in terms of the conflict between the "One-nation" and "two-nation" theories. Joseph Korbel observed: Kashmir, Indian apologists say, involves the struggle between the 'Medieval' Islamic theocracy of Pakistan and the modern secular State of India.[3] Alastair Lamb, in Kashmir problem, elaborates: The argument between the "One-nation" and "two-nation" theories is really concerned with the problem whether Pakistan has a right to exist at all. To the "One-nation" school Pakistan is an affront and an absurdity. It should never have been allowed to be born alive, and it would be best if it was brought to an end as rapidly as possible. Most "one-nation" men have, in fact, refrained from advocating the destruction of Pakistan, but their philosophy contains a firm challenge to the basis of its very being. In the Kashmir issue the "One-nation" School has seen the last case which, if it will not affect the future continuance of Pakistan as a State, will atleast guarantee that the communal basis of Pakistan does not contribute to the State's further territorial expansion at India's expense.[4]

The two-nation theory was never heard even during the eight hundred years intermittent reign of Muslim kings. But the British ruled India for about two hundred years and scissored the Indian sub-continent.

Undoubtedly, Kashmir problem is the lethal combination of Islamic fundamentalism and Pakistan's political adventurism. Kashmir is an unfinished agenda of partition,[5] and outcome of two-nation theory. The moment myth of two nation theory explodes, the Indo-Pakistan differences will melt in thin air. The two countries will devote themselves to the task of storming the fortress of poverty, and economic backwardness. Ultimately the people may feel and realise that they no longer need two countries and unite.

Pakistan on its creation included an eastern wing comprising mainly the eastern half of Bengal province and parts of Assam. It was proclaimed an Islamic republic on March 23, 1956. Sheikh Mujibur Rehman proclaimed the People's Republic of Bangladesh on March 26, 1971 and the east-west war ended on December 16, 1971 when a document of surrender was signed in Dacca by Lt. General A.A.K. Niazi, Commander of the Pakistani Army in Bangladesh, and Lt. General J.S. Aurora G.O.C.-in-C, Eastern Command, who accepted the surrender.[6] The prediction of Lord Mountbatten that East Bengal would be out of Pakistan in a quarter of century, came to be true.[7]

Pakistan controls the northern and western parts of the State of Jammu and Kashmir, an area of about 84,160 square km is still a disputed territory.[8] The seat of Government of Azad Kashmir is Muzaffarabad.

Kashmir is noted for its beauties and bounties. It has been for centuries the object of attention of poets, painters and philosophers.[9] Francis Young husband has immortalised its grace and beauty in superb words: "The beautiful Greece, with its purple hills and varied contour, its dancing seas and clear blue sky, produced the graceful Greeks. But Kashmir is more beautiful than Greece. It has the same blue sky and brilliant sun shine, but its purple hills are on a far grander scale, and if had no sea, it has the lake and river and still more impressive snowy mountains.[10] The climate of the valley until the end of May is similar to that of Switzerland. The old men of the valley declare that the climate is changing and they are very positive that there are now no such winters as they remembered as boys. In Maharaja Gulab Singh's time the snow was upto a man's shoulders, in Maharaja Ranbir's time upto the knees but now winters pass without any snowfall.[11] Enclosed by high mountains, the valley presents a picture of a world in itself. Swami Yogananda in his Autography depicts Kashmir as a paradise land of lotus lakes, floating gardens, gaily canopied house boats, the honey-bridged Jhelum river and flower-strewn pastures all encircled by Himalayas. Kashmir's high mountains, which for the greater part of the year are covered with snow; and all the rest of the valley is a beautiful plain clothed in verdure diversified with snows, orchards, gardens and well-watered by springs and rivers a very pleasant land for those who dwell therein.[12] However, in rigorous winters whole life comes to a standstill. On such occasions the mighty snow-covered mountains confine the starring Kashmiris within rock-bound prison which renders escape difficult. Such conditions of life and environment framed the character, traditions and institutions of Kashmiris.[13]

Lord Birdwood depicts the people of Kashmir valley as the people known as Kashmirs distinct from their co-national of district inaccessible areas, a gentle friendly people of little stamina who in trouble bark loudly, but who seldom really bite.[14]

The State of Jammu and Kashmir which had earlier been under Hindu rulers and Muslim Sultans became nail of the Mughal Empire under Akbar: after a period of Afghan rule from 1756. it was annexed to the Sikh kingdom of the Punjab in 1819. In 1854 Maharaja Ranjit Singh made over the territory of Jammu to Maharaja Gulab Singh. After the decisive battle of Sahroon in 1846 Kashmir was also made over to Maharaja Gulab Singh. The State of Jammu and Kashmir came into being as a single political entity in 1846 under what is called "Treaty ol Amritsar." The British Government vide The Treaty concluded on May 16, 1846 transferred possession to Maharaja Gulab Singh and the heir male of his body, all the hilly or mountainous country, with its dependencies, situated to the Eastward of the river Indus and Westward of the river Ravi.[15] The British supremacy was recognised over in respect of State of Jammu and Kashmir until the Indian Independence Act. 1947. When all the princely States decided on the question of accession to India or Pakistan—there being no third choice provided under the Act, Kashmir through its ruler Maharaja Hari Singh asked for stand still agreements with both India and Pakistan. In the meantime, the State became the subject of an armed attack from Pakistan.

The Pakistani force which crossed into Kashmir on October 22, 1947 comprised of regular troops in disguise. Mahsuds and Afrids from NWFP and others and was led by army officers. The invaders, alter an unopposed thrust, accompanied by pillage and murder were about to seize Srinagar. It was then that the Maharaja ol Jammu and Kashmir stopped dithering about the future of the State and signed the instrument of Accession to India.[16] The instrument of accession was executed by Maharaja Hari Singh on October 26, 1947 and acceptance of Accession by the Governor General of India, Lord Mountbatten, in third paragraph of the instrument ol accession, the Maharaja writes about his position and epithets as under.

"Now, therefore, I Shriman Indra Mahendra Rajeshwar Maharajadhiraj Shri Hari Singh Ji. Jammu and Kashmir Naresh Tatha Tibet adi Deshadipathi, Ruler of Jammu & Kashmir State do hereby execute this my instrument of Accession....."

The State of Jammu and Kashmir, as was seen, till the partition of the country as the creation of Dogra rulers, 1846-1947: K.M. Panikkar, in the *Founding of the Kashmir State* wrote: "The State thus assumed its present shape. An area consisting of more than 80,000 square miles including part of Tibet as well as part of the Pamirs, besides the genuinely Indian Kingdoms of Jammu and Kashmir, came into Gulab Singh's possession. This area had never been effectively united under one ruler before and much of it, with, of course, the exception of valley of Kashmir had never known settled government. The work of consolidation and of Government remained, and this, in view of the diversity of population, interests, climate, and lack of continuity in the past, was by no means an easy task. It is to the great credit of Gulab Singh that to this all-important task he now bent his energies, and though he was already fifty-three when he became the sovereign ruler, his efforts in this direction were crowned with success."[17] During the heyday of Hindu power its territorial limits extended beyond its natural boundaries. It included the hill State of Punch, Rajauri, Bhimbar, Kishtwar, certain districts of Jammu and Hazara. The conquests of Lalitaditya 724-760, extended as far as Central Asia in the northwest and the Punjab in the South. After the death of Jayasimha, 1155, the Hindu sovereignty receded considerably owing to a series of weak rulers and increasing domination of the Turks in Afghanistan and the Punjab.[18] The condition had not much altered .when in 1320 the Buddhist Rinchan embraced Islam and proclaimed himself Sultan assuming the title Sadr-ud-din, and laid the foundation of the independent Muslim Kingdom of Kashmir.[19]

Hari Singh, Maharaja of Kashmir in his deed of accession to India, used "Tatha Tibet Adi Deshadhipathi", as an ephithet.[20] In the Seventh Century, the Tibetan king, Srong-tsen Gampo, set up a impressive empire extending from west China to north Burma-Mynmar and including large parts of Nepal. The king married the daughter of the Emperor of China, exacting this as a tribute and took a second wife from Nepal when he subjected it. Both these queens were Buddhists and converted the king to their faith, and in the years that followed he extended the Buddhist religion throughout Tibet. By the ninth century Tibet was a successful and strong military power. In the thirteenth century Tibet became a vassal State of Mongols under Genghis Khan but later Kublai Khan appointed a favourite priest as Priest-King of Tibet.[21]

In the Seventeenth century when the Great Fifth Dalai Lama visited Peking, Tibeian records claim that he was received as an independent sovereign. The Thirteenth Dalai Lama during 1910, took refuge in India because of the mutiny by the Chinese garrison in Lhasa. The Tibetans resisted the Chinese, who had to surrender. Thirteenth Dalai Lama returned to Tibet, during July 1912. The peace talks with Chinese resulted in an agreement dated August 12, 1912, which provided for formal surrender and expulsion of all the Chinese troops from Tibet. His Holiness, the Thirteenth Dalai Lama, issued a proclamation on February 13, 1913. that Tibet was an independent country.[22] Tibet had all the attributes of an independent State and had conducted so till the execution of Seventeen Point Agreement executed on May 23, 1951. The Tibetan way of life, their traditions and their culture is deeply influenced by[22] Indian culture.

Since cease-fire, the Pakistan is in forcible occupation of one-third of the State of Jammu and Kashmir, called by it as "Azad Kashmir." Azad Kashmir is, in fact, occupied enslaved Kashmir and is virtually quasi-State in Pakistani held sector of Jammu and Kashmir, in the north-western part of the Indian sub-continent. It is-not only protected by but is economically and administratedly controlled by Pakistan. It has an area of approximately 1680 square km, according to *Britannica Encyclopaedia*[23] but the area of occupied Kashmir is about 84,150 sq. km.[24] It consists of an arc-shaped stretch of territory bordering the State of Jammu and Kashmir on the east, the Pakistani States of Punjab on the South and South-West and NWFP on the West; and Gilgit and Baltistan agencies of Pakistan on the North.[25] The population of Azad Kashmir was about 2.8 millions in 1985.[26] One-third of the State of Jammu and Kashmir has been usurped by Pakistan and is still under Pakistani occupation.[27] This part of Kashmir had remained most unstable. The economic condition of the people is terrible. The government there changed every two or three months. The administration, in fact, was conducted by Pakistani officials.[28] Rajesh Kadian's solution to Kashmir issue lies in occupation of Azad Kashmir. He asserts that a hypothetical Indian plan should concentrate on capturing the whole of Azad Kashmir. He explains that, as long as the Azad Kashmir Government, dejure or Pakistan de facto remains in physical occupation of some land in the State of Kashmir there are in effect two competing governments of Kashmir in the minds of Kashmiri people and much of the world. However, the capture of the Azad Kashmir salient gives India a naturally defensible border along the Kishenganga and the Jhelum rivers.[29] Rajesh Kadian elaborates: The occupation of the Azad Kashmir salient would also allow India to permanently dominate the 180-mile road and rail link between Lahore and the Rawalpindi-Islamabad region. In addition Pakistan's nuclear facilities at Kahutta and hydro-electric resources of Mangla Dam would be threatened. Under such circumstances Pakistan's future adventurism would be severely restricted.[30] Though India has no plans for such a campaign, some Pakistani military strategicians and thinkers are highly cognisant of such a possibility. Brigadier Abdul Rehman Siddiqui, Retd. asserts : "In a major future flare-up in Kashmir, India need not look southward for a general war but would rather concentrate on Kashmir itself to liquidate the Azad Kashmir 'Salient' and clinch the issue once and for all. Hypothetically India should concentrate all its military resources and power in Kashmir.[31] We must remember that even enemy sometimes teaches a lot. In fact he is a great educator. We must be ready and equipped to learn, and in turn teach the enemy a lesson. Kashmir has been late since sixteenth century to live in misery-downtrodden, poverty stricken and backwardness. Inscrutable are the ways of man. History may tell the story, but it cannot unravel the tangled story of his life. He himself is to avail the opportunity.

## An Unprecedented Crisis

Kashmir is in crucible and its future complexion is in the process of being built up. History has confounded the Kashmiris with an unprecedented crisis which also provides them with a rare opportunity. The crisis can end in a disaster or unique triumph depending upon the attitude that is adopted by to meet the situation. Mahatma Gandhi hoped and prayed that Kashmir should become a beacon light of the sub-continent.[32] The nation expects immediate and viable improvement in the Kashmir situation. There is too much murk now in the erstwhile valley of mirth.[33]

The regions of Gilgit and Baltistan in PoK, have since been merged by Pakistan into its northern territories and directly administered by the federal government without any representation in the "PoK assembly".[34] The Baltistan areas of district Ladakh-Jammu and Kashmir State included sub-divisions of Kharmang, Khalpus, Shardu and Rondu. The entire Baltistan area is now in unauthorised and forcible occupation of Pakistan.[35] Alastair Lamb in his historical survey of Kashmir problem, regarding Ladakh and Baltistan writes: The region of Ladakh and Baltistan is often treated as if it were a single district. In fact, it represents a fusion of two quite separate tracts which the Dogra rulers of Jammu acquired in the first part of the nineteenth century. Baltistan, with its administrative centre at Skardu, is overwhelmingly Muslim. Ladakh proper, with its capital at Leh, was once a Buddhist kingdom with the closest ethnic, cultural and political ties with Tibet. Its sparse population of 40,000, in 1961 was overwhelmingly Buddhist.[36]

The North-Eastern ranges of mountains, encloses Kashmir from the North and North-East and separates her ethnically and culturally from the surrounding regions of Ladakh, Baltistan and Dardistan, which can be reached after crossing the Zoji-La-Pass and Burzil Pass. The Burzil Pass, elevation: 10740 ft. connects Kashmir valley with Astore, Chilas and Bunji and farther still with Gilgit, Chitral, Yasin, Punial, Darel, etc. All these States are now held by Pakistan.[37] The route over Zoji-La Pass, Elevation: 11,300 ft. links Kashmir with Ladakh, Baltistan and Tibet, and Central Asian region of Badakhshan, Samarqand, Khutan, Bukhara, Kashghar, etc. Since ancient times this route had been an important thoroughfare and influenced the political history of the country during the fourteenth and fifteenth centuries. The Buddhist Rinpocha, who proclaimed himself the first Muslim ruler of Kashmir, entered the valley by this route. The route has also been an important commercial highway between Kashmir and Western Tibet.[38]

The most striking feature in the physical aspect of Ladakh is the parallelism of its mountain-ranges, which stretch through the country from South-East to North-West. This general direction of the mountain chains determines the courses of the rivers as well as the boundaries of the natural divisions of the country. The general aspect of Ladakh is extreme barrenness.[39] Seen from above, the country would appear a mere succession of yellow plains and barren mountains capped with snow, and the lakes of Pangkong and Tshomo Riri would seem like bright cases amidst a vast desert of rock and sand. No trace of man nor of human habitations would meet the eye: and even the large spots of cultivated land would be but small specks on the mighty waste of a deserted world. But a closer view would show many fertile tracts along the rivers, covered with luxuriant crops, and many picturesque monasteries, from which the chant of human voices ascends on high in daily prayer and praise.[40] The territory of Ladakh is one of the most elevated regions on the earth. Its different valleys lie along the head-waters of the Indus, the Sutlej, and the Chenab; and the joint effects of elevation and of isolation amidst snowy mountains produce perhaps the most singular climate in the snow world. Burning heat by day is succeeded by piercing cold at night, and everything is parched by the extreme dryness of the air.[41]

The Ladakh region is vast, strategically important but poor. It is situated on the Tibetan-Chinese border and has a small population of about 69,000. The demand for an autonomous structure for the district of Leh was mainly inspired by the regional aspirations for all-round development. In the current atmosphere of terrorism in the rest of the State of Jammu and Kashmir this shining outpost of tranquillity deserves full attention.[42] The Jammu and Kashmir Government and the Centre have agreed in principle to grant autonomy to the Leh area of the Ladakh district. The announcement made by Home Minister S.B. Chavan in the Lok Sabha on 4th March 1994 regarding the Government's decision to set up an autonomous hill council for Leh is welcome. The step will mark the beginning of a new chapter in one of the three parts of the large northern State—Jammu, Kashmir and Ladakh.[43] The provision for autonomous hill council has its roots in the Sixth Schedule of the Constitution which stresses the agricultural and environmental aspects of development, giving a proper opportunity to the people to charter their course of progress. The provision specifically mentions "the allotment, occupation or use, or the sitting apart of land, other than any land which is a reserved forest, for the purpose of agriculture or grazing..... and likely to promote the interests of the inhabitants of any village or town." The land of lamas, will now have the freedom to form district and regional council with administrative units in villages to give every citizen a chance to realise his and his neighbourhood's potential.[44]

The process of change began in right earnest in Ladakh in 1974 when the Indian Government threw the area open to tourism, a move that was probably intended to place Ladakh firmly on the map in Indian territory. At about the same time, concerted efforts were initiated to develop the district. To date, development has been concentrated primarily in Leh and its immediate surroundings and roughly 70 per cent of the population still lives more or less traditionally. But the psychological impact of modernization has been felt throughout the entire region.[45] The autonomous council has to take the economic needs of the area into consideration in the light of the cultural values of the district civilisation. There is no need to worry about "the extinction of a way of life." A pro-change climate of opinion is evident in Ladakh. The changes brought about now will have absorbing effect on the rest of the State. The new administrative process must start immediately.[46]

Ladakh, which is nearly six times the size of the Kashmir valley and has an overwhelming Shia presence in Kargil district and are profoundly pro-India, is devoid of any separatist tendency.

Shia religious leaders, including Sheikh Mohammadi had repeatedly been preaching that militants in the valley by their deeds, were going against the tenets of Islam. The people of Kargil have maintained peace and tranquillity despite the turbulence in the valley.[47] Despite resilience of Kargil people against militancy and their repeated, undettered commitment to the Indian State, Kargil ironcially remains neglected. Sheikh Mohammadi asserted, "We have helped our army in the three Indo-Pak wars, resisted against Pakistan-inspired militancy and continue to render help to the army deployed along the Line of Control. We have considered this as our duty being the citizens of the country."[48] Kargil is the capital of district called Puril, and is inhabited by Mohammedans of Shia sect.[49]

In fact, so embittered are the Ladakhis with political economic domination by the Kashmiris that they have urged the Central Government to directly administer the region. Hence the demand for Union Territory status.[50]

Aksai Chin has been the part of Ladakh. Even the Chinese Government has now admitted that in 1956 they built a highway from Tibet to Sinkiang running for about a hundred miles through this territory. In September 1957, it was announced that this road had been completed.[51] The Sino-Pak boundary agreement of 1963 seeks to link up Pak-occupied area to that held by China in Aksai Chin. The area is vital to Ladakh because the Nubra takes its origin from the "spout" of Siachen and Shyok from another glacier close by. In the event, Aksai Chin and Siachen are the water life line of Ladakh alongwith the Indus whose tributaries they are.[52]

It was "not correct", as Zhou Enlai claimed in 1960, that Beijing had been in possession of the table land and adjoining areas "for several years" and that the Chinese needed Aksaichin, for providing the "only route" from Yarkand to Gartok in Western Tibet. The fact is that an alternate route from Keriya to Gartok did exist and has already been made use of. In the event, "there seems little justification, even from the Chinese point of view" for the road through Aksai Chin.[53] As to the Beijing's claim on Aksai Chin, these stoutly contested by three redoubtable explorers in this country alone. Younghusband commenting on Fielding's report in 1907: P.Z. Nazaroff, a Russian emigree from Tashkent who travelled along the India-China frontier in 1924. And the eminent German geologist Eriv Trinkler who travelled, 1927-28 and later wrote in 1931 on the "Western-Post" plateaux of Tibet.[54] Alastair Lamb, in historical survey of Kashmir problem claims that while the Aksai Chin was absolutely valueless to India, yet India could not accept Chinese ownership of it without making suitable cartographical acknowledgment. Any change in Indian map would hardly escape the sharp eyes of Pakistani bureaucrats ever on the watch for any signs of an Indian intention to alter the status of Kashmir.[55]

Lamb elaborates : The Indian agreement regarding Aksai Chin could have been interpreted in Pakistan as an Indian cession of Kashmiri territory.[56] India cannot afford to concede any territory of Kashmir either to Pakistan or China. No part of Indian territory by any stretch of imagination can be said to be of no value to India. Every particle of the Indian land is worth worship for Indians.

## An Important Formulation

An important formulation often missed about Tibet is its access to the world outside is "far easier" from India than through the Aksai Chin road. In the event, border trade between India and Tibet makes much more economic sense than hauling goods and services all the way across the Chinghai-Tibet road that "snakes along" for more than 1400 miles across the world's most impossible terrain.[57]

On Siachcn, Sahdev Vohra, in his published work *The Border Dispute with China*, makes the point that attempts by Pakistan to attack Indian positions on the glacier were on the old track route from Khapalu along the Saltoro Valley to Sinkiang, which could only benefit the Chinese position in the trans-Karakoram area that acts as a buffer between China and Russia. The British Raj involved Afghanistan to act as a buffer between the Indian empire and Tsarist/Soviet Russia; China today was attempting to use Pakistan in a similar role.[58]

Siachen glacier is completely under Indian control. Since 1983, the Pakistan and Indian troops are holding positions on the Saltoro ridge, which is west of the Siachen glaciers. Incidently, this is roughly along the high crest dividing the watershed between the Siachen group of glaciers to its east, and Saltoro-Kondus-Bilafond glaciers on its West. This position held by two sides is also in consonance with the accepted international norms for locating frontiers in high mountain regions, and implements in practice the Karachi Agreement signed between India and Pakistan in 1947.[59]

Siachen glacier is one of the world's largest mountain glaciers, lying in the Karakoram Range system of Kashmir near the India-Pakistan border, extending 70 km from north-northwest to south-southeast. It has a number of fast-flowing surface streams and atleast 12 medial moraines. It is the source for the 50 miles long Nubra River, a tributary of the Shyok, which is part of the Indus River system.[60]

Karakoram Range system occupies about 207,000 sq. km. The Karakorams consist of a group of parallel ranges with several spurs and are characterized by craggy peaks, steep slopes, and heavy glaciation. The range forms one of the highest mountain systems in the world, with an average height of about 20,000 feet. The international boundaries of the Soviet Union, China, Pakistan, Afghanistan and India all are covered within the highest mountains of the system. Surrounded by a number of other very high mountains ranges with immense glaciers, the glaciers, the Karakorams are virtually inaccessible. Mountain passes are situated at elevation of about 16,000 feet and are open only for five or six months of the year. The completion of the Karakoram Highway in 1978 improved transportation in the region. Owing to severe natural conditions, the mountain population is very sparse. In the south the inhabitants are concentrated mainly in a few small towns; while on the northern slope Tibetan farmers live in villages at elevations upto 14,800 feet. Most engage in subsistence agriculture and livestock raising. Wild animals of the region include the snow leopard, wild Yak and Tibetan antelope.[61]

Kashmir, undoubtedly, is land of surpassing natural beauty. The Himalayas have many other beautiful valleys and countless other places from which the great snow ranges and peaks can be seen, but none of these have the same combination of mountain and meadow, river and lake, glacier and forest, that are afforded by Kashmir.[62] James P. Ferguson, in *Kashmir: An Historical Introduction* depicts Kashmir, a meeting-place of three great cultures—Hindu, Muslim and Buddhist. The splendid epochs of each of these cultures all have their connection with Kashmir. But the distinctive feature of Kashmir is that these three cultures are not merely stages of past history but are living, co-existent forces. The Kashmiri Pandit is one of the most distinguished representatives of Hinduism today. No one follows the five-fold injunction to prayer more piously than the Muslim of the Valley, while in Ladakh the larger rocks crowned with gompas-Buddhist monastery and prayer wheels; chortens-Buddhist cenotaph and mane walls-prayer wall are evident in every village. In Kashmir one finds a spector of the three great religious systems of Asia, existing side by side and ruling the lives of their followers with unabated power.[63] Kashmir needs such a revival, and once again its people living in amity and peace.

## REFERENCES AND NOTES

1. Alastair Lamb, *The Kashmir Problem*, (1986) pp. 11-12.
2. Ibid., pp. 12-13
3. Joseph Korbel, *Danger in Kashmir* (1954).
4. Alastair Lamb, *The Kashmir Problem*, (1968) p. 14.
5. "Some Rights other Wrongs", *Indian Express*, February 11, 1994, p. 8.
6. *The Times of India* and *New York Times*, December 16. 1971. Also see Gulab Mishra "Prabhakar", *Indo-Pakistan Relations* (1987) p. 360.

7. Manorama Year Books, (1994) p. 221.
8. Gul Mohd Wani, *Kashmir Politics: Problems and Prospects*, (1993) p. 11.
9. Francis Young Husband, *Kashmir*, Edinburg, (1909) p.161.
10. Gul Mohd Wani, *Kashmir Politics: Problems and Prospects* (1993) p. 13.
11. Dr. R.K. Parmu, *A History of Muslim Rule in Kashmir*, 1320-1819, (1969) p. 50.
12. Ibid..p. 52.
13. Lord Birdwood, *Two Nations and Kashmir*, (1956) p.13.
14. *Treaty of Amritsar*, 1846, Article.1.
15. G.M. Telang, "Myths about Kashmir", *Indian Express*, October 27, 1993.
16. K.M. Panikkar, The Founding of the Kashmir State, first published 1930, under the "Gulab Singh", (Second) Impression (1953) pp. 124-125.
17. Kashmir Imbroglio : Diagnosis and Remedy
18. Dr. R.K. Parmu, *A History of Muslim Rule in Kashmir*, 1320-1819, (1969) p. 389.
19. Ibid.
20. See Accession Agreement dated October 26, 1947.
21. Sukant Gupta, "Tibetan's never-ending Struggle", *The Tribune*, March 19, 1994, p.8.
22. *Tibet: Proving Truth from Facts*, (April 1993) p. 17.
23. *The New Encyclopaedia Britannica*, Vol. I, Micropaedia, Chicago, (1992) p. 753.
24. Manorama Year Book, (1992) p. 192.
25. *The New Encyclopaedia Britannica*, Vol. 1, Micropaedia, Chicago, (1992) p.753.
26. Manorama Year Book, (1992) p. 192.
27. Ibid.

28. Bakshi Ghulam Muhammad, "Kashmir and the Plebiscite". *The Modern Review*, (May 1954) p. 347.
29. Rajesh Kadain, *The Kashmir Tangle: Issues and Options*. (1992) pp. 166-167.
30. Ibid.,p.l67.
31. Ibid., p. 169.
32. Prem Nath Bazaz, *Kashmir in Crucible*, (1967).
33. "Testing Time in Kashmir", *The Tribune*, February 1. 1994, p. 8,
34. Ramesh Khazanchi., "Follies of Plebiscite in Kashmir". *The Times of India*, March 9, 1994, p. 12.
35. Dinanath Raina, *Unhappy Kashmir*, (1990) p. 4.
36. Alastair Lamb, *The Kashmir Problem: A Historical Survey*, (1968) p. 19.
37. Dr. R. K. Parmu, *A History of Muslim Rule in Kashmir*, 1320-1819, (1969) p. 44. Ibid., pp. 44-45.
38. Ibid., pp.44-45
39. Alexander Cunningham, *Ladakh Physical, Statistical and Historical* (1970) p. 16.
40. Ibid.
41. Ibid.,y.l7.
42. "Right Step in Ladakh", *The Tribune* dated March 8, 1994, p. 8.
43. Ibid.
44. Ibid.
45. Helena Norberg-Hodge, "Ancient Futures: Learning from Ladakh"; Sierra Club Books, (1991).
46. "Right step in Ladakh", *The Tribune* dated March 8, 1994, p. 8.
47. Dinesh Kumar, "Kargil Fatwas against militancy", *The Times of India*, January 31, 1994,p.7.

48. Ibid.

49. C.E. Tyndale Biscoe, *Kashmir in Sunlight and Shade*, (1971) p. 203.

50. Ramesh Khazanchi, "Follies of Plebiscite In Kashmir", *The Times of India*, March 9, 1994, p. 12.

51. The Chinese Threat, Publications Division, Ministry of Information and Broadcasting, Govt. of India, (1963) p. 47.

52. Sahdev Vohra, *The Border Dispute with China*, (1994).

53. Parshotam Mehra, "Well drawn border study with China", *The Sunday Tribune*, March 13, 1994, p. 8.

54. Ibid.

55. Alastair Lamb, *The Kashmir Problem: A Historical Survey*. (1968) p. 96.

56. Ibid.

57. Parshotam Mehra, "Well drawn border study with China", *The Sunday Tribune*, March 13, 1994, p. 8.

58. Ibid.

59. Jasjit Singh, "Defusing Siachen: Clear definition of Line of Control is crucial", *Indian Express*, December 27,1993, p. 6.

60. *New Encyclopaedia, Britannica*, Vol. 10, Micropaedia, Chicago, (1992) p. 774.

61. The New Encyclopaedia Britannica, Vol. 6, Micropaedia, Chicago, (1992) p.738.

62. James P. Ferguson, *Kashmir: An Historical Introduction*, (1961) p. 9.

63. Ibid., p. 10.

PART — VII

# Demand for Autonomy

## Chapter 19

# A Case for Greater Autonomy

On 9th July 2000, at New Delhi, Justice R. S. Sarkaria, who headed the commission on Centre-state relations, said that it is possible to give Jammu and Kashmir greater autonomy under the Constitution. He accused the Centre of having failed in adhering to the true spirit of the federation.

In an interview to a TV channel, Justice Sarkaria referred to the Kashmir problem and said, "The solution lies within the present Constitution. The Centre can easily delegate more powers under the Concurrent List to the states without needing to go in for a Constitution amendment, not just for Jammu and Kashmir but for every Indian state."

Except for certain key areas like national security, defence and external affairs, he said "the Centre can easily give more powers to the states, at least in practice. The moment you do this, everything will be resolved. Article 370, other separatist demands in the north-east, nothing will matter."

He described as unfortunate and even dangerous the demand of the Rashtriya Swayamsevak Sangh-Bharatiya Janata Party combine for abolition of Article 370 at this stage.

He said this could only cause more trouble and even lend Pakistan a propaganda weapon. He said the Article has in any case been "watered down" over the years and J&K did not have many powers under this Article today.

He found it amusing that those politicians who had scoffed at and violated his report earlier were now citing it as a solution to the Centre-state disputes. A case in point was the misuse of Article 356, he said, which had been misused by all parties.

The Constitution of India envisages a federal structure with unitary bias. The word federalism appeared nowhere in the Indian Constitution despite the presence of substantial provisions. To quote Dr. Ambedkar, "Although the Constitution is a federal Constitution as much as it established what may be called as dual polity which will consist of the union at the Centre and the States at the periphery, each endowed with sovereign powers to be exercised in the field assigned to them repetitively by the constitution yet the Constitution has avoided the tight mould of federalism...... and could be both unitary and federal according to the requirements of time and circumstances." This ambiguity has been cause of varied tensions, debates, conflicts and controversies increasing with the actual working of the political system in India.

Till 1967 as the Congress Party was ruling both in the Centre and in the States the relations between the Centre and the State were by and large smooth. In the post-1967 developments different parties came to power in different states. This has been compounded by the overall changes in the political process and consequences of socio-economic developments.

## Deviation from the Path

The framers of the Indian Constitution were in favour of a strong and united India vis-a-vis fissiparous forces and other parochial tendencies as also to undertake the tasks of national defence, planning, removal of poverty and backwardness, consolidation of democracy and freedom and performing an effective role in world affairs. However, there was sincere desire for a federal spirit. On August 3, 1949, Dr. Ambedkar had insisted that it was a federal polity which the Constitution would establish. "The States under our Constitution are in no way dependent upon the Centre for their legislative or executive authority. The Centre and the Sates are co-equal in this matter. In spite of this pious intent the reality today is very different. Four decades of the working of India's federal system reveals flaws and weaknesses both at the structural and the functional levels." Since the adoption of the Constitution the trend has been relentlessly, mindlessly towards amassing of power by the Centre, crippling the autonomy of the States. This process of centralization has brought two interrelated phenomenon to the fore. One, tension in Centre-State relations and demand for autonomy for states; second, Regionalism.

## Major Areas of Tensions in Indian Federalism

1. Role of Governor as a representative of the Central Government with regard to appointing and dismissal of State Ministries and dissolution of the Sate Assemblies.

2. Misuse of powers of imposition of President's Rule Under Article 356.

3. Reservations of Bills for the consideration of the President under Article 201.

4. Fiscal matters including sharing of finances and Central approval of State projects.

5. Use of Electronic media.

Within these five major areas there are several other issues of administrative and political processes.

## Role of Governor

Since 1967, when the monopoly of the Congress Party was shattered, the role of Governor assumed great significance. This has been aggravated because of nature of multi-party system and prevalence of the phenomenon of defections. The ruling party at the Centre found in the office of Governor an effective instrument to recapture power for itself. As Soli J. Sorabjee puts it. "It will not be exaggeration to say that no institution or constitutional office has suffered greater erosion or degradation than the office of Governor. The public today generally regard the Governor as an employee of the Central Government and in some cases as a spy of the Centre. The unfortunate fact is that few incumbents of this high office have any clear conception of their role in our constitutional scheme and in fact regard themselves as the lackeys of employees of the Central Government and readily act according to its behest."

The office of Governor was used to topple down the State Governments on one pretext or the other during seventies and eighties. As early as in 1953 Gian Singh Rarewala led coalition ministry in PEPSU was dismissed on the ground of law and order. Dr. Ambedkar, then a member of the Rajya Sabha, called it "a rape of the constitution." Then again in 1959 Namboodripad led communist government enjoying majority support in Kerala was dismissed likewise. Thereafter it has been done more than 80 times in various states.

During Mrs. Gandhi's regime the trend of appointing Governors after consulting State Chief Ministers was relegated. Mr. Rajiv Gandhi followed the same pattern. The practice of sacking of Governors for partisan reasons has also been followed.

Apart from toppling or dismissing ministries the governors have been used to interfere in the State

Government's affairs in the name of their discretionary powers. The attitude of Ms. Kumudben Joshi towards the TDP Government in 1980s in Andhra Pradesh was manifest in a variety of activities she undertook in the name of social service. Her refusal to clear some appointments and deletion from Cabinet prepared addresses were criticised as indications of her non-cooperative stand against the norms of parliamentary form of government. Similarly in 1988-89. Mrs. Ram Dulari Sinha, Governor of Kerala was almost on a confrontationist line with the CPI(M) led left Democratic Ministry. Since 1967 Governors have been used to dissolve or suspend State Legislative Assemblies to help the ruling party at the centre to form governments at its convenience.

Governor's abuse of their powers and interferences in State Government affairs for partisan reasons has been giving rise to a sense of insecurity among States and a demand for settling the issues of appointment and dismissal of Governors themselves, their compulsion to act on the advice of Council of Ministers, and definite code for the exercise of discretionary powers.

## Misuse of President's Rule

The provision for imposition of President's rule in States under Article 356 was made to deal with serious situations as a life saving device to be used as a measure of last resort. However, in practice, this article has been frequently used for purely partisan interests.

***Imposition of President's Rule***—The use of Article 356 rests on the subjective satisfaction of the President. President's rule can be imposed either on the recommendations of Governor or even without that, purely for the satisfaction of President himself. The Prime Minister can also make use of Article 356 to ensure that the administration in State is carried on in accordance with the provisions of the Constitution, and otherwise, dissolve the State Government on the basis of his own assessment of the representative character or otherwise. In practice these provisions have been misused by :

(i) Dismissing the State Government and on partisan consideration;

(ii) Suspending and dissolving the Assemblies on partisan consideration;

(iii) Not giving a chance to the opposition to form government when electoral verdict was indecisive;

(iv) Denying opportunity to the opposition to form government when ministry resigned in anticipation of the defeat on the floor of the House;

(v) Not allowing the opposition to form government even after the defeat of the ministry on the floor of the House.

Drawing attention to the repeated abuse of Article 356, The Sarkaria Commission has pointed out that during the period 1951 to 1987, of the 75 occasions when the President's rule was imposed, only in 26 cases was it inevitable. Soon after coming to power in 1977, the Janata government dismissed Congress Governments in nine States at one go. In 1980 on returning back to power Mrs. Gandhi repeated the performance in nine States governments by the Janata Party. The use of Article 356 was made so frequently during Mr. Rajiv Gandhi's tenure that it showed an intolerant attitude of the Central Government towards the non-Congress (I) State Governments. President's Rule continued for almost five years (May 1987 to February 1992) in Punjab at a stretch.

***Deployment of Central Forces***—The deployment of central forces in the States to maintain law and order has been made many a time without consulting the State Governments and sometimes against the wishes of the State Governments. "Public Order" is exclusively a State subject. Neither the Centre's legislative nor its executive power can transgress into this sphere of State authority. Only if "public order" is flouted on such a large scale in a State as to constitute "internal disturbance." does the Centre's duty get activated as defined in Article 355, Ramakrishna Hegde points out that read together, the provision means that it is necessary to invoke the services of any Central force "in aid of the civil power", if the situation gets out of the exclusive control of state, though its primary responsibility for "public order" remains. In the exceptional situation, however, the Centre shares the responsibility, since its forces are being used besides the State Police.

Deployment of any the Centre's force "in aid of the civil power" is exclusively a union subject. The 42nd Amendment (1976) had inserted in the Constitution Article 257-A which empowered the Union to deploy a central force "for dealing with any grave situation of law and order in any State." During Janata rule this provision was deleted in 1979 by the 44th Amendment. "A grave situation of law and order" is basically different from the "internal disturbance" envisaged in Article 355.

However, in recent years, after any disturbance of law and order, Central Ministers have felt free to roam in any State for sheer partisan ends, making orders directly to State officials, ignoring the State Ministers, and at times insulting them as well. For instance, on July 25, 1988, the then Union Minister of State for Home, Mrs. Ram Dulari Sinha, declared after a visit to Karamihedu in Andhra Pradesh, "If such incidents continue, the Centre will have to intervene."

The obvious meaning of Centre's intervention is imposition of President's rule. Hegde points out that far graver incidents have occurred in Congress (I) ruled States without either of these steps in redress. A situation in which the State Governments exist and function at the sweet will of the Centre reflects a total negation of federalism.

The provision for imposition of President's rule is not in conformity with federal as well as democratic principles. Frequently used for part is an ends, it has become an irritating contention between Centre-State relations. Hence, there has been a persistent demand for the deletion of the Article 356 from the Constitution.

## Reservation of Bills

The power of the Governor to reserve a bill, passed by the State Legislature, for the President's assent is another cause of tension between the Centre and the State. This has especially been so in case where, presumably under the direction of the Central Government, the governor has reserved a bill against the advice of the State Ministry.

Through this provision, contained in Article 200 and 201, the Centre wants to keep watch on the activities of the States. However, Governors have used Articles in most of the cases to serve the interest of the ruling party at the Centre which led to a good deal of controversy. Several examples can be cited in this regard.

On September 23, 1990, *Sunday Mail* reported that the President had yet to give assent to as many as 74 Bills referred to him by different State Governors. Of these, two had been pending for seven years, three for six years, two for five years, seven for three years and 58 for the past one year. The report further says that the Home Ministry has a stock reply to any queries regarding the fate of Bills. Thus after making the

Karnataka Government wait for six years, the Home Ministry wrote to the State Government that its Education Bill, 1983 was under examination.

The opposition ruled states have from time to time raised their voice against the misuse of Article 200 and 201. In its memorandum to Sarkaria Commission, the Bhartiya Janata Party alleged that the bills have been reserved for consideration of the President in order to create difficulties for the State Governments. In its reply to the Sarkaria Commission's questionnaire, The West Bengal Government felt that Articles 200 and 201 have to be deleted or a constitutional amendment should clarify that the Governor would not act in his discretion but only on the advice of the State Council of Ministers. At the opposition conclave held at Srinagar in 1983, all the opposition parties demanded the removal of the power of the Centre to veto through the President the laws passed by the State Legislature. In 1983 the four Chief Ministers from Southern States demanded legislatures to enact laws on subjects for which constitutionally they have executive responsibility without having to seek the President's assent.

## Fiscal Matters

The most controversial and ticklish problem between the Centre and the States in a federal system is that of financial relations. The demand of the State for greater fiscal autonomy has become one of the most debated issues of the Indian Federation. The tension between Centre and States with regard to fiscal relations arises because of comparative powers of taxation, statutory versus discretionary grants, and economic planning.

***Comparative Power of Taxation***—As against those of the States, sources of revenue of the Centre are relatively elastic and expensive. The Centre also controls vast resources generated through deficit financing, loans from organised money-market in the country as well as huge funds of foreign aid. The residuary powers of taxation are also vested with the Central Government. The Constitution also authorizes the Centre to collect surcharges on taxes to raise additional funds in times of emergency. In practice surcharge has become a permanent feature of income tax structure. The corporate tax, which keeps on expanding is in the exclusive purview of the Centre. Given the taxation powers the States do not have sufficient resources of their own to discharge their responsibilities. The gap between State revenues and their expenditure has been increasing, partly due to State's own inability to mobilise even these resources which they can, as also incurring wasteful expenses in populism. The states are therefore dependent on central assistance.

***Statutory vs. Discretionary Grants***—There are four methods for devolution of funds from the Centre to the States— (a) obligatory sharing of union taxes on income; (b) permissive sharing of Union excise duties; (c) assignment of certain union duties and taxes wholly to the States; and (d) provision for giving financial assistance to the States in the form of grants and loans. Articles 280 and 281 provide for the appointment of an independent statutory finance Commission every fifth year or earlier as the President of India desires. With regard to sharing of resources and assignment of certain resources entirely to the States, Finance Commission was to regulate, co-ordinate and integrate the finances of the Government of India and the State Governments. Originally, it was intended to cover all the financial transfers from the Centre to States. However, slowly Planning Commission has been brought in for the purpose and now it plays a more important part in devolution of resources from the Centre to the States. As a completely Central institution the Planning

Commission is politically influenced and the states have a sense of discrimination in allocation of grants. The Planning Commission's authority to determine the scope and pattern of a major portion of Central assistance to States has relegated the role of Finance Commission to a subsidiary one. The Centre does not seem to be much serious even about the reduced role of Finance Commission. In addition provision for grants-in-aid by the Centre is purely a political and arbitrary means of devolution. The Centre has been making use of this more and more and that too in a controversial manner.

Under article 281, centre gives grants-in-aid to States on its discretion for undertaking welfare schemes, meet natural calamities or for removal of disparities, etc. The centre discriminates between States being ruled by different political parties. H.A. Ghani points out that a close scrutiny of the Central relief to the States affected by natural calamities indicates that no well-considered norms were followed in this regard. Preoccupied by political considerations, the Central teams have always assessed the damage done by droughts, flood, etc, in an ad hoc perfunctory manner.

***Economic Planning***—The process of planning in India has tended to push the political system to greater centralization due to the central control over resources for development and the preponderance of the centralised planning machinery. R.K. Hegde points out that the gravest and most harmful consequence of the atrophy of the state's domain in the economic field is in regard to industries and economic planning. For example, according to the Constitution, industries are essentially a state subject. Only those industries are to be regulated by the Centre, the control of which by the Union is declared as expedient in the public interest by Parliament. More than 90 per cent of the organised industries in terms of value output have been brought under of the Union. The regulation of industrial activity by the Union

Government has on several occasions inhibited the setting up of new industries.

In the name of national planning, the centre has been inordinately delaying for political consideration viable and important state projects. On the other hand, Centre has been super-imposing its schemes on the States which were deemed by State government to be irrelevant to the conditions prevailing in the States. Hence, the opposition conclave held at Srinagar in October, 1983 said in a consensus statement that the present authority of the Planning Commission and Union Ministry of Finance offering discretionary grants to the States must be drastically reduced.

## Use of Electronic Media

In the recent past the use of electronic media for political purposes has also become a serious tension area in Centre-State relations. According to the Constitution all laws and regulations concerning Broadcasting emanate exclusively from the Central Government. But during the 1980s the media has been systematically used by the Central Government to black out anything critical of its performance. The opposition was not only almost totally ignored but unfair and uncalled for charges were hurled against it. Everything that the Centre did not like was censored. Broadcasting of radio and television has become Delhi-centred.

The opposition parties have from time to time protested against the misuse of AIR and Doordarshan. The official media came in for universal criticism at the conclave held at Srinagar in October 1983. The participants alleged that from the very beginning the media had been a "mouth piece" of the Union Government. It had virtually became the "Voice of Congress (1)." To save the radio and television from the increasing misuse by the ruling party at the Centre, the conclave called upon the Central Government to set up a statutory central communication council.

## Demand for Autonomy

In the last four decades all consensus and cooperation has been eroded and replaced by a growing politics of confrontation. The states have been developing a sense of deprivation on the ground that the Centre has denied them the autonomy that has been guaranteed under the Constitution. The trend towards centralization has not been weakened despite changes in government. The demand for a greater and more meaningful devolution of power has been assertively and more stridently articulated over the years. Immediately after 1967 elections there emerged a general criticism on the issue of Centre-State relations in view of Congress losing power in eight States and office of Governor becoming controversial. In view of the widespread criticism, the Union Government asked the Administrative Reforms Commission (appointed in 1967) to look into the Centre-State administrative relations. The Commission recommended that powers should be delegated to the maximum extent to the States. It also opined that centralized planning had tended towards excessive interference in the freedom of States to work out their policies and programmes. The Commission made recommendations with regard to the office of Governor and suggested the need to establish an Inter-State Council under Article 263 of the Constitution. However, the process of centralization continued.

## Tamil Nadu

In 1969, the Tamil Nadu Government took the initiative and appointed Rajamannar Committee, to go into the question of Centre-State relations. The Committee submitted its report in 1971. The recommendations made by it included readjustment in Scheduled VII of the Constitution to transfer residuary powers to the states; repeal of Article 249 and modification of Article 252; repeal of Article 200 and 201 and reorganisation of Finance Commission and Planning Commission.

### West Bengal

In December 1977, the West Bengal Government published a memorandum on Centre-State relations, according to which in a country like India, with such diversities in race, religion, language and culture, national integration could be achieved only through conscious voluntary efforts and devolution of powers to ward off fissiparous tendencies. The West Bengal Memorandum inter alia demanded that the word 'Federal' should replace the word 'Union' in the Preamble of the Constitution. It also suggested the repeal of Articles 356, 357 and 360. According to it, the State's consent should be made mandatory for the formation of new States and alteration of areas, boundaries or names of existing States.

### Punjab

In Punjab in 1978, Akali Dal released the revised version of Anandpur Sahib Resolution, originally adopted in 1973. This resolution demanded greater State autonomy and wanted to leave very little with the Centre. According to it, Centre's authority should be confined only to Defence, Foreign Relations, Communications, Railways and Currency, and the entire residuary powers be vested in the States.

### Post-1980 Period

In the post-1980 period the opposition increasingly became regional in its orientation. It put forth the demand of State autonomy. Some prominent leaders including Farooq Abdullah, Karunanidhi, Barnala, Hegde, Rama Rao and

Mohanta attended the conclaves arranged for discussion in autonomy at Vijayawada, Delhi and Srinagar. To articulate the demand of greater State autonomy, a good number of seminars were arranged including the one held at Bangalore from 5th August to 7th August, 1983. After seven hours of deliberation at Vijaywada conclave of opposition parties, a lengthy statement was issued attacking the Central Government for encroaching upon the powers of the States. The three-day opposition conclave held at Srinagar in October, 1987 called upon the people to save the country from disintegration by halting the 'dangerous drift' due to the centralization of power and distortion of the Constitution. It issued a consensus statement seeking a full review of Centre-State relations, checking the unitary overtones which overshadow the federal features of the Constitution and change the centralised pattern of economic and financial administration. It added that to end the tensions and disputes between the Centre and the States, it was necessary to curtail the arbitrary powers of the Centre with respect to the States. It suggested that Article 356 which enabled the President to dissolve the State Government or assembly should be suitably amended. In case of a constitutional breakdown, it should be obligatory for the Centre to hold elections within six months.

The supporters of decentralization of powers and autonomy for States argue that the preservation of national unity and the process of consolidating the forces of national integration presuppose the acceptance of the manifold diversities, present in the nation and the urgent need for realistic and logical attempts to handle these diversities at the local level, by harnessing local initiative and utilizing local talent. Any attempt to tackle these diversities from a central point of control would only serve to heighten the tensions in the system. Contrary to this those who advocate greater consolidation of the powers of the Centre opine that providing an impetus to the forces of nationalism was critical to strengthening national integration. They are emphatic in their belief that any step in the direction of weakening the Centre would only open the flood-gates to eventual "balkanisation." A strong Centre is the only panacea to stem the institutionalisation of sub-national loyalties. According to this viewpoint the Centre is believed to protect and project national integration while other centres of power would only encourage and abate the rise and growth of divisive forces.

However, events both in India and in other parts of the world have shown that whereas decentralization aims at fulfilling the hopes and aspirations of the people in a more purposive and meaningful manner, it is the process of centralization which triggers off the process of disintegration.

## Sarkaria Commission

In this background the decade of the eighties in particular witnessed a struggle to get the federal issue on the nation's agenda. When the political challenge assumed new dimensions and tensions between the Centre and the State grew in sharpness, it became necessary to ease the situation somewhat. In this context the Government of India announced on March 24, 1983 the appointment of a Commission to examine and review the working of existing arrangement between the Union and the States in regard to powers, functions and responsibilities in all spheres and recommend appropriate changes and measures. The Commission came to be known as the Sarkaria Commission on Centre-State Relations after the name of its Chairman, Justice (Retd.) R.S. Sarkaria. The Commission was asked to keep in view the social and economic developments that have taken place over the years as also the scheme and the framework of the Constitution and the need for preserving the unity and integrity of the country.

## Tension Areas in Union-State Relations

*Opposite Trends.* From the replies to the questionnaire and memoranda submitted by the State Governments and political parties the Sarkaria Commission identified certain major issues in Union-State relationship. Some issues are from the way the constitutional institutions have been utilized, others from the gap between the theory and the practice or the spirit and substance. Some arise from political differences between the Union and the State Government and others from a general notion of uniformity in "the standard of administration through centralization. Therefore, while there were certain common grievances regarding the intrusion of the Centre into the States, there were specific grievances regarding the individual experience in inter-governmental relationship.

According in its report submitted on October 27,1987 the Sarkaria Commission observed :

"The survey of the developments of the past 37 years brings out clearly the diametrically opposed trends. On the one hand, a number of facts, primarily centripetal economic forces, have stengthened the impulses of centralization, modernization, growth and development. On the other, very strong centrifugal forces have been unleashed in the country on account of break-up of the old political order, split of national parties, ever increasing exploitation of populist slogans and caste, language, money and muscle power in elections. Corruption in many walks of life, emergence of linguistic chauvinism and fissiparous tendencies..,. .all these point to increasing rush weather ahead for our ship of state."

*A Strong Centre without Centralization.* As the only safeguard to national integrity which was being threatened severely in the light of recent fissiparious tendencies in the body politics, however, the Sarkaria Commission favoured a strong Centre. The Commission did not equate strong Centre with centralization of powers. In fact, it viewed centralization as dangerous for national integration. The Commission observes :

"Those in power at the centre, have been obliged to use diverse strategies and tactics which were not always sound from long-term interests, to maintain their control over state-level forces. Many a time, the actions of the centre, its discriminatory approach towards some states, its lack of understanding of local problems, its abject insensitiveness and the blunted misuse of authority vis-a-vis the states have all distanced it from the people. This, in turn has, it is believed, reversed the process of national integration. The divisive tendencies have been further compounded by such a short sighted approach."

The Commission noted : "There is considerable truth in the saying that under centralisation leads to blood pressure at the centre and anemia at the periphery. The inevitable result is morbidity and inefficiency. Indeed, centralisation does not solve but aggravate the problems of the people."

*The Premise of Recommendations.* The Sarkaria Commission's recommendations are primarily based on the premise that the existing constitutional principles and arrangements are sound and what is needed is to build a mechanism to ensure a system of collective decision. It was not concerned with the politics of Centre-State relations but only with the "administration." The total of 265 recommendations were classified subject wise under twenty areas. Underlying all these is an assumption of the superior calibre of the central institutions and personnel over those of the States.

However, it did emphasise the need for a real understanding between the Centre and the States and make amendments to allow the Indian polity grow on federal principles.

## Salient proposals of the Sarkaria Commission

1. More extensive and generous use of Article 258 which gives powers to Union government to confer powers, etc., to State governments should be made than as hitherto being done.

2. Any move to disband the All India Services or to permit the State government to opt out the scheme must be regarded as retrograde and harmful to the larger interest of the country. The All India Services should be further strengthened and greater emphasis laid on the role expected to be played by them.

3. Whenever, the Union proposes to undertake legislation with respect to a matter in the concurrent list, there should be prior consultation not only with the State governments, individually, but also collectively. There should be regular consultations on the management of All India Services between the Union and the State governments.

4. The Planning Commission and the National Development Council are to be reformed assuring at the same time of full and effective consultation with the States at all stages of the planning process so that they feel that their role in it is not that of a supplicant, but of an equal participant.

5. Before the Union government deploys its armed and other forces in a state in aid of the civil power otherwise than on request from the State government or declares any area within a State as 'disturbed', it is desirable that the State government should be consulted, wherever feasible, and its

cooperation sought, even though prior consultation with the State government in not obligatory.

6. Close and fullest involvement of the States at all stages of plan formulation is very essential for the successful implementation of the same.

7. Convention as to consultation with State governments in concurrent list individuals as well as collectively should be strictly adhered to except in extreme emergency.

8. Governor should not, on demitting his office, be eligible for any other appointment or office of profit under the Union or State government.

9. As a matter of salutary convention Bills reserved for President's assent should be disposed of within 4 months.

10. As a matter of convention, President should not withhold assent on the consideration of policy differences on matters in the State list except on grounds of patent unconstitutionality.

11. Article 356 (emergency provisions) should be used very sparingly in extreme cases as a measure of last resort when all available alternatives fail.

12. The healthy convention that as a principle High court judges are not transferred except with their consent should continue. As a matter of healthy practice, the Chief Justice of India before formulating his opinion on the proposed transfer of a Judge take into confidence two senior Judges of the Supreme Court.

13. An over all comprehensive review of Centrally Sponsored Schemes should be made periodically by the Planning Commission and it should be placed before the NEDC for consideration.

14. It will be in the best interests of the concerned governments to take explicitly into account the high opportunity cost of populist Schemes and to examine whether any important programmes of development are compromised due to such diversion of resources.

15. Finance Commission Division should in cooperation with the States, organize comprehensive studies on trends in growth of public expenditure in the States.

16. An expert committee with representatives from the States may be appointed by the Union government to recommend reforms in taxation and inter Alia consider the potential for resource mobilization by the Union and the States.

17. National Development Council (NDC) should be renamed and reconstituted as the National Economic Development Council (NEDC) by Presidential order. It should be made to function more effectively and emerge as the highest political level inter-government body for giving a direction and thrust to planned development of the country.

18. A Standing Committee of the NEDC should be constituted consisting of the Prime Minister, Finance Minister and three other Union Ministers, six Chief Ministers, and others.

19. An expert committee should be constituted to enquire into and revive from time to time in consultation with the States the operational feasibility of the scope for leaving taxes and duties under Article 269 and the complementary measures, the State government would be required to take. (Taxes levied under this article are collected by the Union Government and assigned to the States).

20. All matters which need to be sorted out between the Union Government and a Union Territory with legislature

may be discussed by a Standing Committee for Union Territory.

21. Norms and standards in education are to be determined by the Union and professional bodies like the University Grants Commission, while the implementation is left to the States.

22. In order to ensure effective consultation with the State Chief Minister in the selection of a person to be appointed as Governor, the procedure of consultation should be prescribed in the Constitution itself by suitably amending Article 155.

23. Residuary powers of legislation in regard to taxation matters should continue to remain exclusively in the competence of Parliament while the residuary field other than that of taxation should be placed in the concurrent list.

24. Clause (2) of Article 252 may be substituted by a new clause providing that an act passed by Parliament under clause (1) may be amended or replaced either by Parliament, or by the Legislature of the State to which it applies after receiving the assent of the President.

25. Safeguards should be incorporated in Article 356 to enable Parliament to review continuance in force of a proclamation.

26. By an appropriate amendment of the Constitution the net proceeds of the Corporation Tax may be made permissible shareable with the states, if and as Parliament may by law so provide.

27. The Constitution should be suitably amended to add the subject of taxation of 'advertisement broadcast by radio or television' to the present Entry 92, List (Union list) and Article 269 (1) (f) relating to duties and taxes leveled and collected by the Union assigned to States.

28. There is a case for providing appropriate safeguards against the misuse of powers under 45 of List III (concurrent area) in the Commission of Enquiry Act itself. (The item relates to enquiries and statistics specified in State list or concurrent list).

29. Inter-State River Water Disputes Act may be amended to make it mandatory on the Union government to constitute a tribunal within one year of receipt of an application from a State and should be amended to empower the Union government to appoint a tribunal when it is satisfied that a case exists, to require States to furnish necessary data to the tribunal, to make the award of the tribunal effective within 5 years to give the award of the tribunal the same sanction and force as that of a decree of a Supreme Court.

## Inter-State Council

On top of this elaborate scheme of establishing a cooperative Union-State relations through extensive arrangements for consultation, discussion and participation, is the recommendation relating to the setting up of a permanent Inter-State Council under Article 263 of the Constitution. It would discuss many of the problems of common Union-State interest. It would consist of a General Body with Prime Minister as Chairman and all Union Cabinet Ministers and all Chief Ministers as members. It will have a Standing Committee with the Prime Minister as Chairman, Six Union Cabinet Ministers and Six Chief Ministers one from each zone as members. The Inter-State Council is expected to provide a forum for discussion in camera among senior statesmen, to promote proper understanding and mutual confidence among the Chief Executives of the Union and the States.

The Commission also provided for a permanent secretariat for the Council.

## More Radical Suggestions

Judged from the standpoint of Centre-State relations, the net result of the working of our present constitution has been the growth of regionalism, separatism, centre-state disputes and violence. Therefore more radical suggestions mooted by some political parties and several citizens and experts, for improving Centre-State relations, involve certain structural modifications in the constitutional provisions. These include the proposals to :

(i) Amend Article 248 to provide the legislature of the state with exclusive power to make any law with respect to any matter listed in the Union List or Concurrent List. That is, the residuary power of the federation should lie with the states.

(ii) Delete Article 249 that gives power to Parliament to legislate on the State List, by the concurrence of the Rajya Sabha on a matter deemed by it to be of national interest. This short-circuits the amending process laid down in Article 368, and unilaterally transfers a subject from the State List to the Concurrent List. A better and more equitable alternative is any how available in Article 252(1) even if it be cumbersome and time-consuming.

(iii) Amend Article 280 (regarding the Finance Commission), and provide for the transfer of seventy-five per cent of the total revenue raised by the Centre from all sources, to the States.

(iv) Delete Article 302 (regarding the power of Parliament to impose restriction on trade and commerce with a State or between the States).

(v) Delete Articles 356 and 357 (Emergency provisions, giving right to the Centre to dissolve a State Assembly and impose Presidential rule).

(vi) Delete Article 360 (Financial provision) that empowers the President to interfere in State administration, on ground of threat of financial instability.

(vii) Delete Article 200 and 201 which empower the Governor to withhold assent to bills, and reserve them for Presidential approval.

(viii) Amend Articles 368, to ensure that no amendment of the constitution is possible without two thirds majority of the members of Parliament, present and voting.

(ix) Amend Article 3, to ensure that the name and area of a state cannot be changed by Parliament without the consent of the state legislature concerned.

(x) Retain Article 370 appertaining to the special status of Jammu and Kashmir, against which demand is made by the BJP and its associates.

## Proposals to Restore Balance

Six proposals have been made to restore balance in the federal arrangement :

(i) The Centre should only retain portfolios of national importance like Defence, Foreign Affairs, Foreign Trade, Currency, Communication, Economic Coordination and National Planning, etc.

(ii) The States should be adequately represented on the National Development Council (NDC).

(iii) NDC and the Planning Commission should be given statutory position by insertion of an Article in the Constitution.

(iv) In the Rajya Sabha equal representation to the Sates (except those with a population of less than three million) should be provided, to enforce the basic federal principle of equality of federating States. Further, there should be direct elections to the Rajya Sabha, and both the Houses of Parliament should have equal powers.

(v) The All India Services like IAS, IFS, etc., should be abolished, and only the union service and the State services should be instituted, to which recruitment should be made respectively by the Centre and the States concerned. Further, the Centre should have no jurisdiction over the personnel of the State services.

(vi) The Seventh Schedule and the three lists should be suitably amended to promote state autonomy and its greater jurisdiction.

## Article 263

Anticipating problems in Union-State relations the founding fathers of the Indian Constitution provided for a mechanism to ensure cooperation among the various units of federation through the provision with respect to an Inter-State Council by Article 263 of the Constitution.

The Article provides, "If at any time it appears to the President that the public interests would be served by the establishment of a council charged with the duty of (a) inquiring into and advising upon disputes which may have arisen between States; (b) investigating and discussing subjects in which some or all the States or the Union and one or more of the States have a common interest; or (c) making recommendations upon any such subject and, in particular, recommendations for the better coordination of policy and action with respect to that subject, it shall be lawful for the president by order to establish such a council and to define the nature of the duties to be performed by it and its organization and procedure."

## ARC Recommendation

*The Past.* Due to the uniformity of party in power both at the Centre and in almost all the States till 1967, there were not very significant disputes between the two levels in India. But after 1967, the situation changed. On its report in 1969, the Administrative Reforms Commission, reviewing the post-1967 situation, recommended the setting up of an Inter-State Council. The Commission felt that an unnecessary onus came to be placed in the case of many inter-state disputes, such as those about respective borders, on the Central Government and any action or inaction on its part could be misunderstood by a contending party. But the Central Government did not hear this warning and as such no Inter-State Council was established till 1990.

*A Major Complaint.* One of the major complaints of various States before the Sarkaria Commission was that President has not adequately used the power given to him by the Constitution to establish a permanent forum having comprehensive jurisdiction for mutual consultation and coordination of policy and action on all matters of common interests falling within the purview of clauses (b) and (c) of Article 263. The Sarkaria Commission, in its Report, recommended that an Inter-State Council should be formed charged with duties set out in clauses (b) and (c) of Article 263. The Commission felt that it was essential to avoid repeated references to the President for piece-meal orders under Article 263. The Council should be authorized to deal with specific issues as and when they crop up.

*Congress under Rajiv Gandhi.* As the Congress (I) Government headed by Rajiv Gandhi remained lukewarm to the Sarkaria Commission's recommendations in general, no efforts were made to establish such a council.

*The National Front Government.* In its 1989 Election Manifesto the National Front promised to. undertake a comprehensive review of Union-State relations, in consultation with all Chief Ministers and having regard to the reports of the Commission and committees on the subject and the representations made to them by the States and political parties. In pursuance of this promise the National Front Government got established. The Inter-State Council through a presidential notification on May 25, 1990. The Council was to consist of the Prime Minister, Chief Ministers of all States, Chief Ministers or Administrators of Union Territories and six ministers of cabinet rank of the Union Government.

*Present Inter-State Council.* The council is now headed by the Prime Minister and in his absence, by the Union Minister of cabinet rank nominated by him. The Council prepares guidelines for identifying issues to be brought before it and meets at least thrice every year. Its meetings are held in-camera. It arrives at decisions by consensus which are final and binding. It shall have its own Secretariat comprising of officers as the chairman may determine.

## Councils Sub-committee

*Congress (I) Govt. in 1991.* The Congress (I) Government which came to power in June 1991 also accepted the continuation of the Inter-State council for its effective functioning. The Inter-State Council has constituted a sub-committee consisting of some Union Ministers and Chief

Ministers. In the subcommittee's meeting held on September 26, 1991, S.B. Chavan, chairman of the meeting announced the Government of India's acceptance of the Sarkaria Commission's recommendation that before the Centre sponsors legislation on a subject in the Concurrent List, there should be prior consultation with the State Government's "individually as well as collectively".

Though this was one step towards normalization of Union-State Relations, but the fact remains that till now India is a highly centralised state. From the appointment of Governors and the imposition of President's rule, or in the Concurrent List, India is basically a centralised structure. In political parlance, the strength of the Indian State is often equated with the existence of a strong Centre.

No reasonable person will dispute the need for a strong Centre if State remains weak. Because of its authority in decisive fields the Centre is bound to remain strong. However, State autonomy in other fields would help the strong Centre to pay undivided attention to its work in decisive fields.

Federalism is essentially a political culture, an outlook on national life. The question is whether in a land of India's continental dimensions, of rich diversities, regional, linguistic and other profound cultural traditions, does Indian nationalism require suppression of the diversities or whether the national well-being will be fostered by encouraging and allowing the diversities to have full play within the national framework. As Khushwant Singh wrote in *The Hindustan Times* dated 15th July 2000 :

"Most states have been demanding more autonomy for a long time much before the demand of Kashmir became strident. As soon as Dr. Abdullah had a resolution passed in its favour by the Kashmir Assembly, Akalis in Punjab began to clamour for it and Subhas Ghising revived the call for a separate, autonomous Gorkhaland. Undoubtedly, similar demands will erupt in different parts of the country.

The Central Government should have been prepared for this development. Its thinking on the subject has been very confused and often contradictory. At one time when Farooq raised the issue, ex-Prime Minister Narasimha Rao responded with great generosity. "Sky is the limit," he proclaimed. But no sooner Kashmiris spelt out what they wanted, the Central Government cried "foul" and vetoed their move. It is wrong in thinking that giving more autonomy to the States will lead to disintegration of the country. On the contrary, a truly federal government will strengthen the country's unity. This has been fully established by the experience of Canada, the United States and Australia."

To conclude with the observation of Nikhel Chakravarty. "If more autonomy is granted right to all the States and the Centre is diverted of its overload of powers, retaining only the very minimum, why should that lead to the disintegration of the country ? Rather, the very concept of the Union of India will come into its own. The durability of our present state structure depends on the willing cooperation of all regions. The Centre is strengthened when the parts are willing partners. There lies the dialectics of our polity today."

Chapter 20

# Assembly Resolution

Following is a brief summary of some main recommendations of the Autonomy Resolution by J & K Assembly.

**Main Recommendations of The Autonomy Proposal**

## 1. Temporary, Transitional and Main Provision (Section 2)

The word temporary should be removed from the heading of Section 21 of Indian Constitution. The word "special" should be used in place of "temporary".

## 2. Constitutional Relations (Section 11)

Subjects in the Central list, not concerned with defense, foreign affairs and communication should be removed from applicability in the State.

All changes made in the Article 246 after 1950 should be rejected.

Articles 248, 249, 250 and 251 should not be applicable to the State.

The lists second (state) and third (concurrent) of the VIIth Schedule should not be applicable in the State.

Article 254 should be restored to its original state as it was applicable in the State in 1954.

Articles 262 and 263 should not be extended to the States.

### 3. Elections (Section 15)

All the changes introduced in this section should be rejected.

### 4. Emergency Provision (Section 18)

Sub-article 6 of the Article 352 should work with States consent. Its section B should be abolished.

Articles 355, 356, 357, 358, 359 and 360 should not be applicable to the State.

### 5. Fundamental Rights (Section 3)

This section should be deleted. There should be a separate chapter on Fundamental Rights in the States Constitution.

### 6. The Union (Section 5)

Articles 72 (1) (d), 72 (3), 133, 134, 135,136, 138, 195 (1) (d) and 151 (2) should not be applicable to the State.

Articles 149, 150 and 151 should be used in the State in the same form as they were in 1954.

### 7. State (Section 6)

Article 218 should not be applicable to the State. Articles 220, 222 and 226 should not be applicable to J & K.

### 8. Finance, Property, Agreements and Cases

These should be discussed by the representatives of the Centre and the State.

### 9. Services under Union and States (Section 14)

The words "Including the State of J & K" should be deleted from Article 312.

### 10. Special Provisions concerning some classes (Section 16)

Articles 338, 339, 340, 341- and 342 should not be applicable to the State.

### 11. Amendment to Indian Constitution (Section 20)

Sub-section (4) of Article 362 should be removed. Its sub-article (2) should be applied while its sub-section (1) should be removed.

### 12. Schedules

Entries of seventh schedule of the Union list which were not applied to J & K by the Constitutional Order 1950 should be removed. The concurrent list not applicable to the State in 1950 should be removed.

### 13. Changes in the State Constitution

J & K Constitution Act, 1959 (First Amendment) and J & K Constitution Act 1965 (sixth Amendment) should be taken back and the original provisions of J & K Constitution should be continued.

### The Most Unacceptable Parts

V. Sudarshan writes in *Outlook,* July 10, 2000, "What the Farooq government wants is to put the recommendations of the J & K State Autonomy Commitee through a mechanism that ensures speedy scrutiny — perhaps through a ministerial level committee. The posturing on the autonomy recommendations is being done with the assembly elections, due in September 2002, in view. But between now and the polls, political developments in J & K could impact on the manner in which the proposals are considered."

Though the Centre and the state have varying opinions on autonomy, the precise details vis-a-vis the proposals haven't been spelt out. However, despite this, it is possible to arrive at a general assessment with respect to some of the recommendations. The most difficult wrangling is likely to be over the following recommendations.

All amendments in the J&K Constitution made vide the Constitution of J & K (first Amendment) Act insofar as they relate to superintendence, direction and control of elections to the state legislature and to the state high court be repealed and original provisions of J & K Constitution be restored.

This could be a non-starter.

The Centre would find it impossible to concede a separate chapter on fundamental rights to J & K.

The proposition that the Election Commission has no role whatsoever in J & K may not get off the drawing board.

The State Autonomy Committee recommendations with respect to the Emergency provisions could well run into a brick wall.

The following areas could yield results with which both parties to the issue can live confortably with :

Considering the financial arrangements between the Centre and the state and considering that the 1952, Delhi agreement was not the conclusive word on this matter there is scope for discussion. It doesn't, however, appear that the role of the Comptroller and Auditor General with respect to J & K can be easily or radically redefined. Unless the matter is dicussed, it won't be apparent as to why the Centre should give up it claims with respect to provisions of financial emergency vide Article 360.

There could be give and take on the policy of deployment of All-India Services.

Article 356, which relates to provisions in case of failure of constitutional machinery in the state, is a matter of fierce debate even outside the scope of its applicability in J & K.

The impasse with respect to nomenclature of Head of State and Head of Executive (Sadr-e-Riyasat and Wazir-e-Azam) is a reheated out-take from point 6 of the Kashmir Accord of 1975, which, noting the lack of agreement on this point, remitted the matter to the principals. Does nomenclature really matter ? Remember that Narasimha Rao had taken a very lenient view on this.

On the matter of other powers to the state, it would be pertinent to point out to paragraph 4 of the 1975 accord "with a view to assuring freedom to the State of J & K to have its own legislation on matters like welfare measure, cultural matters, social security, personal law and procedural laws, in a manner suited to the special conditions in the state, it's agreed that the state government can review the laws made by Parliament or extended to the State after 1953 on any matter relatable to the Concurrent List and may decide which of them, in its opinion, needs amendment or repeal..." How many reappraisals under this clause have actually been carried out by J & K ? It's another matter that around 250 articles apply to J & K and some of them may not be the most relevant. For example, provisions relating to maritime laws and lighthouses. There are many others. A process of rationalisation is always possible. But feasibility is another matter.

**What's Controversial in the Report**

- Substitute the word temporary in Article 370 with 'special'.

- Centre to look at defence, foreign affairs communication and ancillary subjects.
- Head of state to be renamed Sadr-e-Riyasat.
- Article 356 not to apply to State.
- External emergency only with concurrence of state,
- Separate chapter on fundamental rights to be included in J & K constitution.

## Delhi Agreement, July, 1952

*Jawaharlal Nehru and Sheikh Abdullah 24, July, 1952*

- The head of State of J&K shall be recognised by the President on the recommendations of the Legislative Assembly of the State.
- Residuary powers would vest with the State as provided in Article 370.
- The State legislature would have the power to regulate the rights and privileges of permanent residents.
- Explanations and modifications to the Fundamental rights chapter of the Indian Constitution in the State.
- The Jurisdication of the Supreme Court would extend to the state.
- The national flag will enjoy the same status as in others parts of India, the state flag, however, would be retained for historical and sentimental reasons.
- Article 352 be modified to provide for promulgation of Emergency in case of external aggression; in case of internal disturbance only at the request of or with the concurrence of the State Government.

- The Election Commission would conduct elections to Parliament, and for President and Vice-President.
- A financial arrangement between the Union and the State be evolved.

## View of Ladakh Buddhists

Ven Kushok Bakula, the octogenerian head Lama of Ladakh, may be feeling his age, but his zeal to fight for the rights of the people of this backward region of Jammu and Kashmir has not died out.

After his 11-year stint as India's Ambassador to Mongolia, 84-years-old Lama has experienced little transformation in the region since its annexation with India. He thinks that the State and the Centre had always ignored Ladakh despite its strategic importance on all fronts. "I was always unhappy the way Srinagar and New Delhi looked upon the people of Ladakh," Bakula said.

Extending his whole-hearted support for the ongoing agitation in support of a Union Territory status for Ladakh, Bakula, a legendary Ladakhi figure, made it clear that the Buddhists would not accept anything else.

The week-long agitation has been launched in protest against the Jammu and Kashmir Government's move on the restoration of pre 1953 administrative status to the State.

"The Ladakhis will not allow the National Conference to proceed with the autonomy move. The Assembly can only ratify the autonomy report after killing all of us," Bakula told an IBA-sponsored meeting.

Indeed, the Ladakhis' opposition to the 'rule from Srinagar' is traced back to Bakula's time, when he was a member of the Kashmir Constituent Assembly. The Buddhist leader then had made it clear that "the rule from Srinagar was unpalatable".

Recalling his days in Srinagar, Bakula said : "There was not a single example where Srinagar gave us something without our constant pleading .and threat of agitation."

Asked why the Ladakhis were demanding a Union Territory status instead of statehood, he said : "Pakistan-occupied Kashmir is under the direct control of the federal government. New Delhi should take the cue and make Ladakh a Union Territory, in view of its strategic position."

Bakula is upset over the policies of the Central Government on the region. "Despite the Ladakhis playing a significant role in the Kargil war, little acknowledgment came from the Government." he said.

The grievances have culminated over the years, the head Lama said, adding that a step-motherly treatment was meted out to the Buddhists from the time when Sheikh Abdullah was the head of the state in the 1950s.

Bakula, who was a minister and a parliamentarian from 1953 to 1976, lamented that both the State and the Centre were equally responsible for the state of affairs in the region.

He shares the concern of the Ladakhis that the proposed step for the restoration of pre-1953 position will destroy the interests of the indigenous people.

"The Buddhists never believed in violence. But with the passage of time, we might not have full control over the young generation who are heading the movement," the Lama said.

## Farooq Isolated

Jammu and Kashmir Chief Minister Farooq Abdullah's insistence on a pre-1953 status for the State as a means to resolve the lingering Kashmir crisis has given a new twist to the oft-repeated demand for grant of greater autonomy to the State.

Unnerved by stiff opposition to the recommendations of the State Autonomy Committee, which has sought to put the clock back, Dr. Abdullah's action in convening a special session of the State Assembly to discuss the controversial report, is being viewed in political circles as a desperate attempt by the beleaguered Chief Minister to hold his ground.

Dr. Abdullah stood isolated on this issue as neither the Centre nor the majority opinion of the State spoke in favour of the Comittee's report. It has forced Dr. Abdullah to look for some kind of legitimacy for his autonomy proposal through seeking a stamp of approval from the Legislative Assembly. The ruling National Conference enjoys a brute majority in the House.

The Jammu and Ladakh regions are already up in arms against Dr. Abdullah's move, while the displaced Kashmiri Pandit community has equivocally rejected any proposal aimed at resolving the Kashmir crisis without their involvement.

"Proposals like autonomy, trifurcation of the State or starting a dialogue with the All-Party Hurriyat Conference, are irrelevant until Kashmiri Pandits were involved in the process," felt Kashmiri Samiti Chief C.L Gadon.

The Autonomy Committee's report, among other things, has suggested repealing all matters in the Union List, save defence, external affairs and communications, so as to provide greater autonomy to the State.

Significantly, it wants Jammu and Kashmir to be kept out of the ambit of the Supreme Court and Election Commission while recommending reversion to the pre-1953 nomenclature of Sadr-e-Riyasat in place of the Governor and the Prime Minister for the Chief Minister.

The Committee, which was headed by State Works Minister Ghulam Mohiuddin Shah— who assumed the charge after Dr. Karan Singh had resigned— has gone a step further by suggesting that Article 370 of the constitution providing a special status to J & K be accorded permanence, which was originally enshrinted only as a temporary measure.

## Discussions on J & K Autonomy Resolution

The Autonomy resolution passed by the Jammu and Kashmir Assembly reportedly figured prominently at separate meetings, Prime Minister Atal Behari Vajpayee had today with his party colleagues Mr L.K. Advani and Mr. Khushabhau Thakre, and a section of the NDA allies.

Mr. Vajpayee's joint meeting with the Advani-Thakre duo was his first since the passage of the resolution, about which he had heard while travelling abroad. During the hour-long discussions, the BJP president is believed to have conveyed to Mr. Vajpayee and his Home Minister the party rank and-file's strong opposition to the autonomy demand.

Significantly, Mr. Thakre also thought it prudent to share with Messrs Vajpayee and Advani the BJP's strong reservations about the manner; in which the Government has thus far responded to the developments in Srinagar. The point he drove home was that the two leaders, as the party's representatives in the coalition regime, should take a "firmer stand" against the resolution.

Mr. Thakre told them that the party viewed the autonomy resolution as a very dangerous trend, which could help divisive elements take advantage of the situation. In such a scenario, the BJP cadres were totally opposed to any kind of dily-dallying on the leadership's part.

Shortly, after the in-house BJP parleys, if they could be described as such, leaders of certain other NDA partners also called on the Prime Minister. Among them were Union Agriculture Minister Nitish Kumar (Samata), Communications Minister Ram Vilas Paswan (Janata Dal-United) and HRD Minister Murili Manohar Joshi and Power Minister Rangarajan Kumaramangalam (both BJP).

The Prime Minister's meeting with Advani and Thakre also triggered speculation about the possibility of talks between him and J & K Chief Minister Farooq Abdullah.

Among the other issues that came up during Thakre's parleys with the Premier and Advani was the outcome of the recent Panchayat polls in Uttar Pradesh. On his part, the BJP chief maintained that contrary to the general impression, the party has managed to retain its 1995 tally, which in other words meant that things haven't turned from bad to worse for the BJP.

## Badal, Vaiko Critical of Farooq Govt

Kashmir Chief Minister Farooq Abdullah and his National Conference were getting isolated within the NDA as two constituents of the ruling coalition opposed the resolution on Kashmir's autonomy.

MDMK leader Vaiko said categorically, 'We do not fully agree with resolution on Kashmir autonomy. We're not a party to that decision and that resolution has to be studied clause by clause," while replying to a question from reporters. He also stated that his party's two-day conference was virtually an NDA conclave.

At Chennai, Punjab Chief Minister Prakash Singh Badal also took a similar line stating that the autonomy sought by Akali Dal and other parties like the DMK amounted to more powers to the states within a federal set up. "Many countries have given powers to their states within their federal set up and that is the form of autonomy we have in mind. We do not ask for the autonomy that has been sought in the resolution (on J & K)," he said.

It would he interesting to watch how Mr. Abdullah would react when he is scheduled to address the conference on Sunday. In fact Mr. Vaiko made it clear that the MDMK, toed the DMK line while seeking autonomy for states. "For us autonomy means devolving more powers but within a federal set up that actually strengthened the unity of the country and did not weaken it," he explained. It is for this reason that his party supported the decision to review the constitution since that would give more powers to states without compromising on the country's unity.

## Ex-PMs Against J &K Move

On July 1, 2000 three former Prime Ministers, V. P. Singh, Chandra Shekhar and I. K. Gujral, criticised the Kashmir Assembly autonomy resolution.

Both Mr. Gujral and Mr. Singh, speaking at a seminar, warned that the division of the State on the basis of religion could give a fillip to communalism in the already troubled State.

Addressing another seminar on national security, Mr. Shekhar lashed out at Prime Minister A. B. Vajpayee and Home

Minister L. K. Advani for stating that the Government would consider the issue of more autonomy to Jammu and Kashmir.

He said these statements would encourage demands for autonomy from other States like Punjab, Tamil Nadu and Assam. "Instead of making such remarks the Government should have clarified that these issues are not negotiable," he maintained.

Even as the three former Premiers were critical of the autonomy move, Union Law Minister Ram Jethmalani, speaking in Chennai, said the autonomy resolution had negated Pakistan's claim that accession of the region to India was vitiated by force and fraud. Describing the resolution as a view of the Kashmir Assembly, the Minister said it would duly be considered by the Centre.

While criticising the recent autonomy resolution. Mr. V.P. Singh said any demand for autonomy linked with the division of the State on the basis of religion or community would destroy the uniqueness of Kashmir. Supporting his views. Mr. Gujral said. "Autonomy linked with a plan to bifurcate or trifurcate the State will give a big jolt not only to the country but also to the people of Kashmir who have already suffered so much."

Both Mr. Singh and Mr. Gujral supported an all-party dialogue on the issue adding that the discussion should take into consideration the aspirations of the common people in the State without tampering with 'Kashmiriyat.

Meanwhile, senior Congress leader Manmohan Singh, speaking in Bangalore said the 1975 accord signed by Mrs. Indira Gandhi and Sheikh Abdullah should be the basis of any autonomy package for J&K.

"We recognise that J & K has special problems and the State needs autonomy. But the question is the extent of autonomy. We think that a lot of these issues were settled in the 1975 accord which should be the basis of any package." he added.

## Farooq Stalling Peace Process : Mufti

Former Home Minister Mufti Mohammed Sayeed charged J & K Chief Minister Farooq Abdullah with trying to stall the peace process by raising the bogey of autonomy and has suggested that the Centre should extend a formal invitation to the All Parties Hurriyat Conference for peace talks.

Strongly favouring a meaningful dialogue with the APHC, Mr Mufti said, "The Vajpayee Government should not allow the peace process to be aborted or subverted by the machinations of the entrenched ruling political establishment of the State."

Talking to the media persons, the J & K. People's Democratic Party chief supported the Centre's policy to hold talks with separatists. "The APHC leaders, in turn, should acknowledge Centre's initiative by prevailing upon militants silence their guns for creating an atmosphere conducive for the dialogue," he said while maintaining that there was no harm in involving Pakistan in the peace process at a later stage.

Coming down heavily on Mr Abdullah for raising the spectre of Autonomy Mr. Mufti felt that the discredited National Conference Government, which was the outcome of a "rigged poll", will not be able to deliver the goods even if the autonomy demand was conceded. "Nothing will happen even if you give Farooq the moon as his Government is seethed in corruption and welfare of the people is his last priority," he said.

## Farooq Accused of Trying to Divide the Country

Panun Kashmir an organisation of the displaced Kashmiri Panditis, has demanded creation of a separate "homeland" for the Pandits in Kashmir Valley with Union Territory status. It lambasted Chief Minister Farooq Abdullah 'for pursuing an agenda similar to the Muslim League'.

Talking to the newspersons, the organisation's political affairs committee chairman Ajay Chrangoo said, "The Farooq Abdullah-led National Conference is pursuing an agenda aimed at the second partition of the country, as is evidenced by the passing of the autonomy resolution by its government in the Jammu and Kashmir Assembly where it enjoys a brute majority."

Mr. Chrangoo felt that the autonomy resolution was aimed at limiting the Centre's authority in Jammu and Kashmir and had nothing to do with actual devolution of power.

## Congress on NDA Stand

Prime Minister Atal Behari Vajpayee's views and the Bharatiya Janta Party's stand on the Kashmir autonomy issue came in for sharp criticism from the Congress which said that there was a "sharp contradiction" between the two.

"We want the National Democratic Alliance Government to clarify its position on the Kashmir Assembly resolution. The BJP has vociferously opposed the autonomy package but both Mr. Vajpayee and Home Minister L.K. Advani are talking about a discussion on the package," All India Congress Committee spokesperson Anil Shastri said. He was responding to the Prime Minister's call for an all party meeting on the issue.

The party pointed out that the issue of autonomy has had a cascading effect and similar demands were now being made in Panjab and Tamil Nadu, which went against the interests of the nation.

"The demands for autonomy are being raised in States governed by NDA partners. Still, the Home Minister has agreed to attend a conference in Tamil Nadu being organised by LTTE supporters which is not a good sign," Mr. Shastri said.

He also wondered whether the National Conference, which is at present a part of the NDA Government, would continue to be a part of the coalition if the BJP opposed the Kashmir autonomy resolution in Parliament.

Terming the autonomy resolution as recipe for disaster, Congress spokesperson Anand Sharma said, the NDA Government was resorting to such gimmicks in order to detract the people's attention from its non-governance.

Mr. Sharma alleged that individual ministers in the Union Cabinet were pursuing their own agenda and the Prime Minister was becoming a prey to their populist tactics.

## Consensus on J &K Need of the Hour

The Nationalist Congress Party (NCP) criticised the Sangh Parivar for its belligerent posturing on Kashmir. The Prime Minister should restrain the parivar as the need of the hour was to evolve a national consensus on the issue

"The pre-1953 status sought in the autonomy report (endorsed by the J & K. Assembly) is a pipedream in its fullness. On Kashmir, we should have a national view and not a BJP or a Congress view," averred NCP general secretary Devendra Nath Dwivedi.

The NCP leader also criticised Home Minister L.K. Advani for his statement that the autonomy question would be decided by Parliament. "Instead of clarifying the Government's position, he has only tried to pass the buck. Parliament decides what the Government determines," he remarked. Mr. Dwivedi said, that it has become necessary to do away with the transitional and temprorary description of Article 370.

**Rejection by RSS**

Proceeding on predictable lines, the two-day meeting of the RSS leadership at Gandhinagar on July 2, described the autonomy resolution of the Jammu and Kashmir Assembly as fraught with dangerous consequences.

The meeting of the RSS Akhil Bharatiya Karyakari Mandal (All India Executive Committee) vehemently opposed the autonomy resolution and argued the BJP-led National Democratic Alliance Government to stop it from implementation.

Briefing newsperson after the conclusion of the meet at this village near the state capital. Joint General Secretary Madandasji said such a serious situation would not have arisen if Article 370 were abrogated earlier.

He said even before the autonomy resolution, Hindus had to leave the Valley and become refugees in their own country. The RSS spokesman said that the idea of two Prime Ministers, two laws and two apex courts would not be acceptable.

The resolution on Kashmir autonomy observed that it would give encouraging signals to separatist forces in the country, especially in the northeast.

The RSS document stated that the autonomy proposed was not acceptable to the people of Ladakh and the Centre must reject the resolution.

Madandasji also said that dismissal of the Farooq Abdullah Ministry or removal of National Conference from the NDA were not demanded in the resolution, but these would be the viable options.

**Badal for Devolution of More Powers**

Punjab Chief Minister Prakash Singh Badal today said his party, Shiromani Akali Dal supports the devolution of more powers to the States within the limits of a true federal system.

Badal told reporters here that the time had come to give more powers to the States, as their financial status was very poor.

"We are for one country. Nobody wants to separate from India," Badal replied to a question on the autonomy resolution in Jammu and Kashmir assembly.

He said the Akali Dal and the DMK were the only parties, which voiced the need for true federalism in 1962, as it was the only way for progress and prosperity. But, we were branded as separatists, he said.

"We are for more powers under a true federal structure. The State Government has to serve the people directly. The development of the people is mainly dependent on the financial resources in the States, " he pointed out.

Blaming the Congress for the poor conditions of the States the Chief Minister said during its rule all the powers were vested with the Centre, as the "nominated' Chief Ministers could not raise their voice against the high command.

Stating that federal system was the only way to progress, Badal said the policy now was that the states would hold certain subjects while the powers remained with the Centre.

Though agriculture is the main source of income for people in various states, the pricing of agriculture products were vested with the Centre, he observed.

Unless and until states remained strong and economically sound, Centre would remain weak in all aspects, Badal said.

## 'Centre Adopting Different Yardsticks'

Hurriyat Conference leader Mohammad Yaseen Malik said that autonomy was not what his organisation wanted and accused the Centre of adopting 'different yardsticks' in regard to talks with separatists in Nagaland and Kashmir.

Terming the recently adopted autonomy resolution by the National Conference-dominated Jammu and Kashmir Assembly as of "no consequences," Malik, who is also the chairman of the Jammu and Kashmir Liberation Front (JKLF), said the Union Government should strive towards a permanent solution of the Kashmir issue.

"While peace talks with separatist Naga leaders are being held without any conditions in neutral countries," Union Home Minister L.K. Advani is putting "pre-conditions" for talks with Hurriyat leadership, he said. "Prime Minister has gone abroad to meet NSCN (IM) leaders in third countries (without preconditions), while Advani is asking us to hold talks within the framework of Indian Constitution," the Hurriyat leader said.

While emphasising that Hurriyat conference was for talks, Malik said no conditions should be atached to these. "Everyone must come to the table with his own agenda," he said. Stating that all parties concerned with the Kashmir issue — India, Pakistan and people of Kashmir—should be at the table for talks, Malik said a 'conducive atmosphere" should be created for a dialogue. He accused the BJP leadership of "back-tracking" on Kashmir by "falling prey to electoral and political compulsions."

## Alleged 'Disinformation'

Recently a senior minister of Jammu and Kashmir had alleged that a "disinformation campaign" had been launched over the state government's demand for greater autonomy and said the resolution could "in no way be termed as secession".

"Even major political parties, like BJP and Congress have not gone through the autonomy report properly and were casting aspersions on it," State Finance Minister Abdul Rahim said who is a member of the autonomy committee which had prepared the report.

He said the resolution, adopted by the state assembly last week, was "the letter and spirit" of three agreements—Instrument of Accession, 1950, Presidential Order and 1952 Delhi Agreement—signed between J & K Government and the Centre.

Charging that a 'disinformation campaign had been launched by "interested parties" over the autonomy issue, he said the report never sought setting up a separate Supreme Court for the state.

"We have already accepted Article 131 of the constitution, which empowers the Supreme Court's jurisdiction over the state," he said.

Asked whether the report would be opening "Pandora's box" with other states making similar demands, he said "the case of Jammu and Kashmir is different as we have signed the Instrument of Accession while other states have signed the instrument of merger with the Union of India. And, what we are asking for is only restoration of the powers, which were taken away during the past 50 years."

"Some political parties say that we have shown disrespect to the Constitution but they should first check the facts. It is only a resolution and not a law," the minister said.

He said the state assembly passed a resolution so that discussions could be held with the Centre over implementation of recommendations made by state autonomy committee headed by State Works Minister Ghulam Mohammed Shah.

He said, by passing the resolution, the state government had performed its basic duty as restoration of autonomy was on the agenda of the party since 1975.

The minister said that some leaders were "tampering with facts" by citing the example of an agreement between then Prime Minister Indira Gandhi and then Chief Minister Sheikh Abdullah in 1975 as the final agreement between the state and the Centre.

"The first clause of the agreement is that Article 370 must be restored to its earlier glory," he claimed.

"We are open for negotiations but whatever is implemented should be in consonance with the recommendations made by the State Autonomy Committee," he added.

"Either the Centre will convince us or we will convince them," he said.

Asked whether the autonomy resolution could send wrong signals to radical elements, he replied "I don't think so .. we are aiming for powers within the framework of the Indian Constitution."

## Autonomy Flayed

BJP General secretary, M. Venkaiah Naidu said his party was for more devolution of powers to states, but not for granting autonomy to any state. Addressing, a news conference in Visakhapatnam, Mr Naidu said that the BJP wants a strong Centre and strong states. Referring to the Jammu and Kashmir Assembly possing a resolution for autonomy, Mr. Naidu made it clear that his party's "stand was very clear that there should be no question of going back to the pre 1953 state".

## Chapter 21

# Debate on Autonomy

In 1999, the report of the J & K Committee on Autonomy was tabled in J & K Assembly House. On 19th June, 2000 a special session of the J & K Assembly started to discuss the report.

### The Autonomy Debate

The ruling National Conference believes that greater autonomy is the only solution to the problem of militancy in the state. At a meeting of the NC's legislature party the demand for a return to the pre-1953 position was reiterated.

The NC's autonomy plank hinges on accepting Indian sovereignty over defence, external affairs and communications.

Significantly, the BJP and Congress are against greater autonomy. The common viewpoint of the two national parties is that the clock cannot be set back. They feel that a situation wherein Jammu and Kashmir gets back its greater autonomous status of 1952 will weaken the country's bonds with the state.

Some call the state autonomy report a document of secession, others simply a ploy by National Conference to "hoodwink' the people.

Given its two-thirds majority in the legislative assembly, the NC could be expected to carry the day. But given the hostility of the militants represented by the All Parties Hurriyat Conference (APHC), the political voice of secessionists, such an easy option for the ruling party would not be without its grave pitfalls.

The Hurriyat is getting shriller by the day in its opposition to the cause of greater autonomy. The militant groups are determined to stall anything that reinforces India's sovereignty in Kashmir

Legal and constitutional experts say that greater autonomy to Kashmir would require constitutional amendments that may not be possible immediately. It would require the convening of another session, or the prolonging of the session.

Also, the Ladakhis were against the autonomy as "Srinagar rule". They, therefore observed a "black week".

The militants would be seeking to flex their muscles diabolically in an effort to overshadow the debate on restoration of greater autonomy.

Whatever be the outcome of the session's debate, the fact is that it has stirred hectic political, media, security and militant activity in Kashmir. Security forces are on maximum alert and the common man is caught between hope and apprehension.

## Where They Stand

**Hurriyat**—Rejects the greater autonomy concept. Is fighting for either aazadi and sees role for Pakistan in any dialogue.

**National Conference**—Wants Indian sovereignty to be confined to defence, external affairs and communications.

**Congress and BJP**—No further autonomy. Feel that if the State gets back its status of 1952, the country's bonds with the State will weaken.

## Views of Political Parties

Major Political formations have strongly opposed the Jammu and Kashmir autonomy package that calls for the return to the pre-1953 situation. While the BJP is totally against any move that smacks of autonomy, parties like the Congress and the CPI are ready to discuss the issue if it is based on the 1975 Indira Gandhi-Sheikh Abdullah accord, which maintains the country's secular traditions and upholds national interests. The CPI-M. on its part, made it clear that it was for greater autonomy for the state within the framework of Article 370 of the Constitution.

Charging that the autonomy package mooted by the National Conference is "politically motivated" to detract attention from the state government's failures, most of these parties have already instructed their legislators to vote against it. They have also strongly opposed the division of the state along communal lines.

Although one of its own NDA allies was behind the latest proposal, BJP vicepresident J.P. Mathur emphasized that "the mistake committed by Jawaharlal Nehru by granting special status to the state cannot be allowed to be repeated." He recalled that his party has systematically demanded the abrogation of Article 370 until it decided to keep it in abeyance of the interests of the NDA.

"Since there is already a parliamentary resolution that calls for reclaiming Pakistan occupied territory, the BJP cannot support any measure which will encourage divisive forces and give a further fillip to terrorism," Mr. Mathur said. While reacting to the issue, AICC treasurer in charge of Kashmir affairs Ahmed Patel stressed the need to end militancy and give an impetus to development. He emphasised that any talk of autonomy should be based only on the 1975 Indira

Gandhi-Sheikh Abdullah accord. It should be people-oriented, reinforce the country's secular traditions and safeguard its national interests. "The autonomy committee report is not in the interest of the people of Kashmir," Mr. Patel said, pointing out that not a single Congress legislator or central leader was included in the committee which looked into the crucial autonomy issue.

The CPI vehemently opposed to the return to the pre-1953 situation, with Mr. Atul Anjaan pointing out that there has been a qualitative change in the situation since then. Instead, he said, the 1975 accord could be the basis for discussing the issue of autonomy and the problems of the people.

While going along with the issue of greater autonomy for the three regions of the state, the CPI however, was against the proposal that calls for its subdivision into that zones because that is based on "communal lines."

## Stormy Kick-off

The much-awaited debate on the State Autonomy Committee report, that calls for the pre-1953 autonomous status of Jammu and Kashmir, began on a stormy note in the State Assembly.

The ruling National Conference passionately backed the restoration of greater autonomy. The NC felt it was a historic "Opportunity to rectify mistakes of the past".

For the Opposition, it was a "ploy to deflect from the real issues facing the State."

The Opposition blamed the ruling party for its three-and-a-half years' performance ; timing of the special session and on the financial aspects of the autonomy.

As soon as the House assembled, BJP legislature party leader Shiv Charan Gupta and others were on their toes terming the autonomy debate a "farce."

"This is a moment of truth when the House should debate what mistakes were made and what lessons need to be learnt," he said.

"Instead we are discussing autonomy that can only "counter secessionism. And all those who support secessionism are militants" He added. The BJP members later staged a walkout.

One of them, Ashok Khajuria, wore a black scarf to demonstrate what he called a "black day in the history of Jammu and Kashmir".

Moulvi Iftikhar Hussain Ansari, who recently joined the National Conference, said, "East India Company go back."

Congress MLAs also staged a walkout for different reasons. They said that the NC-BJP combine was in alliance at the Centre and here they were "staging a drama of opposing each other."

The tone for the debate was set by Housing and Urban Development Minister Ghulam Mohi-ud-Din Shah, who headed the State Autonomy Committee panel that submitted the report in April last.

"Had the constitutional arrangement stayed intact, the situation would not have come to such a pass today," he said and highlighted why it was important for the state to have greater autonomy to save Kashmir that had rejected the two-nation theory in 1947.

### VHP Opposes Greater Autonomy

The Vishwa Hindu Parishad has strongly opposed the National Conference move for more autonomy.

Calling it a retrograde step, VHP central secretary Mohan Joshi said, that greater autonomy would end unity, the people of Jammu and Ladakh would feel alienated.

By pressing for a pre-1953 position the Farooq Abdullah government was only sending wrong signals to separatists, he said. Asked if the VHP would demand the dismissal of the J & K government, Mr. Joshi said it was up to the Centre to decide that.

## National Debate Sought

On June 21, 2000, Jammu and Kashmir Chief Minister Farooq Abdullah, asserted that his party, which enjoys two-third majority in the State Assembly, can pass the resolution on autonomy without any further delay but first would like a nation-wide debate on the issue. Intervening in the discussions on the State autonomy committee report, during the special session of the Assembly, Dr. Abdullah said he can "pass the resolution just now. But I want a debate and discussion not only in Jammu and Kashmir, but in the rest of India as well".

"We are not anti-Indians but better Indians than you," he told the Opposition members. The Chief Minister, without naming the Hurriyat Conference said, "the Government of India is ready to discuss 'azadi' (freedom) with the people who want 'azadi'. But why do you hesitate to listen to our plea for autonomy within the parameters of the Constitution."

Meanwhile, during the second day of the session, the NC unleashed its star speakers from three regions - Jammu, Kashmir and Ladakh - to take on opposition stalwarts over the autonomy issue.

"It is unfortunate that the autonomy issue is being debated again, But what was agreed in the Instrument of Accession should not have been tampered with (theory forcing the current debate)." said Mr Ajat Shatru Singh, son of Dr Karan Singh who was the first chairman of the State Autonomy Committee.

## Autonomy Vs. Aazadi

The people of Kashmir are bone weary. Caught between unrelenting militancy and a state machinery that looks at each one of them as a possible suspect, they have forgotten to live as free citizens. They want peace. They yearn for freedom. As one travels across the Valley, the refrain is : peace and freedom.

Judging by the sudden burst of political activity in Srinagar in the Summer of 2000, now something is brewing. Over the past one month, the town has been flooded with dogooders, each ready with his own wonder prescription for the wounded Valley.

Vidya Subramanium writes, "For Kashmir, the choice is broadly between autonomy and azadi, represented respectively by the Farooq Abdullah-led National Conference (NC) and 23-member All-Pary Hurriyat Conference (APHC). But the two are locked in a fierce combat, making any break through difficult. For Farooq Abdullah, autonomy is vital for two reasons. One distillusionment with his government is growing. Though today there is barely any support for Pakistan in the Valley, the mood is visibly against India and the National Conference. If Abdullah defaults on autonomy, his own cadres will not forgive him. The local media, which has been editorially urging him to take the plunge will turn against him. And the people will never again vote for the NC. Second, autonomy is the only card he has against the Hurriyat, his sole weapon to squash negotiations between the Centre and the Hurriyat. For Hurriyat leaders, who for the first time are enjoying a measure of legitimacy with official India, it is as important that Abdullah doesn't steal their thunder."

## The US Pressure

Vidya Subramanium argues that an unseen hand is nudging the many parties to the dispute towards some sort of a settlement. The U.S. Hurriyat leaders say it openly, N.C. ministers admit it in private as do sundry others—intelligence sources, political busy bodies and nongovernment activities.

There is no other explanation for the BJP and the Hurriyat—two ideologist opposites—sending signals to each other. Officially the BJP is opposites to Article 370. So, it is logical to assume that the party's offer to negotiate with the Hurriyat—whose constituents are either pro-Pakistan or in favour of complete independence—happened under pressure.

There is circumstantial evidence to suggest this. President Clinton completed his South tour on March 25. On April 3, the first batch of Hurriyat leaders was released. Around the same time, Pakistan's former foreign secretary Niaz Naik reportedly arrived in Delhi for a bit of Track-II diplomacy. Hurriyat leaders say they were released under US pressure. They also concede that they have been talking to Farooq Katwan, the American-Kashmir Study Group.

There are solutions floating around too. Hurriyat spokesperson Abdul Ghani Bhatt says he has one that would be acceptable to India. Pakistan and the Kashmir. Topping the list is one of half a dozen formulae advocated by the Kashmir Study Group in a paper titled Kashmir—A Way Forward.

This involves creating a "Muslim majority entity with its own constitution, citizenship, flag and a legislature which would legislate on all matters other than defence and foreign affairs. Both India and Pakistan would be responsible for the defence of the Kashmir entity..."

Bhatt mentioned variations of this as well as another one involving a step-by-step approach. Cessation of hostilities, softening of borders between the two Kashmirs, trade among Pakistan, the two Kashmir and India, and finally joint elections under UN supervision.

## War of Words

The autonomy report excited passions in the special session of the J & K assembly. But no flying of chapels. No use of mikes as missile. The speakers just threw words at each other. The BJP called the ruling National Conference antinational and the latter accused the BJP of planning to balkanise the state.

## Soft-pedalling Autonomy Issue

In what appears to be an attempt to softpedal the controversy over the ongoing J & K Assembly debate on the autonomy report, on June, 22, 2000, Chief Minister Farooq Abdullah called for a national consensus over the issues.

Going by the tenor of the CM's observations there is every likelihood that the resolution on autonomy presently under discussion in the Assembly, may not be put to vote.

"The report is being discussed in the Assembly to reiterate the known stand of the National Conference", Dr. Abdullah said after detailed discussions with Prime Minister A.B. Vajpayee at his Race Course residence in Delhi.

The Chief Minister is understood to have explained to the Prime Minister the reasons leading to his Government's decision to convene a special Assembly session.

Responding to pointed queries over the implication of the Assembly debate, Mr Abdullah maintained that there was nothing novel about it. "We have fought the Assembly elections over the autonomy plank and followed it up with ratification of the report at the level of the Cabinet", he said.

"We have never sought third party intervention", he remarked, saying there was nothing wrong in seeking a better deal from "within the family" (Indian Union).

Asked whether the sudden introduction of the Autonomy resolution in the Assembly was a ploy to scuttle the proposed Centre-Hurriyat talks, he clarified that the Centre was free to hold talks with any one. "We do not want to stand in the way of such parleys", he asserted.

Dr. Abdullah also chose to question the authenticity of allegations over his Government's move to shift focus from the failures of his administration by convening a special session of the Assembly.

Dr. Abdullah recalled that the Congress Government headed by P.V. Narasimha Rao and the UP and the NDA had not objected to greater autonomy for the state.

## Hurriyat's Sword

According to reports, there was an war in Srinagar— but between autonomy and aazadi, between chief minister Farooq Abdullah and the All-Party Hurriyat Conference. One left for Delhi early this Thursday morning amidst speculation that the Centre hadn't taken kindly to his autonomy battle cries. The other let it be known that it would do everything in its power to mobilise the people of Kashmir on the aazadi plank. The official explanation for Abdullah's sudden dash to Delhi is that it was for a previously scheduled meeting of chief ministers on sales tax. But would sales tax take precedence over a session of the assembly devoted to the all-important autonomy issue ? Reports suggest that the National Conference may be readying itself for a showdown. Either okay autonomy or, we'll pull out of the government.

Abdullah's track record shows, however, that he is not so reckless. When asked why the National Conference was supporting a party that was against Article 370, state education minister Mohammed Shafi said, "We thought cooperation with the Centre was pragmatic and in the larger interest of the state. Abdullah is under tremendous pressure, though. The shadow of the Hurriyat looms large on his government and if he does not prove his commitment to autonomy—by adopting the autonomy committee report in the House his own party cadres will bay for his blood. Even as Abdullah pleads his case in Delhi, his party MLAs made rabble-rousing speeches in the assembly. This is the last chance for democratic forces. If we let this go, the state will pass into the hands of gun-wielding militants."

Indeed, autonomy is Abdullah's best and last weapon to counter the Hurriyat. If he can get the centre to go along on autonomy, that will automatically end all prospects of talks between the Vajpayee government and the Hurriyat. For the same reason, the Hurriyat is under compulsion to loudly denounce autonomy. At a hurriedly called press conference, Hurriyat leader Abdul Ghani Lone said that the Hurriyat condemned autonomy "With all the vehemence at our command". The basic issue, he said, was self-determination.

Lone admitted that the Hurriyat leaders had met the Kashmir Study Group's Farooq Katwari. He also said that Hurriyat had a solution to the Kashmir problem. But he would not say what it was. Lone attacked home minister L.K. Advani "for offering to talk to the Hurriyat on the one hand and for encouraging custodial killings in Kashmir" on the other. He said the Hurriyat had asked JKLF leader Yasin Malik to postpone his hunger strike against continuing atrocities in the Valley by a fortnight. "If by then the killings do not stop, we will supplement the hunger strike with other strong measures," he said.

**BJP's Stand**

On June 23, the BJP emphatically rejected the National Conference demand for allowing J&K to revert back to the pre-1953 status. However, the party said it was willing for discussions on greater devolution of powers to the State. Party general secretary K. Venkaiah Naidu stated that while the Centre had yet to formulate its stand on the demand raised in the Jammu and Kashmir Assembly special session, the BJP had decided that such a thing would never be acceptable to it.

"One can't turn the clock back nor will it help anybody," the leader stressed. He also stated that the party was unable to understand what the National Conference meant by talking of autonomy for the state. If they wanted greater decentralization of powers, the party was all for discussion on the matter, he said. "We are ready for devolution of powers up to the zilla parished and panchayat level," Mr Naidu added.

Pointing out that the country had come a long way since 1953, Mr Naidu said the focus of attention in the state should now be on development, good governance and better facilities to improve the living conditions of the people.

Adequate powers were available to the Jammu and Kashmir Government under the States List to take care of matters such as health, education, social welfare, roads, communications, agriculture and other allied activities, he stated. In view of the special status enjoyed by the state, additional resources were made available to it by the Centre to meet all its needs.

## Union Minister Dared Farooq

Union Minister and BJP leader Chaman Lal Gupta dared Jammu and Kashmir Chief Minister Farooq Abdullah to go to polls with "greater autonomy" issue and claimed that National Conference would be swept out of power. "No one else than Abdullah knows better that if elections are held tomorrow with autonomy as an issue, he will not even get two seats, He will be the last man to recommend polls." After addressing a symposium on "Autonomy and Minorities" Gupta said that Abdullah was a seasoned politician and he could see the writing on the wall. He knew very well how his son Omar Abdullah, a minister in the NDA Government, could win the last Lok Sabha poll with a meagre percentage of votes, Gupta said.

## Designed to Hog Limelight

Ninety-year-old Swami Umeshanand, who was associated with Kashmir politics for several decades in his capacity as political adviser to Maharaja Hari Singh, is appalled by Farooq Abdullah's autonomy package. "Farooq is afraid that he is losing touch with the people. He is worried that the Hurriyat leaders may grab the limelight. In the hope that both the people of Kashmir and the Central Government will blindly follow him in their search for a solution to the Kashmir problem, he has floated this ridiculous package," Swami Umeshanand said.

He strongly believed that when Maharaja Hari Singh signed the accession treaty in 1948, it meant that Kashmir had become an integral part of India. "Can the problem of Kashmir be solved by separating it from India ? Autonomy would mean reversing the accession treaty signed over 52 years ago," he argued.

What is the solution to the unending bloodbath in Kashmir ? While he vociferously debunked Farooq Abdullah's 'Save Kashmir' formula, he felt that the solution may lie in the trifurcation of the State. "Even historically the Kingdom of Kashmir has had three provinces—Jammu, Ladakh and Kashmir and was governed by independent officials," he said. But he quickly added that trifurcation on communal lines would unleash still more blood bath. "For trifurcation to happen the State would have to be divided on the basis of boundaries and not religion," he said.

## Hurriyat's Tower of Babel

Hurriyat leaders form an unlikely coalition. Yasin Malik is not for Pakistan, he is for azadi. Spokesperson Abdul Ghani Bhatt is pro-Pakistan, but he wants a decision that will take along the Hindus, Muslims and Buddhists. Hurriyat chairman Syed Ali Shah Geelani believes in the two-nation theory. Young Omar Farooq insists that the Indian Kashmir can never be separated from PoK. Yet these and 19 others together form the All-Party Hurriyat Conference. What they share in common are hard feelings about India, or to be more precise, the Indian administration. How will they come to a common decision ? "We have got together on one plank and that is : Let the people decide."

## Kashmir Ki Awaaz

Manoj Joshi writes, the Kashmiri politician's life is not an easy one. He is compelled to tread carefully across the strife-ridden land. In the past 10 years or so, over 20 former legislators and ministers have been killed. Last month, the Hizbul Mujahideen assassinated state power minister Ghulam Hasan Bhat. Not surprisingly, moderate politicians do not advertise themselves too much.

But benighted Kashmir doesn't really lack leaders. Besides those owing allegiance to democracy and the Indian Constitution, there are a number of others grouped under the All Party Hurriyat Conference. In addition, scores of former 'chief commanders' and 'area commanders' of the now defunct militant bodies or militants turned-counter-militants also see themselves as practising politicians. Then, of course, there are the militants whose political context is defined by the Kalashnikov and the bomb.

But then who speaks for the Kashmiri ? The influence of almost all parties in the Hurriyat, barring the Jammat-e-Islami, does not extend beyond Srinagar. The militants are a motley lot, many not even Kashmiris. Actually the one organisation that has roots across the Valley is the National Conference. Imagine for a moment that the violence had ended, the security forces are withdrawn and a fresh election held. The chances are that Farooq Abdullah's National Conference would sweep it.

Most Hurriyat leaders who once backed militancy have now abandoned that path or say they have. But they have yet to prove their credentials as democrats. They have shown little skill beyond the politics of protest. Given its varied background—it ranged from pro-independence JKLF to pro-Pakistan Jamaat-e-Islami—they cannot have a uniform position to negotiate with the government of India. Though their current chairman Syed Ali Shah Geelani belongs to the Jamaat-e-Islami (Kashmir), it is not clear whether that outfit is fully behind him. In 1998, he was replaced as the Amir of the outfit by Ghulam Mohammed Bhat who declared that they did not believe in armed struggle. However, officials say that the Hizbul Mujahideen and the Al Badr maintain their links to the Jamaat.

The Hurriyat's other senior leader, Abdul Ghani Lone, has had a chequered career as an MLA—with the Congress and National Conference governments—before founding the People's Conference. Thereafter, he became a militant leader and allegedly founded his own group called Al Barq, staffed with foreign militant. Even the venerable Prof. Abdul Ghani Bhat has, in the past, had his own militant outfit, the Muslim Mujahideen.

The secular part of the APHC comprises the Jammu and Kashmir Liberation Front led by Yasin Malik. The JKLF announced a unilateral cease fire in 1994, and possesses no armed wing. But this outfit was responsible for the outbreak of militancy.

The most engimatic figure in the grouping is the young Mir Waiz Omar Farooq whose father was assassinated by Pakistani agents in May 1990. Farooq has been a consistent votary of tripartite talks among India, Pakistan and the Kashmiris to resolve the problem.

So for the moment, the ball remains where it has been for the past several years, in the court of Farooq Abdullah and the National Conference.

## Stands on Autonomy

*Home Minister L.K. Advani*—I do not want to foreclose any option by commenting on the matter. We will discuss the matter within the four corners of our Constitution.

*Congress Spokesperson Anand Sharma*—The 1975 accord alone should form the basis of any autonomy package. Time is not ripe for raising the autonomy question as the State is in the grip of large-scale terrorism.

*BJP President Kushabhau Thakre*—It is a retrograde step and would nullify all measures taken to integrate the State with the rest of the country over the past 50 years.

*CPI Secretary D. Raja*—There is a need to discuss the quantum of autonomy being sought. We are agreeable to the demand for devolution of powers but a national debate on autonomy should be initiated.

*Former PM Chandra Shekhar*—Farooq Abdullah should have discussed the autonomy report with the Centre before introducing the resolution in the Assembly. This is not the right time for raising the issue.

*J & K People's Democratic Party Leader Mehbooba Mufti*—It is one more gimmick and probably the last one on the kitty of Farooq Abdullah to blackmail the people of the State and the Centre.

*Hurriyat Leader Sheikh Abdul Rashid*—Passing of a resolution has not solved the Kashmir issue nor is it going to do so in future.

## Motion on Autonomy Adopted

On June 26, 2000 the Jammu and Kashmir Assembly adopted the recommendations of the State Autonomy Committee (SEC) and demanded that the Centre and the State Government take "Positive and effective steps for its implementation." The motion was adopted amid a protest walkout by Opposition parties.

State Chief Minister Farooq Abdullah said the motion's approval was aimed at removing "blots of mistrust created due to erosion in the State's special status in the past."

During his 100-minute speech, Dr. Abdullah appealed to those opposed to the greater autonomy demand not to "push us to the wall" and made light of the Ladakh Buddhist Association's apprehension over conversion to Islam, saying a single instance of conversion was a case of "love affair".

"We are Indians. We are not Pakistanis," the Chief Minister asserted, urging the Opposition parties to "see things in the right perspective."

The adoption of the autonomy report — which was moved by Law and Parliamentary Affairs Minister P L Handoo was greeted with joy by treasury benches as the BJP, Janata Dal (United) and a lone member of Jammu and Kashmir Awami League staged a walkout. The Congress, CP1-M and BSP, however, did not join the protestors.

Initially, the National Conference had limited the scope of discussion on the autonomy report and the resolution's passage were considered a remote possibility. But mounting pressure forced the ruling party's hand and it decided last evening to carry it through the Assembly with a voice vote.

Earlier the entire Opposition had staged a walkout protesting a remark attributed to National Conference MLA Mohammed Shafi Bhat who allegedly had said : "Burn the Indian Constitution". The Chief Minister was forced to intervene in the matter and take Mr. Bhatt to task to pacify the agitated Opposition.

Speaking in the autonomy motion's favour, Dr. Abdullah said : "It was our commitment to the people at the time of elections that we would restore their dignity and honour".

The autonomy report demands that the State be given control over all subjects of governance except foreign affairs, communications and defence. It also seeks restarting of the titles of "Sadar-e-Riyasat" for head of the State and "Wazir-e-Azam" or Prime Minister for head of the State Government.

The Chief Minister also hinted that he had the backing of Prime Minister AB Vajpayee over the issue. "Vajpayee is a democrat beyond his imagination despite being an RSS man," he said, adding that "the media had wrongly speculated that the Prime Minister had asked him not to go ahead with the motion."

The weak-long high voltage debate on the motion had veered around two main points. While the NC wailed over Centre's 'broken promises' with some speakers going to the extent of saying that had tribal raiders not invaded Kashmir the State would not have acceded to India, the Opposition described the autonomy move a step towards secession and a crude attempt by the ruling party to deflect attention of the people from the "real" issues.

BJP Legislature Party Leader Shiv Charan Gupta opposed the motion and alleged that the ruling party had launched "an anti-Indian and anti-security forces" campaign while debating on the issue.

However, Congress Legislature Party leader Tara Chand saw it as "a drama being enacted by the BJP and NC to arouse communal passions for vote politics".

## Opinion of Home Ministry

Home ministry sources discounted the passing of the greater autonomy motion in the Jammu and Kashmir assembly with a majority vote.

"It means nothing," a senior official said. Officials in the ministry say there are no real takers for the greater autonomy concept in J & K.

"The Congress party, which is responsible for all the agreements with the state government (since accession), cannot agree to it. The BJP which still firmly believes in the abrogation of Article 370, whatever its leaders in the government may say, can under no circumstances accept the autonomy card," an official said.

He added that even the constituents of the All-Party Hurriyat Conference (APHC) "don't give a damn about autonomy. Azadi for them is the main goal." As for Kashmiri Pandits, he said, "they are dead against it. They see it as a threat to the sovereignty of the country. So who will accept this proposal ? The National Conference alone cannot do it."

Of the 27 proposals contained in the state autonomy committee's report, most would be unacceptable to the Centre, home ministry sources point out.

The autonomy committee report — which was handed over to the Centre several months ago — is still being examined by an expert committee of bureaucrats. Thereafter, a committee of Union ministers is also expected to study it.

Bureaucrats are certain that the report will never see the light of the day, as it "contains proposals which no Central government in its right senses can accept. The concept of greater autonomy is simply a ploy for the political survival of chief minister Farooq Abdullah," said an official.

For instance, the provision for national emergency will not be applicable in J & K and if the need arises—like in the case of the Kargil attack—the Centre would have to seek permission from the state government to take appropriate action.

All -India services like the IAS and the IPS will not be applicable to the state, as the autonomy report seeks to have a Kashmiri administrative service to run the state.

Article 356 of the Constitution under which President's Rule can be imposed by the Centre in states in case of a failure of constitutional machinery there, would not be applicable to J & K. Nor would the writ of the Supreme Court, Election Commission of India and Comptroller and Auditor General of India apply. However, official sources conceded that there were a few things which could be acceptable, such as the redrawing of a fresh list of Scheduled Castes and Schedule Tribes, as the autonomy report insists on the state having its own SC/ST list.

## Unacceptable Act

- Congress, BJP and even Hurriyat will not accept the autonomy card. Hurriyat wants only 'aazadi'.
- Moreover, most of the proposals in the report would be unacceptable to the Centre. It is still being examined by an expert committee of bureaucrats.
- The passing of the Bill is simply a ploy to ensure Farooq Abdullah's political survival.

## Parliament Say on Autonomy to be Final

Union Home Minister L. K. Advani has said that a final decision on the resolution passed by the Jammu and Kashmir Assembly, demanding greater autonomy for the State, would be taken by Parliament.

Virtually endorsing his party's point of view on the autonomy issue, Mr. Advani said : "Whatever needs to be done (on the resolution) has to be done by Parliament. Everyone knows its composition and the views of those who constitute it."

He further said that the Centre would take a "considered view" after receiving the report from the State Government.

"I presume the report (on the resolution) will be sent to the Union Government. We will then take a considered view," he commented.

Mr. Advani said that a Cabinet meeting to discuss the developments relating to the autonomy issue would be held immediately after Prime Minister Atal Behari Vajpayee returned from abroad. Mr. Vajpayee is at present in Lisbon to attend the first Indo European Union Summit.

He refused to comment on Dr. Abdullah's reported remarks that the Prime Minister had welcomed the autonomy move during his recent meeting with him here. 'I will not comment on it. If at all anything has to be said on it, the Prime Minister will say it."

While denying that the passage of the resolution by the J & K Assembly has caused any embarrassment to the Centre, he said that the National Conference (NC) is still a part of the ruling National Democratic Alliance (NDA) "Nowhere has the Chief Minister talked about severing links with the alliance," Mr. Advani responded to a question regarding likelihood of NC parting ways with the NDA.

The Home Minister further said that the Centre favoured more devolution of power to the States. In any case, Jammu and Kashmir already enjoys more powers, he added when asked if the autonomy resolution would give rise to similar demands from other States as well.

In Srinagar, Farooq Abdullah ruled out the possibility of any confrontation with the Centre, saying that "we believe in dialogue and discussions".

Meanwhile, the Jammu and Kashmir Legislative Council adopted the motion on autonomy seeking approval of the report of the State Autonomy Committee and its recommendations.

The motion was passed by voice vote. The lone BJP member voted against it. The State Assembly adopted the motion yesterday.

The resolution on autonomy adopted by Jammu and Kashmir Assembly has been sent to the Centre for follow up action, Speaker Abdul Ahad Vakil said:

"Copies of the resolution for restoration of autonomy to Jammu and Kashmir have been sent to Secretaries General of Lok Sabha and Rajya Sabha," he said. It is now up to the Centre to initiate action, Vakil said.

Dismissing apprehension on the autonomy report, he said the report would rebuild trust and confidence between the State and the Centre.

## Farooq for Talks with Centre

On June, 27, 2000 Jammu and Kashmir Chief Minister Farooq Abdullah ruled out the possibility of any confrontation with Centre saying that "we believe in dialogue and discussions, not confrontation," even as opponents of autonomy in Jammu and Ladakh organised protest marches and demonstrations.

Speaking in the Legislative Council, before the Upper House approved the motion on autonomy with a thumping majority, the Chief Minister said that he would send his ministers to all the State capitals to discuss the matters. "It is a question of either you convince us or we convince you".

He said that his party had the two-thirds majority and could have passed a bill on autonomy. "But we have not done that, because we do not believe in confrontation." He reiterated that "those painting the National Conference as anti-Indian were doing a dis-service to the nation. We are

Indians, believe in the territorial integrity of the country. Our future lies with India and not Pakistan".

Mr. Abdullah said, that this was a false propaganda that "we want to revert back to 1953, we are in 21st century and have no intention to look behind."

Meanwhile, protest marches were organised in Leh and Jammu against the autonomy resolution. The BJP led a demonstration up to Raj Bhawan in Jammu and burnt the copies of the autonomy resolution to show their anger and protest over the issue.

The protesters said that the National Conference government was fuelling secession and it was unacceptable to them.

Former Chief Minister Ghulam Mohammad Shah in a statement here has complemented the National Conference MLAs for having passed the autonomy resolution seeking the restoration of Article 370 in its original form. He said that this was a bold step but short of the situation that could deliver a lasting solution and which could end the problems of the people in Kashmir suffering torture, harassment and wanton killings every day.

Mr. Shah said that the tripartite talks alone could bring a lasting solution to the Kashmir crisis. He urged the National Conference MLAs to take 'one more bold step to seek tripartite conference for the resolution of Kashmir problem, then at that time they will truly deserve to be congratulated'.

In the meantime, Mr. Raman Bhalla, senior Youth Congress leader, has decried the autonomy resolution. He said that the best solution to the Kashmir crisis lies in the 1975 Indira-Sheikh accord. He said that the National Conference had adopted the autonomy resolution to hoodwink the people when its performance on all fronts is nil.

## BJP Grappling with Autonomy

The autonomy resolution passed by the Jammu and Kashmir Assembly appears to have left the ruling BJP thoroughly confused.

While party president Kushabhau Thakre said removing the National Conference from the NDA would not be a good idea, the state BJP unit has planned torch-light processions in protest against the resolution.

Mr. Thakre told reporters here this morning that the BJP leadership, including the Prime Minister, would try to make Chief Minister Farooq Abdullah understand that such a resolution is not advisable as it would open the floodgates of similar demands from other-parts of the country.

He said the National Conference remains a part of the NDA and there is no proposal to ask them to quit the Union Council of Ministers. The BJP president said dismissal of the Abdullah Ministry would not solve the problem. Instead, he said, the people of Kashmir should be made to understand that such an autonomy resolution will ultimately be detrimental to their long-term interests.

Mr. Thakre pointed out that a similar demand has already come from Punjab and there is likelihood of such demands coming from the North-Eastern States.

Meanwhile, in Chennai BJP general secretary M. Venakaiah Naidu said the J &. K autonomy resolution will be defeated in Parliament since most of the parties, including the BJP and the Congress were against it.

"The BJP and the National Democratic Alliance (NDA) government are willing to consider greater devolution of powers to states including J & K, but if they want to revert to pre-1953 position then no party will back it. Parliament will definitely reject it," he said.

He wondered why Kashmir could not develop despite getting 16 times more the central financial assistance than Bihar.

The BJP spokesman refuted the charge that the autonomy issue had come alive exploiting the softness of the BJP government. "Autonomy has been discussed for the last fifty years, but it is the scope of autonomy that has to be considered. If it means greater powers to the states then were already on the way. We recently shared 19 per cent of central revenue with States. But if they want separation then they're not going to get it under any circumstances," he said.

## Thackeray tells Centre to Dismiss J & K Govt

Shiv-Sena supremo Bal Thackeray urged the Centre to dismiss Dr. Farooq Abdullah-led Jammu and Kashmir Government for passing the controversial resolution seeking restoration of greater autonomy in the state and thereby "threatening the territorial integrity of the nation."

"By passing a resolution for greater autonomy for J & K, Abdullah has taken a step to secede from India", Thackeray was quoted as saying in the party mouth-piece *Saamna*.

## Autonomy Issue Top on RSS Agenda

The autonomy resolution passed by the Jammu & Kashmir Assembly recently was on the top of the agenda at the annual meet of the Rashtriya Swayam-sewak Sangh (RSS) which began at Gandhinagar on Saturday.

Though the original agenda of the RSS annual meet included discussions on the contentious issues like the conversions and the internal security scenario, the latest development in Jammu & Kashmir was been made a top priority at the meet.

It is not clearly known as yet whether the parent body of the Sangh Parivar would go to the extent of asking its political wing to drop the National Conference from the National Democratic Alliance (NDA) and demand the dismissal of the Farooq Abdullah ministry in Jammu & Kashmir. The RSS meeting as usual, was a closed-door affair, but it has been learnt from reliable sources that the Vajpayee led NDA, Government's economic policies might come in for heavy criticism.

It may be mentioned here that the Swadeshi Jagaran Manch, another constituent of the Sangh Parivar, has never missed an opportunity to condemn the policies of globalisation and liberalization of the BJP led Union Government.

The two-day meeting of the All India Executive Committee of the RSS, held at village Koba near here, was attended by around 230 'Prant Pracharaks' and 'Kshetriya Pracharaks' from all over the country.

Many top leaders of the RSS, including its chief K.S. Sudarshan, have been holding informal discussions in small groups. Former RSS chief Raju Bhaiya and veteran Nanaji Deshmukh were among the notable absentees for health reasons.

## Leh, Jammu Strike

Jammu and Leh observed a general strike to protest the recently passed autonomy resolution in the Jammu and Kashmir Assembly.

The Jammu Bar Association had given the bandh call. The association itself has been observing a four-day strike since Wednesday. The strike has crippled the work in courts in Jammu. Commercial activity came to a stand-still in 'the walled city where shops remained closed. However, there was no report of any violent incident from anywhere. Other areas of the city responded partially to the bandh.

## Autonomy Vote

Resolution will be considered within Constitution, says PM.

On June, 30, 2000, Prime Minister Atal Behari Vajpayee said, that the Government was willing to consider autonomy to Jammu and Kashmir but within the framework of the Constitution. He was talking to newsmen on the way back home after a five-day tour of Europe.

Asked whether he was surprised at the passage of the autonomy resolution, he said, "We were not told about it." Some officials also expressed surprise that the resolution was piloted by the National Conference-led government at a time when the Prime Minister was abroad.

Mr. Vajpayee said he himself would undertake the consultation process and it would be completed by the year-end.

As a first step, an analytical note on the J & K Assembly resolution with various options would be put before the Union Cabinet. Later, Mr. Vajpayee will seek the views of constitutional experts, political parties, Kashmiri Pandits and those actively associated with the issue.

After these talks, the issue is likely to be taken up in Parliament for a debate in the monsoon session beginning third week of July.

The Prime Minister said before he left for Europe, that Chief Minister Farooq Abdullah met him in New Delhi and indicated that there would be a discussion on autonomy in the Assembly. But he said that the Centre did not feel that the J & K Assembly would adopt a resolution.

On various aspects of the resolution, he said he had not yet studied the details of the debate and the decisions of the Assembly. The Prime Minister maintained that consultation with the Hurriyat Conference would continue.

Asked to comment on Akali leader Gurcharan Singh Tohra's demand for autonomy for Punjab too, he said, "Indian democracy is resilient and strong enough to withstand any threat."

The Prime Minister ruled out any talks with Pakistan as long as cross border terrorism was being encouraged, abetted and aided by the neighbour. When pointed out that the EU and the US were pressuring India to have talks with Pakistan, he shot back, "I don't agree with them."

The Prime Minister said, that there were no differences within the various constituents of the National Democratic Alliance on economic reforms. He however, conceded that the Swadeshi Jagaran Manch (SJM) differed with his government's policies.

Chapter 22

# Centre's Reaction

## Autonomy Rejected

On July 4, 2000, the Union Cabinet rejected the controversial Jammu and Kashmir Assembly resolution seeking restoration of the pre-1953 status on the ground that it sought to reverse application of Constitutional provisions to the detriment of the country's integrity and interests of the people of the State. The Cabinet also disfavored presentation of the report in Parliament.

"The Government is of the firm conviction that national integration and devolution of powers to States must go together," the Cabinet resolution said.

The resolution adopted at the Cabinet meeting, presided over by Prime Minister A.B. Vajpayee, noted that "acceptance of the (J & K) resolution would set the clock back and reverse the natural process of harmonizing the aspirations of the people ... with the integrity of the nation."

Later in the afternoon, Home Minister L.K. Advani spoke to news persons to spell out the reasons for the Cabinet's rejection of the autonomy resolution. He said that most of the recommendations of J & K's autonomy panel had sought to reverse application of Constitutional provisions which "may not only adversely affect the interests of the people... but would also tantamount to removal of some of the essential safeguards enshrined in the Constitution."

Mr. Advani, however, kept the doors open for devolution of more financial and administrative powers to States, including J & K.

The discussions in the Cabinet were reportedly stormy with at least three Ministers advocating a soft line to afford Chief Minister Farooq Abdullah an "escape route" in the face of militant posturing by a large number of his party legislature. But Parliamentary Affairs Minister Pramod Mahajan later claimed that the Cabinet decision was unanimous.

The dissenting Ministers are understood to have cautioned others against the possible political implications in the Valley.

Hours before the Cabinet met, Mr. Vajpayee is reported to have summoned Dr. Abdullah currently in Delhi, for a one-to-one meeting at his Race Course Road residence. The Prime Minister is believed to have used the opportunity to express his strong disapproval of the manner in which the contentious resolution was adopted in the State Assembly despite Dr. Abdullah's assurances to restrict the matter to a debate.

The PM is also reported to have taken exception to the Chief Minister's diatribes against the Sangh Parivar, the RSS in particular, in Bangalore yesterday.

Emerging from the brief meeting. Dr. Abdullah uncharacteristically avoided news persons who were keeping a vigil outside the PM's residence.

Efforts to contact the Chief Minister later proved futile as he remained incommunicado. He instead let his senior Cabinet colleagues to do the talking.

Denouncing the Union Cabinet's decision as a challenge to the country's secular democratic forces, J & K Minister for Law and Parliamentary Affairs, Mr. P.L. Handoo told

*The Hindustan Times* that the National Conference would continue with its "ideological struggle." for restoration of the pre-1953 status..

However, Mr. Handoo, who had moved the autonomy resolution in the State Assembly, ruled out any NC move to break ties with the NDA.

**Cabinet Stand Welcomed**

BJP president Kushabhau Thakre welcomed the Union Cabinet's rejection of the autonomy resolution passed by the Jammu and Kashmir assembly.

"The Indian Constitution strikes a right balance between regional aspirations and national integrity." Thakre said reacting to the unanimous Cabinet decision.

He said that the autonomy decision, if accepted, would have "dangerous potential of sowing the seed of secessionism and ultimate Balkanisation of the country."

Stressing that its stand on the J & K autonomy issue had been vindicated, the Congress said that the Union cabinet's decision had "exposed the flip-flop-flip of the Vajpayee government."

Congress spokesperson Ajit Jogi said that first the National Conference, an integral part of the NDA, "passed a completely unsuitable and untenable resolution." Then, both the Prime Minister and the home minister said that the resolution "could be considered and discussed, even by Parliament." Finally, "in yet another somersault the idea of consideration in Parliament was dropped and the Cabinet took up the issue and rejected it."

## Wild Jubilation in Jammu

In Jammu, there were scenes of wild jubilation, as groups of people, led by various political parties and other organisations, took out processions to the beat of drums and setting up of firecrackers as the news of the Union Cabinet rejecting the NC-sponsored autonomy resolution spread through the city.

The news was greeted with exchange of sweetmeats at the BJP headquarters here, which had been in the forefront of organizing the "black week" during the autonomy debate in the state assembly and a massive region wise bandh after the autonomy resolution was passed. Sweets were also exchanged in the market places as the shopkeepers, their customers and the passersby congratulated one another over what they called "timely action" of the Centre.

Reports of celebrations were also received from other major towns of the region like Udhampur, Kathua, Rajouri, Poonch, Bhaderwah and Doda. Participating in the jubilations were workers of all non-NC parties, students, Panun Kashmir activists, workers of the Ladakh Buddhist Association, traders and others.

Chairman Thupstan Tsewang of the Ladakh Autonomous Hill Development Council, which on Friday unanimously passed a resolution demanding Union Territory (UT) status for Leh, said on Tuesday, it would continue to press for it despite the Union Cabinet's rejection of the resolution which had in the first place provided the stimulus for the UT demand.

Tsering Samphel, president of the Ladakh Buddhist Association who has been spearheading the on-going protest against the NC government resolution, also said that the struggle for UT status for Leh would continue. A large number of villages on Tuesday converged on Leh and took out a procession through the town demanding UT status for the district.

State BJP chief Daya Krishan Kotwal said, "The Centre's timely action has prevented the country from moving toward disintegration." He said it also "exploded" the myth of a "nexus" between the BJP and the NC with regard to the autonomy report and the resolution. He however, reiterated his party's demand for regional councils for the three "natural" regions of the state for equitable political and financial powers.

Congress leaders and former MP Dharam Pal said that the Union Cabinet had kept in view the fact that the autonomy report had been opposed by various non-NC parties in the Valley including the Hurriyat, and the people of Jammu and Ladakh.

Two senior ministers of the J & K government said that autonomy report would be taken up again and the central working committee of the National Conference would meet in Srinagar in a couple of days to work on a future strategy. The state's law and parliamentary affairs minister Pyare Lal Handoo said that the rejection of the report by the Union cabinet did not mean the end of the chapter. The fight would continue.

The J & K food and civil supplies ministers Ajay Sadhotra said that the National Conference would "fight to the last" on the autonomy issue.

When the Centre short-circuited the Jammu and Kashmir autonomy move on July, 4th, 2000, there were none to shed tears for Chief Minister Farooq Abdullah in his own State.

While the people of Jammu region saw the autonomy move as one aimed at further fuelling the separatist movement, those in the Valley dubbed it as a "political gimmick" by Dr. Abdullah to strengthen his position in the state.

"It's an attempt to divert the attention from the State Government's failures," was the common refrain.

Hurriyat Conference leaders, said Dr. Abdullah is a "puppet" in the hands of the Centre — a term synonymous with the Chief Minister even among the common man. Interestingly, there was near unanimity over the "no autonomy" slogan despite differences in perception.

As against Hindus in Jammu who dubbed the moves as a step towards "Islamization of the Valley", Kashmiri Muslims in Srinagar interpreted it as "concentration of power in the hands of a select few".

Needless to say, the credibility of Dr. Abdullah and his Government is at an all time low in the State. The fact that the ruling National Conference is an ally of the "RSS-backed BJP" and younger Abdullah, Omar, is a Minister in the Centre, made matters worse for the Chief Minister.

"The agenda", agitated residents of Gandhi Nagar and Jawahar Nagar in Jammu told *The Hindustan Times,* "is to convert the valley to an Islamic State" on the bandwagon of autonomy.

Others saw the autonomy move as the "first step towards complete Islamizations of the State."

"Autonomy means that the hold of the Kashmiri Muslims will increase."

In this context, a mention was made about the "demographic transition" that is taking place in Jammu—a visible increase in the percentage of Muslim population in what is traditionally regarded a Hindu stronghold.

But while the people in Jammu are "dead against" the autonomy, their counterparts in Srinagar seem hell-bent on accepting nothing short of "aazadi" (freedom).

"No India, no Pakistan... only freedom," seems to be the underlying feeling here. They dismissed all talk about autonomy as "mere humbug". Even though somewhat far-feteched, Yusuf Tarigami, MLA, felt that there were only two alternatives to work on : autonomy or azadi.

"And the autonomy alternative", he told *The Hindustan Times*, "is any day better than the secession of Jammu and Kashmir."

## Different Strokes

Opposition Parties reacted sharply, though differently, to the Union Cabinet's rejection of the Jammu and Kashmir Assembly Resolution endorsing the demand of Autonomy for the State.

The Congress asserted that the Cabinet decision had vindicated its stand on the J & K Autonomy issue. Left parties felt that the Cabinet had too abruptly "disposed off" the issue. The AIADMK wanted the imposition of the President's rule in the State following the passage of the "condemnable resolution".

Congress spokesman Ajit Jogi said that the Vajpayee Government was guilty of "gross inconsistency of conduct on a vital and sensitive issue of national significance like J &K". He said that the Government's conduct was not only deplorable but "is also a blatant and crude attempt to escape the Government's undeniable guilt by association since the unprecedented resolution was passed by its own integral constituent in the first place."

Criticizing the "flip-flop-flip" performance of the Government, Mr. Jogi said that the Assembly Resolution was completely "unsuitable and untenable." In the immediate aftermath of the resolution, "both the Prime Minister and the Home Minister said that the Resolution could be considered and discussed, even by Parliament. In yet another somersault, he said, the idea of consideration in Parliament was dropped and the Cabinet took up the issue and rejected it.

CPI general secretary A.B. Bardhan said that the Cabinet's decision was a "wrong way of disposing a national issue." He said that this was not a question of rejecting what Chief Minister Farooq Abdullah was demanding or of accepting what the BJP had stated. This out of hand rejection could send a confrontationist signal.

Mr. Bardhan said that if the issue of autonomy was to be considered, it should have been discussed at an all-party meeting. Pointing at inconsistencies in the Government's stand, he said that the Cabinet had rejected the Kashmir Assembly Resolution while Home Minister L.K. Advani was recently talking about a dialogue with Hurriyat leaders.

In Chennai, AIADMK leader Jayalalitha demanded dissolution of the J & K Assembly following the passage of the Autonomy Resolution. She said if the Centre did not act against the Farooq Abdullah Government, the demand for autonomy would spread like wild fire and lead to the country's fragmentation. The AIADMK leader accused the BJP led Government of adopting a "free-for-all' approach towards questions concerning the country's integrity.

Her party was steadfast in its commitment to the country's integrity even though it favoured greater devolution of power to the states. Her party believed in the position : "We will not live as slaves, but at no time will we seek separation."

Jammu and Kashmir National Panthers Party president Bhim Singh said in the interest of the people of Jammu and Kashmir, the Farooq Abdullah Government should be dismissed forthwith for free and fair elections. At the same time, he said, Statehood be granted to Jammu province, democracy to Kashmir and status of Union Territory to Ladakh. Mr. Singh said that the Department of Jammu and Kashmir should be shifted to the Prime Minister's Office to resolve the various problems of the State.

## JD (U) on Autonomy

Janta Dal (United) strongly opposed the autonomy demand raised by the J & K Assembly, saying it had "dangerous implications" and announced its decision to raise the issue at the National Democratic Alliance coordination committee meeting this month.

Party spokesman and national secretary, M. Raghupathy told reporters that the Janata Dal (United) was in favour of devolving more powers to the states in accordance with the recommendations of the Sarkaria Commission on Centre-State relations.

Emphasising that his party was against the autonomy demand, he said that any solution to the Jammu & Kashmir problem should be found within the Constitutional framework and "nothing should be done which may jeopardise the country's unity and integrity".

Meanwhile in Hyderabad, BJP general secretary, M. Venkaiah Naidu welcomed the Union Cabinet's decision to reject outright the Jammu and Kashmir Assembly Autonomy Resolution.

The BJP general secretary said in Hyderabad that the decision was right and taken at an appropriate time.

"The National Democratic Alliance (NDA) Government led by Atal Behari Vajpayee has once again shown that it can take hard decisions as and when necessary in the interest of the country." He added.

## Government Move

The Politburo of the Communist Party of India (Marxist) maintains that the Vajpayee Government can not evade the issue of greater autonomy for Jammu and Kashmir and must consult all political parties on the matter. In a detailed reaction on the Union Cabinet's rejection of the Jammu and Kashmir Assembly resolution on autonomy, the politburo stated that the Cabinet move could not end the matter. The party has rejected the contention, which equates autonomy with separatism.

The party said that in the case of Jammu and Kashmir, the demand for autonomy had a specific background. The State had a special status. It was a fact that over the years, Governments at the Centre had eroded and whittled away the scope and content of autonomy within the ambit of Article 300. This was recognized in the Indira Gandhi-Sheikh Abdullah Accord of 1975.

The CPI (M) does not subscribe to the scope of autonomy as defined in the resolution adopted by the State Assembly, which is going back to the pre-1953 status. Over the decades, developments in the political system and the political administrative structure in the country have warranted certain changes that are justified.

"It is not possible to accept the definition of autonomy which assigns the Centre only External Affairs, Defence and

Communications. However, the reality is that even within the ambit of Article 370, there was a steady erosion of the rights of Jammu and Kashmir," the party spokesperson said.

**Cabinet Decision a Non-issue**

The All parties Hurriyat Conference (APHC) described the hullabaloo over the J&K Assembly resolution, which the Union Cabinet rejected today, as a "non-issue" as far as the permanent resolution of the Kashmir problem was concerned.

"We in the Hurriyat attach more significance to the Vajpayee Government's approach on Kashmir and not what Dr. Farooq Abdullah does, as the people of Jammu and Kashmir have lost trust in his Government," former APHC chairman Umar Farooq told *The Hindustan Times*.

He said that the Hurriyat was not interested in any arrangement aimed at transfer or devolution of more powers.

The dialogue should focus on the core issue and not the grant of greater autonomy, which was "totally irrelevant" in the present context.

Mr. Farooq said that the APHC never attached any significance to the development as greater autonomy for J & K was never on its agenda.

There was nothing new in the theory propounded afresh by the Chief Minister, he remarked. According to him, Kashmir's autonomy has been systematically eroded over the years.

Responding to the Cabinet's rejection of the Assembly resolution, Mr. Farooq observed that the Kashmiris were clamoring for a permanent solution to the problem, which cannot be achieved through the autonomy route. "When we speak of a solution to the Kashmir problem, our focus is on the entire State (including parts under Pakistan's occupation). The grant of autonomy touches only a fraction of the problem," he argued. The Hurriyat leader further remarked that the APHC would favourably respond to any unconditional offer for talks by the Vajpayee Government provided the proposal reflected a genuine desire on the Centre's part to find a lasting solution to the festering dispute." It is for New Delhi to reduce its ever-growing dependence on the armed forces and create a congenial atmosphere for dialogue." Mr Farooq exhorted the Government to start on a positive note and express its willingness to address the core issue of the Kashmir problem. Such an approach would also help the Hurriyat to convince the people of Kashmir about the utility of engaging with the Centre.

Meanwhile. J & K. Democratic Forum Chairman Bhushan Bazaz said that Dr. Abdullah should have taken all regions of the State into confidence before raking up the autonomy issue.

## Assam on Autonomy

The Autonomy resolution by the Jammu and Kashmir Assembly has sparked off an intense debate in the Northeast, particularly in Assam where the ruling Asom Gana Parishad (AGP) had advocated autonomy for the State in its 1996 election manifesto.

"Demanding autonomy is certainly not anti-national or secessionist as some political parties including a section of BJP maintain" told Chief Minister Prafulla Kumar Mahanta. "But yes, autonomy must be within the purview of the Constitution."

In its 1996 election manifesto, the Asom Gana Parishad said it would strive for Assam's autonomy in all matters.

However, defence, foreign affairs, currency and communication were the exceptions, besides state regulation in all administrative and financial affairs without Central interference.

It differs from the Jammu and Kashmir package on a separate national flag and Constitution.

It also differs in redesignating the Governor and the Chief Minister as per the pre 1953 arrangement.

Mr. Mahanta declined to comment on these aspects of the Jammu and Kashmir package owing to "our limitations as a regional party", but he felt that all items in the autonomy charter were within the scope of negotiation. He, however, hinted at these demands being tools for bargaining with the Centre. "There are two strong reasons why Assam needs autonomy : to tackle insurgency and to control our own natural resources towards development," the Chief Minister said.

"Insurgency in North-east has gone international, and the States of this region need certain powers to take up the issue directly with neighbouring nations where leaders of banned outfits have taken shelter."

Mr. Prafulla Kumar Mahanta regretted that the Centre was not willing to let the North-eastern States to deal directly with the neighbouring countries on the insurgency issue.

"On the other hand, New Delhi insists insurgency is a regional problem that should be solved regionally."

**Track on J & K Autonomy**

Circumstances may have compelled Madhya Pradesh Chief Minister Digvijay Singh to make a slight but crucial amendment to his earlier view that full autonomy should be given to Jammu and Kashmir to defuse the situation in the terrorist infested state.

Asked for a reaction by a cable news network on J & K, Chief Minister Farooq Abdullah's recent remark that the autonomy demand had Digvijay Singh's support, the latter said "Ye sab thik hai" (all this is OK), but only if something could be worked out "within the frame work of the Indian Constitution". The view, said he, was fully in consonance with his earlier demand that all states should ideally have a greater measure of autonomy to promote true federalism. A couple of weeks ago, however, the CM had told some local journalists during an informal chat that he was strongly in favour of full autonomy for J &K to rid the country of a festering problem. No mention was then made of the "framework" within which this ought to be done.

The feeling in political circles is that Digvijay's remarks on J & K were largely aimed at selling a proposition which would indirectly help in strengthening his own political future and standing. A senior Congress leader observed that seven continuous years in power at a time when the party's central leadership was getting progressively weaker had given the "raja" an appetite for greater "independence". "He now hates kowtowing to Delhi for small favours. He now wants to be a real Raja."

## Ineptly Handled Autonomy Issue : Congress

The handling of the Jammu and Kashmir autonomy demand by the Union government shows its monumental failure in dealing with a sensitive issue, Congress spokesperson Anand Sharma said. "The government's inaction and inept handling of the issue has opened a Pandora's box as is evident from the observations of various political parties."

The demand for more autonomy, made by everyone from G.T Tohra to Prafulla Kumar Mahanta, had serious implications. It would make more difficult tackling cross-border terrorism and effectively countering insurgency in some parts of the country, he said.

The demand for more powers by the states was nothing new and the Sarkaria Commission dealt with this issue in detail he recalled.

## Allies as Shield

RSS Chief K.S. Sudershan's demand to annul Article 370 and impose President's rule in Jammu and Kashmir, and effect corrections in the economic policy has drawn a blank response from the BJP.

The party says that the Government will listen to the Sangh Parivar's demands only if they were acceptable to its allies and in consonance with the ruling NDA's agenda.

Responding to the RSS chief's remarks in a TV interview BJP general secretary M. Venkaiah Naidu said the BJP-led Government was not in a position to accept or implement all views of the RSS.

"We cannot thrust our views on our allies on any subject, which is not on the agenda of governance. Only those demands that are acceptable to them can be implemented," he said.

Mr. Naidu said that the BJP would not press its views on Article 370 since it had been out of the NDA's agenda.

The BJP spokesperson said that the RSS had every right to express its opinion on any subject as it was a separate organisation.

"We respect everyone's right to express their opinion. But only what is acceptable to our allies can be considered by the Government."

In an interview to the media, the RSS chief is quoted as saying that the Vajpayee Government's economic policies need to be changed and the Centre must clamp President's rule in Jammu and Kashmir and do away with Article 370.

"Whatever we find unacceptable in the Vajpayee Government's economic policy, we will place before the people. The policy is not beneficial to them in any respect," he was quoted by a news agency.

Mr. Sudershan said that he had urged the Government to withdraw the proposal to allow 100 per cent foreign direct investment in e-commerce as it was dangerous and tantamount to "selling the nation".

On the Government's move to disinvest equity in the PSUs, the RSS chief said purification was no big deal. "We should not hand it over to foreigners in a bid to privatize. This is wrong," he said.

On the construction of Ram temple at the disputed Ayodhya site, the RSS chief said that the Government should hand over the place to the Ram Janmabhoomi Trust or pass a legislation if it was possible. Both, he said, seemed unlikely with cases dragging in the courts. "The only other option is that the Muslims relinquish claim to the place."

Mr Sudershan said that it would be easier to convince the Muslim leadership that there was no mosque on the site and such a piece of land was not acceptable for Muslim place of worship under Islam.

"The Ram temple will be built. No one can stop it," he said.

## Sudershanspeak

- Scrap Article 370, clamp Central rule in J&K.
- Convince Muslims to hand over Ayodhya site for Ram temple.
- Do not hand over nation to foreigners.
- Sheikh Abdullah worked for separation from India.
- Anti-Christian Violence ploy to defame RSS.
- Economic policy not beneficial to the country.
- Allowing 100 p.c. FDI e-comerce is dangerous.

## Hawkish RSS Line

CPI Leader A. B. Bardhan says that the Government, by evading important issues raised by the Kashmir autonomy resolution, has succumbed to RSS and BJP hawks.

In an article in the forthcoming issue of the party organ *New Age*, he said the issue of Kashmir autonomy existed along, but the vital question was the quantum of autonomy. "By pre-emptorily rejecting the demand for autonomy, the Union Cabinet has virtually sent out the message that it is in no mood to discuss and debate the issue" the CPI leader writes.

"We do not agree with the recommendation of the Kashmir autonomy report. There are several points that are not acceptable. For instance, the demand for going back to the position as it existed in 1953 cannot be accepted. This would be to recall the morrow of the accession of the J & K State to India," says the article.

The Cabinet, the CPI leader says, had deliberately mixed up autonomy for Kashmir with the devolution of more financial and administrative powers to the States. The issue of Centre-State relations was also dragged in unnecessarily.

Instead of devolving more power to the States, the Centre has done just the opposite. "The States are being held on a tighter leash, and largesses from the Centre, even when a national calamity in some form or the other overtakes a State, are promised and doled out according to its political caprices and calculations," he wrote.

## Is it End ?

The Editor, *The Times of India*, July 10. 2000 writes : Are the good times coming to an end for the BJP-led government ? The allies as usual are rallying round the prime minister, but that other source of trouble -the RSS - is once again breathing fire. Though somewhat quarrelsome in the beginning, the RSS had become the picture of cooperation under the genteel Rajju Bhaiya. The BJP's once hot-headed spiritual parent seemed to have understood that war-cries of the sort it favoured would only hamper the growth of its favourite child. If the advent of K.S. Sudarshan upset this happy balance, it was not by accident. Mr. Sudarshan is a known hardliner, and indeed, almost the first thing the new RSS chief did on taking charge was to prophecy an epic war between Hindus and anti-Hindus. This was RSS-speak we hadn't heard in some time. After that shrill rhetoric, now the RSS is on specifics. Mr. Sudarshan has a long list of do's and don'ts for the BJP—scrap Article 370, get the Ayodhya temple from the Muslims, forget foreign direct investment, etc. Worse, Mr. Sudarshan makes mince-meat of Sheikh Abdullah by alleging that he alleging that he worked for separation from India. The last bit is ominous for the BJP, especially considering the current sensitivities of its ally, the National Conference. There's lot the Farooq Abdullah-led NC will put up with -including a thundering 'No' on the autonomy proposals - but it will not hear a word said against the Sher-e-Kashmir. And most certainly not from the RSS, which it views with enormous suspicion.

There is no mistaking the signals from Nagpur. The RSS wants the National Conference to be given the boot. RSS sources first merely hinted at this ; later at its conclave in Ahmedabad, the Sangh actually asked the BJP to consider breaking ties with the NC. Mr. Sudarshan's attack on Article 370 and Sheikh Abdullah seems like a deliberate provocation. The idea seems to be to somehow get the NC out : If the BJP won't do the needful—force the NC to bite the bait. However, this is not as simple as it might seem. The significance of the NC goes beyond its two MPs. In other words, while physically the NDA can withstand the exit of the NC, emotionally it cannot. Currently Farooq Abdullah is more than a mere ally of the BJP, in the aftermath of the autonomy struggle he has become something of a martyr, not just within the NC, but also for some of NDA's other constituents. If Mr. Abdullah is shown the door in the manner the RSS wants, the spill over will affect the NDA as a whole. It is crucially important, then, that the Vajpayee government weathers this all new-RSS storm. The RSS, in turn will doubtless remember the destiny of previous non-congress governments- all of them collapsed due to internal trouble rather than because of machinations by a political opponent. The Vajpayee government itself suffered this fate in its first term. It's up to Mr. Sudarshan to ensure that he doesn't take the place of Ms. Jayalalitha this time round.

Chapter 23

# Continuing Dialogue

## Autonomy Issue

Having summarily rejected the Kashmir autonomy resolution, the Vajpayee government found it much harder to satisfy the aspirations of Kashmir-and of other states-with its anodyne promise of "devolution of more financial and administrative powers".

On 6th July, 2000, home minister L.K. Advani promised "suitable steps ... to ensure harmonious Centre-state relations in the light of the recommendations of the Sarkaria Commission". Justice Sarkaria submitted his report in 1988, but his recommendations have yet to see the light of day. Curiously, the Vajpayee government has not thought it fit to expedite the suggestion the BJP itself made to the Commission, such as on financial autonomy and the appointment of governors "from a panel prepared by the Inter-State council" and "in consultation with the concerned state."

The BJP may consider the autonomy resolution secessionist but for several constituents of the NDA- notably the DMK, MDMK, PMK and the Akalis - what the Kashmir assembly is demanding is not that different from what they themselves asked for in the past.

The three Tamil parties are still officially committed to the Raja Mannar committee recommendations, as endorsed by the Tamil Nadu assembly in 1974. The resolution was moved by M. Karunanidhi, then, as now, chief minister of the state. Its content was the same as the Kashmir resolution: "The federal government should have only powers relating to defence, foreign affairs, inter-state communication and currency." Like the Kashmir assembly, the Rajamannar committee wanted the Supreme Court limited to constitutional cases and the Election Commission to conducting national and not state elections.

But in politics, context is every thing. There was no insurgency, no cry for separation. The Union cabinet did not think it proper to reject the Tamil Nadu resolution. Indira Gandhi simply ignored it, as she had the equally radical 1973 Anandpur Sahib resolution sponsored by the Akali Dal. It was only in the early 1980s- with the shattering of the Congress hold on the south that Centre state problems became important. When. the four southern chief ministers met in Bangalore in 1983 to demand equitable sharing of fiscal revenues, Indira Gandhi's reaction was to appoint the Sarkaria Commission. Since then, the salience of regionalism has dramatically increased. What has changed, also, is that the BJP has supplanted the Congress as the main defender of a centralised polity. The irony is that the BJP is forced to rule in alliance with regional parties, all of whom, to some extent want a radical overhaul of Centre-state relations.

## J&K Not Alone

- Autonomy debate is not over yet.
- Several regional parties also have autonomy dreams.
- Many of them are BJP's partners at the Centre.
- Sarkaria commission report on power devolution is still in the cold storage.
- B.J.P. has ignored its own recommendations to the commission.

**Farooq Tough on 'Azadi'**

"The Gods" said Jammu and Kashmir Chief Minister Farooq Abdullah, "are angry with Kashmir and the Kashmiris. Their misfortunes are consequences of their Kufran-e-neemat (not appreciating the bounties of Allah). Gods gave them in abundance but they did not even part with a handful of rice. Today they have lost everything..."

Dr. Abdullah said this while speaking to a delegation of Women's Initiative for Peace in South Asia (WIPSA). The WIPSA team was in the State to take stock of the ground reality and the extent of Kashmiris' alienation with the rest of the country.

In a freewheeling conversation, the Chief Minister refuted the contention that the Kashmiris wanted "azadi" (freedom) and not autonomy. "It is easy to demand azadi but how will the State sustain itself? Where will the money for development come from ? Who will defend the borders from China, Pakistan and even India if azadi became a reality? Then only the rule of guns would prevail," said a visibly irate Abdullah.

The Chief Minister, however, made it clear that Kashmir would never be a part of Pakistan and the demand for plebiscite would never be conceded.

Dr. Abdullah said that peace with Pakistan is impossible and talks between the two countries are unlikely in the backdrop of Pakistan aiding and abetting militancy in the State.

"There are two faces for Pakistan. One is the friendly face and the other that is Kargil scarred," he said.

The Chief Minister said that Kashmir is at the crossroads and fighting a battle for survival. "We are not out of the woods yet, but the situation is not as bad as it was three years ago," he claimed. Dr. Abdullah said, "Delhi must realise this and make an all-out effort to tell the people that they are an integral part of India."

"The people, on their part, must decide whether they want to be a part of India or not. They cannot stay here, accrue the benefits and say that they are a part of Pakistan," he said.

"The Centre at the same should take steps to alleviate the suffering of the people," the Chief Minister added. "The suffering must end. The Kashmiri people must know that there is concern for them coupled with efforts to balm their wounds," he said.

"The Kashmiri Pundits need to be encouraged and brought back to the State. Fear cannot and should not keep them away."

## Government on Promotion of Centre-State Harmony

The Government is committed to the promotion of federal harmony by ensuring a partnership of the Centre and States as laid down in the National Agenda for governance of the National Democratic Alliance.

The National Agenda for Governance of the NDA states in no uncertain terms that "there is a clear case for devolution of more financial and administrative powers and functions to the states". It further states that "suitable steps will be taken to ensure harmonious Centre State relations in the light of the recommendations of the Sarkaria Commission". In the last two years, the Government has taken several steps in this direction. The Government reaffirms its commitment to continuing its endeavour to evolve a broad consensus on the implementation of steps for wideranging devolution of powers to the states that leads to efficiency in administration, acceleration in development and the fullest realization of the creative potential of all sections of our people.

The setting up of a Commission to review the Constitution is also a step in this direction. In the above context, the Cabinet finds the Resolution passed by the State Assembly of Jammu and Kashmir endorsing the report of the State Autonomy Committee unacceptable.

The Cabinet feels that the acceptance of this resolution would set the clock back and reverse the natural process of harmonising the aspirations of the people of Jammu and Kashmir with integrity of the Nation.

Most of the recommendations contained in the report of the State Autonomy Committee seek to reverse the Application of Constitutional provisions to the State of Jammu and Kashmir which may not adversely affect the interests of the people of the State but would also tantamount to removal of some of the essential safeguards enshrined in our Constitution.

Besides, the issue of restoring the Constitutional situation in Jammu and Kashmir to its pre-1953 position had been discussed in detail by Sheikh Mohammad Abdullah with Prime Minister Indira Gandhi in 1974-75.

It is noteworthy that the agreement signed after these negotiations had affirmed that "provisions of the Constitution of India already applied to the State of J & K without adaptation or modification are unalterable".

## Doors Open for Talks

Former Jammu and Kashmir Chief Minister Farooq Abdullah believed that the Centre has not ruled out a dialogue with him on greater autonomy to the State by not accepting the State legislature's resolution on it.

"I believe that the Centre-State dialogue on the autonomy issue will still take place. My understanding is that they have kept the door for dialogue open. When I meet the Prime Minister next, 1 will discuss the various mechanisms for the dialogue with him" Dr. Abdullah said in an exclusive interview to *The Hindustan Times.* Virtually throwing open the discussion on the autonomy issue once again the Chief Minister said that any mechanism for discussing the issue was acceptable to him. He said that as far as he was concerned, each and every clause of the recommendations of the State Autonomy Committee report was open for discussion, dialogue and debate.

The report of the State Autonomy Committee, Dr. Abdullah felt, could still be referred to a committes of legal experts as it addressed constitutional issues. The Union Government could even send it to the Constitution Review Committee that it had set up.

"If they say it is a political issue," Dr. Abdullah said, "why should it not be sent to a political committee of some kind ? These are only mechanisms for discussion. We have no objection to any mechanism so long as the discussion is held with an open mind. A dialogue is essential with people who understand the law and who are concerned with the issue. Only then can we see how best a working relationship can be evolved on the issue. Our primary interest is in reducing the alienation of the people of Jammu and Kashmir, and thereby strengthening Indian democracy. This can only be done. by clearing the disinformation campaign about the autonomy issue."

The Chief Minister seemed to make a clear distinction between the non-acceptance of the autonomy resolution passed by the State Assembly and the State Autonomy Committee Report which, he said, was still under the consideration of the Centre. "I think the Resolution has been pushed out. Some people say that it was not worded properly. Perhaps the Centre took the wording of the Resolution as an affront. That was not our intention. However, the State Autonomy Committee Report is still under consideration. I do not think that they can just push it out," he said Admitting that "they (the Centre) gave it to us as good as we gave it to them," he, however, claimed that he was "terribly upset" with the whole thing.

There is a strong belief that the National Conference is being disingenuous in talking of a dialogue on the autonomy issue now while having substituted a relatively open motion before the State Assembly with a harder resolution in the last minute. The motion originally moved by the National Conference in the legislature talked of the State setting up a ministerial committee to initiate a dialogue on autonomy not only with the Union government but also other States, the convening of an all party meeting on the issue and requesting the Union Government to also set up a ministerial committee to initiate a dialogue on the State Autonomy Committee Report.

However, after three members of the National Conference moved an amendment to this motion, the party itself substituted the initial motion by another that announced the acceptance of the report and demanded effective steps from the Union and the State Government "for implementation" of the recommendations.

Asked why his party had done this, and whether this meant that the National Conference had in effect shut the door for discussion Dr. Abdullah replied, "I am for discussion so that we evolve a solution rather than harp on something that may sound politically correct but may not be workable. However, in a democracy, I can't tell everyone that they should do as I feel. You have to listen to the majority in the party."

"My own people proposed an amendment to the government's motion. Have you heard of this happening anywhere else ? Then the honorable Speaker, in his best judgement, ruled that the amendment also be included in the debate. I was not in the know of it till the last moment."

"Did he have no control over his party and his MLAs ? Could he not have asked them to withdraw the amendment ? I think it is very difficult for me as the President of the National Conference and the Chief Minister to really become a dictator. The mood of the House too had to be taken into account," Dr. Abdullah explained.

Since he had a good relationship with Prime Minister Atal Behari Vajpayee, had he kept him informed of the changing dynamics of the legislative process in the State Assembly ?

Dr. Abdullah claimed that he had told the Prime Minister what was happening and that Mr. Vajpayee was a bit worried with the developments. "I told him that I had gone before the people on the autonomy question and that I could not go before them and say that this is all I could do. I am sure the Prime Minister did not want the whole process to go the way it did."

Did Dr. Abdullah want it to go the way it went ? "Well, it has gone the way it has gone. It is now there," he replied. If this is what the people of J & K wanted, why had Dr. Abdullah not followed the Centre's rejection of the Autonomy Resolution with mass mobilization of the people in the State on the issue ? The Chief Minister said that the "shock is far too recent" and that it would take time for the people to recover from.it and think of the next strategy".

In the worst case scenario — of there being no discussion on the autonomy issue between the Centre and him — did he see himself taking up more extreme positions as time went by ? Dr. Abdullah replied, "I don't know. I think time itself will tell. My people have gone through hell. I don't want to push them into further tragedies. I will try to the very last to ensure that sense prevails in the corridors of power in Delhi. The rest is up to God."

Did Farooq Abdullah see himself as a man who changed the course of history of Jammu and Kashmir - if his father had done it once by opting for India ; had his son now provided the pivot around which the politics of Jammu and Kashmir will have to move henceforth ? "I think I can't be as tall as my father. You haven't produced a Mahatma Gandhi or a Jawaharlal Nehru in the last fifty years. You have not found another JP. So I don't think I can step into the shoes of my father. However, I am certain of one thing — I have made the States realise that India can become a good and strong federal State," Dr. Abdullah replied.

So had Farooq Abdullah finally arrived as a political leader, as it were ? "I don't know about that. But Farooq Abdullah certainly has the most amount of troubles," he said.

How did he feel about the Centre dealing with the All Party Hurriyat Conference, which seeks independence, while keeping him at a distance because he wants autonomy ? Dr. Abdullah replied, "1 would say to the government: Please start talking to the Hurriyat on azadi and the merger of Jammu and Kashmir with Pakistan and then see what the people of Valley, Jammu and Ladakh have to say. Let the nation know where the Hurriyat stands and what the government of India is offering them. You are not willing to give us autonomy, I wonder how you will offer them azadi and merger with Pakistan ?"

"This is why I say that I am open to discussing every clause of the State Autonomy Committee's recommendations.

I want a federal India, not a unitary India. I belong to a secular India, not to an India based on Hindutva. I have never been for confrontation. I am for reconciliation."

How should the people of the rest of India judge him ? Dr. Abdullah replied "There are those who view me through the RSS spectacles they see me as a traitor who ought to be put behind bars. But they are in a minority. The majority knows that I am fighting not for Kashmir but for India, to retain and preserve our way of life within the Indian Union."

## Sharp Differences in NC

Sharp differences surfaced at the crucial National Conference Working Committee meeting on whether to remain in the National Democratic Alliance (NDA) following rejection of Jammu and Kashmir Assembly's autonomy resolution by the Union Cabinet.

Highly-placed NC sources told journalists that several speakers favoured pulling out of the NDA, as the rejection of resolution was linked to the party's political base in the state.

The speakers according to the sources, contended that the Centre's response to the registration and the attack by the BJP, the leading partner of the NDA made it untenable for the party to continue in the alliance

However, leaders of the party had voiced the need for continuing in NDA as they feel that the state government should work in tandem with the Centre to stamp out militancy from the state.

Sensing the mood in the meeting Chief Minister and protective Farooq Abdullah bought time by announcing extension of the Working Committee deliberations by a day to allow all its 31 members to air their views.

So far 10 members had spoken in the meeting.

Earlier, NC general secretary Sheikh Nazir came out of the meeting and told reporters in reply to a question that his party would not go for confrontation with the Centre.

Nazir said it is not BJP which runs the Union Government but the NDA which is at the helm of affairs at the Centre.

Before the start of the meeting, Chief Minister Farooq Abdullah had told reporters that the Working Committee meeting would be over in an hour and mediapersons should be conveyed the decision by this evening itself.

"The working committee session will continue for longer time as only four of the 31 members spoke so far," Nazir said.

To a question whether the NC has softened its stand, he said, "We have a clear stand on autonomy. We have passed the resolution in the Assembly. We have promised people to restore autonomy and initiated the action by passing a resolution in the Assembly."

Earlier, Mr. Farooq Abdullah had asserted that he has not at any point of time diluted the autonomy issue.

During his various stints in office, no constitution amendment order was extended, he said while participating on the concluding day of the two-day seminar on state and regional autonomy.

He said that the accord between him and former Prime Minister Rajiv Gandhi in 1986-87 to fight the elections was to bridge the gulf between people.

**Farooq under Pressure**

Political Punditry is in overdrive here, and the latest test of skill is prophesying the fate of Jammu and Kashmir Chief Minister Farooq Abdullah. The common wisdom of the moment is : "If Farooq is toppled, his party, the National Conference, will descend on Lal Chowk (the epicenter of Kashmiri dissent), demanding azadi (independence)."

"Farooq and his NC are under pressure to take a hard line against Delhi. The NC has already surprised many by speeches of its legislators in the J & K Assembly on autonomy, where they sounded more like the pro-secession Hurriyat," observes academic Bashir Dabia of Kashmir varsity.

The Mirwaiz of Kashmir, Umer Farooq, has a tongue-in-cheek reminder for Farooq Abdullah : "He owes his position to the political legacy of his father, Sheikh Abdullah. Even under the Sheikh, the National Conference won on an anti-India vote," Political scientist Noor Baba agrees, "If Farooq has to survive politically, he has to confront the Centre," he believes.

Today, Farooq's party does not hold political meetings, and is accused of having no public contact in the manner of conventional political entities. Its vote share is dwindling, which is reflected in the fall in the Valley voters turnout from 40 per cent in 1996 to 11.9 per cent in 1999.

"The political activity of the NC can't be equated with the popular will. There is a question mark over the representative character of the party," infers Prof. Dabla.

It seems there's a crisis of legitimacy stalking Farooq's government. He's mercilessly accused of being a "Delhi agent", charged the Mirwaiz:

"Farooq does not represent Kashmir in Delhi. He represents Delhi in Kashmir !"

What, then, explains Farooq's overriding relevance to Valley politics? "Yes, he does matter because he's the Chief

Minister," concedes Prof. Abdul Gani of the Hurriyat Conference, Farooq's bitter rival. But how does he become Chief Minister ? The answer lies in the NC still being the only Kashmiri political party with an organized network. "It has roots in every village," nods Umer Farooq. These roots can be traced back to Sheikh Abdullah's sweeping land reforms, which made all Kashmiri Muslims landlords, the abolition of the Qusuari (money lending) system, and provision of free education to all.

Farooq, as the Sheikh's political legatee, faces virtually no opposition in the electoral arena. Observers attribute this "monopoly" to the division of the political space exclusively in terms of pro and anti-India positions, and their complete appropriation by the NC and the Hurriyat respectively. Thus, with the political space occupied by biggest two forces, and with one of them — the Hurriyat — opting out of electoral politics, the field is clear for the NC.

**No Standoff on Autonomy**

Tempers cooled on both sides of J & K autonomy question. In response to Prime Minister Vajpayee's white flag, J & K law and parliamentary affairs minister P.L. Handoo today told the media, "There is no question of a standoff or. autonomy. Those who imagine a confrontation obviously do not understand J & K."

This puts to rest speculations that Abdullah is under pressure from the National Conference rank and file to walk out from NDA.

Indeed, earlier reports had suggested that NC working committee members — who held an inconclusive meeting — were completely hostile to the idea of staying on in the NDA.

Handoo, seen as a hardliner himself, denied this. Concurrence between the Centre and state was viral for arriving at a solution, he said. "Every workable proposition would have to be based on a common understanding." Would the two sides now climb down from their respective hardline positions ? "Yes, of course. A middle path might have to be taken," he said.

He denied outright that Abdullah had considered dissolving the assembly and going for fresh elections on the autonomy platform : "Why should he ? There are two more years left for elections," he said.

While Handoo didn't specify the acceptable "middle path", other NC sources said Abdullah would be happy if the Centre set up a ministerial committee to discuss autonomy. The state already has such a committee and the two panels could thrash the issue out.

## PM-Farooq Talks

The ruling National Conference announced on July 16, 2000 that the "kind and quality" of dialogue between Prime Minister Atal Behari Vajpayee and Chief Minister Farooq Abdullah in New Delhi on July 17, could determine the future course of action by the party on its ties with the National Democratic Alliance.

The announcement came after an 'inconclusive' extended meeting of the NC working committee. The committee would meet again after the PM-Farooq talks.

But the tone and tenor of the speeches made by the working committee members indicated that the NC was not in a mood to compromise on the state autonomy report which they described as the "political Bible" of the party. Some of the members even threatened "an outright struggle" on the issue. However, the final decision was left to Farooq, who is also the party chief.

State law minister P.L. Handoo told reporters that the outcome of Monday's talks would set the future course of action by the NC on the state autonomy report which was adopted by the state assembly and later rejected by the Union cabinet.

According to Handoo, the state government has not received the letter from the Centre rejecting the assembly resolution. He said, "As the law minister of the state, I will take the Centre's letter to the state assembly for its advice," indicating that the controversy on the autonomy issue was far from over.

He said that the NC still hoped the assembly resolution would be honored as it was a commitment to the people, "be it an outright struggle". According to the minister, the state autonomy report was the political Bible of the NC government and nothing short of autonomy would be acceptable to it. Only the pre 1953 status, and not the 1975 accord between Sheikh Abdullah and G. Parthasarathy, was acceptable, he clarified.

At the working committee meeting, 14 more members spoke. Six members had spoken on the subject at the previous meeting held before the death of Farooq's mother. On Saturday also, the members said that the NC should not dilute its stand on state autonomy.

PART — VIII

# Jammu's Status

Chapter 24

# Demand for Jammu State

The loudest expression of the feeling of disappointment in the Jammu region over the failure of the Congress (I) to get Ghulam Nabi Azad chosen as the Chief Minister of the State is being made by the Bharatiya Janata Party, the Rashtriya Swayamsewak Sangh and parties that were demanding statehood for Jammu.

The new-found support for Azad may not be entirely for partisan reasons. It must be partly due to his newly acquired status as a symbol of Jammu's urge for identity and empowerment. Under his stewardship, the Congress (I) won 15 seats in the region. The BJP's score was reduced to one whereas it led in 31 of the 37 Assembly segments in the Lok Sabha election in 1999.

The consolidation of the secular identity of Jammu is one of the least noticed but most significant outcomes of the elections. It was this consolidation that enabled Jammu to aspire for the post of the head of the government, for the first time.

Whatever be the considerations that influenced the Congress (I) president to offer the chief ministership to Mufti Mohammed Sayeed and whatever be one's view on that, the unmistakable lesson of the recent experience is that secularism alone can ensure Jammu's unity and share in political power. Moreover, a secular and friendly Jammu is in the best interests of the Kashmir Valley.

The question of chief ministership aroused regional sentiments mainly because in the present set-up, too much power is concentrated in that post. While a truce has been brought about this time by an agreement on rotating the post between the two regions, a long-term solution requires a systemic change. Towards this end, the Congress (I) proposal for a change-over to a federal system from the present unitary system provides a way out, provided the party is able to get it implemented.

A unitary constitution, wherever it has been adopted, has led to disintegration. In Pakistan, it caused the split of the country, and in Sri Lanka, it led to a prolonged civil war. Federal constitutions, on the other hand, have established their superiority in ensuring unity among diverse communities. Even a unilingual and uni-religious country like Britain had to switch over to a federal system by granting regional autonomy to Scotland, Wales and Northern Ireland. Jammu and Kashmir, which is the most diverse State of India, can remain united only under a federal Constitution. Some of the provisions of the present unitary Constitution have the potential to create regional tensions, which is the root cause of what is termed the Kashmir problem. Anticipating this eventuality, this writer reminded Jawaharlal Nehru during a meeting with him on April 14, 1952, in a written note, that "the greatest problem of the State is to maintain cordial relations between its constituent units". Again on the eve of the Nehru-Sheikh Abdullah agreement (the Delhi Agreement) on Centre-State relations in July 1952, I reiterated the need for regional autonomy within the State as it was the logical corollary of the autonomy of the State within India. Both leaders agreed to my submissions and Nehru announced at a press conference on July 24, 1952, in the presence of Sheikh Abdullah, that "the State government was considering regional autonomies within the larger state". Later the Sheikh gave an assurance separately to the effect that "the Constitution of the State, when completed will give regional autonomy, particularly in cultural matters, to Jammu and Ladakh".

Again, during a meeting with Nehru on January 6, 1953, Balraj Puri sought his intervention to prevent the dangerous implications of the unhappy situation in Jammu and suggested "political and constitutional changes to remove the present unrest..."

An announcement for the grant of some sort of autonomy to the region would considerably ease the situation. It is the logical extension of what is called "limited accession". The memorandum emphasised that "autonomy to each region would act as a unifying force between peoples of all regions".

As was to be expected, the clash of regional passions culminated in first emotional rupture between Kashmir and the rest of India, which is by now regarded as one of the major causes of the dismissal of Sheikh Abdullah, the architect of the State's accession to India, from power and his detention on August 9, 1953, which was followed by a movement he launched for self-determination under the aegis of the Plebiscite Front. India lost its moral legitimacy on the Kashmir issue and most of the international support it earlier had on the issue.

The Jammu and Kashmir People's Convention, convened and presided over by him and inaugurated by Jayaprakash Narayan, "to discuss the future of the State" unanimously accepted a draft submitted by this writer on an outline of the internal Constitution of the State. It envisaged regional councils, headed by chief executive councillors assisted by executive councillors with executive and legislative powers, limited to the subjects transferred to the regions. The convention was attended by about 300 delegates, mostly from the Kashmir Valley, representing almost the entire spectrum of its population, including Jamaat-e-Islami, Mirwaiz Maulvi Farooq's Awami Action Committee, G.M. Karra's pro-Pakistan Political Conference and Bakshi Ghulam Mohammed's National Conference, besides the Plebiscite Front. Releasing the constitutional document to the press, Sheikh Abdullah said that "it was aimed at putting our own house in order before deliberating on the future of the State... The present outline on the internal constitutional set up is our humble effort aimed at assuring the people that their regional interests would be safeguarded."

Regional autonomy was also an unwritten part of Indira Gandhi's accord with Sheikh Abdullah which brought the latter back to power in the State in 1975. On the eve of his swearing-in as Chief Minister, he told the Jammu and Kashmir Pradesh Congress Legislature Party, on the support of which he resumed office, on February 24, 1975: "I will make sincere efforts to ensure that all the three regions have equal opportunity of development and participation in the political affairs of the State."

The main political resolution adopted at the first session of the revived National Conference in Jammu on April 24, 1976 asserted that it stood for stable unity of the State on the basis of decentralisation of political power among its three regions and at other levels. As the Chairman of the Reception Committee, this writer stated in the welcome address: "The National Conference is committed to a federal constitutional set-up of the State; according to which political power would be decentralised through a five-tier set up at State, regional, district, block and panchayat levels)."

Reiterating the commitment of his father, Farooq Abdullah, in early 1987, appointed a five-member commission to work out the details of regional autonomy with Balraj Puri as its chairman, and those such as N.K. Mukerjee, Prof. Upendra Baxi, Prof. Bashir-ud-Din and Prof. Mathew Kurien as members. Somehow the formal order for the formation of the commission could not be implemented.

In fact, almost every Chief Minister, before coming to power and after relinquishing it, has made a commitment in favour of regional autonomy.

The chief merit of regional autonomy is that it reconciles the genuine aspirations and interests of all regions and communities of the State. While "the integrationists represented by the BJP have badly failed the Jammuites" — as eminent Canadian Professor Reeta Chowdhari Tremblay concludes in her essay on "Jammu: Autonomy within an Autonomous Kashmir?" — in their attempts to achieve a fair share in the State's political and economic life, "except to make Kashmir Muslim population distrustful and suspicious of anyone beyond the Pir Panchal range, regional autonomy has become increasingly relevant in view of a present global disenchantment with the centralised federal structures."

*The Times*, London, had similarly observed: "Mr. Puri argues with justice that until Jammu and Kashmir draw closer, settle their differences and agree to operate as equal partners, there will never be a stable basis upon which relations with India can be satisfactorily settled."

Thus, regional autonomy emerges as the only answer to the grievances of Jammu and Ladakh and as a solution to the alienation of Kashmir. For it ensures protection of regional identity of Kashmir and the spirit of Kashmiryat. Without recognition to the identity and autonomy of the regions, they and their valuable composite heritage would be swamped by the rising tide of communalism and fundamentalism. Broad principles of regional autonomy, based on the report the writer submitted to the Chief Minister, as working chairman of the Regional Autonomy Committee, may be the basis of a discussion on the subject. The report was prepared after the widest possible discussions with and after studying the interests and aspirations of various communities and parts of the State and experiments in other parts of India and elsewhere. Leading scholars in relevant disciplines were also consulted.

## Case for the State

The Jammu State Morcha's demand for statehood for Jammu has lost its first electoral test. Only one out of its 11 candidates has made it to the new State Assembly. The Morcha's chief, Virendra Gupta was among the losers. This might prove to be the last nail in the coffin, although the idea of separating Jammu from the Kashmir Valley is almost 50 years old.

The origins of this demand may be traced to 1952 when the Praja Parishad Movement first raised the slogan of *Jammu Alag Karo* (Separate Jammu). The Praja Parishad was founded by Balraj Madhok on the existing organisational base of the Rashtriya Swayamsewak Sangh (RSS) in Jammu and shared its ideology of Hindu nationalism. Deploying a religious prism to view the State's political realities, it accused Sheikh Abdullah of trying to Islamicise the administration. The Sheikh had broken up the Hindu-majority district of Udhampur and closed down the Sanskrit Research Department. The land and other property of the charitable trust for the upkeep of temples and Sanskrit *pathshalas* (schools) had been expropriated and the rehabilitation of Hindu and Sikh refugees from Pakistan-held areas was opposed. The study of Urdu was made compulsory for all.

Most important, political initiative and power had slipped out of the hands of Dogras to those of Kashmiri Muslims, and it was felt that agrarian reforms would fundamentally alter the pattern of social organisation of the State to their disadvantage. A Praja Parishad pamphlet observed that the Jammu and Kashmir Constituent Assembly consisted of 75 members, of which 50 were Muslims. Clearly, Sheikh Abdullah's Muslim dominance could not and was not to be forced upon the Hindus of Jammu and the Buddhists of Ladakh. The unceremonious dismissal of the Dogra Maharaja, Hari Singh, had further embittered them and Yuvraj (Prince) Karan Singh's decision to become the first Regent of the State was strongly criticised as a 'traitorous act' legitimising the Sheikh's actions and as "tantamount to selling the Dogras out to the Kashmiris".

The Praja Parishad had launched a popular agitation in 1952. The Bharatiya Jan Sangh, the Hindu Mahasabha, the Ram Rajya Parishad, the Punjab Arya Samaj and some Akali leaders supported the movement. The Parishad's eight-point programme demanded the abrogation of Article 370; full integration of the State into the Indian Union; full application of the Indian Constitution; removal of the distinction between 'state-subjects' and Indian citizens; complete jurisdiction of the Supreme Court; removal of customs barriers between Kashmir and India; fresh elections to the Kashmir Constituent Assembly; and investigation of corruption in the State administration by an impartial tribunal.

Stressing the unity of the Indian nation, Praja Parishad leader Dr. Syama Prasad Mookerjee accused the Sheikh: "There cannot be a republic within a republic... Consciously or unconsciously, you are creating a new sovereignty for Jammu & Kashmir... India has been torn into two by the two-nation theory. You are now developing a three-nation theory, the third being the Kashmiri nation. These are dangerous symptoms."

The Parishad harked back to the golden days of the Dogra Maharaja's rule and mobilised the people to get rid of Kashmiri domination in the Muslim-majority State by demanding complete merger into Hindu-majority India. Jammu reverberated with the popular slogan, *'Ek desh mein do vidhan, do nishan, do pardhan, nahin chalega, nahin chalega* (In one country, two constitutions, two flags and two chiefs will not work; will not be tolerated). The Parishad's *prabhat pheris* (early-morning neighbourhood processions) and the RSS *shakhas* (branches) demanded, *'Abdullah hakumat khatam karo'* (Terminate Abdullah's rule) and *''Jammu alag karo'* (Separate Jammu). The urban population of Jammu city, especially students, was effectively mobilised. In the first major demonstration in February 1952, students of Gandhi Memorial College protested against the hoisting of the National Conference flag.

Slieikh Abdullah dismissed the agitation as a reactionary and communal revolt by a handful of feudal landlords and parasitic classes that opposed the agrarian reforms for having removed the social bases of their power. Prime Minister Jawaharlal Nehru appreciated the legitimate grievances of the Jammu people but castigated the narrow communal approach of the Praja Parishad movement. That indeed proved to be the cardinal reason for its failure.

Owing to its limited social base, especially in the rural areas, the movement did not acquire a mass character. The Parishad's identification with Hindu landlords, *jagirdars* and *sahukar,* (money lenders) who had enjoyed a privileged position under the Maharaja's rule delivered a body blow to its social and political appeal. The peasantry in the State (mainly in the Valley, but also in Jammu) had reaped rich dividends from the National Conference's land reform policies. Having made it a Hindu-Muslim issue, the Parishad leadership failed to gain the support of Jammu Muslims, who did not support the National Conference but also rejected the former's communal agenda. The Parishad also failed to mobilise the support of the small but influential Hindu minority of Kashmiri Pandits in the Valley and the Ladakhi Buddhists who shared its antipathy for Sheikh Abdullah.

In the contemporary context, the Jammu Mukti Morcha (JMM, which fought these elections under the banner of the Jammu State Morcha), which revived the demand for the bifurcation of the Jammu and Kashmir State, faced the same dilemma. The demand for separate statehood is rooted in political and regional imbalances that favour the Valley at Jammu's cost. However, when the political mobilisation to seek redress of those grievances adopts a communal approach and makes it a Hindu-Muslim issue (read Hindu-majority Jammu *vis-a-vis* Muslim-majority Valley), it is doomed to failure because the plural character of Jammu's populace exposes its internal contradictions. The Jammu Muslims are in a minority in the Jammu region but form a majority in Poonch, Rajouri and Doda districts. If the key issue is that Jammu Hindus must separate themselves from Kashmiri Muslims and create a new polirical entity to ensure their political and economic development, then why should Jammu Muslims agree to stay with Jammu Hindus in a separate Jammu state?

Let us explain this further. It is the neglect and apathy of successive State governments towards Jammu's political and economic development and the Central government's Valley-centric thinking that has led to the reassertion of Jammu's demand for separate statehood. This is evident from the nature of the grievances outlined by the JMM activists in the early 1990s. Successive Valley-dominated State governments were blamed for Jammu's poor share in the State services. In the Civil Secretariat, Jammu's representation was less than 10 percent. The proportions of employees from the Valley and

Jammu in the State Secretariat and regional services of Kashmir and Jammu were 99:8 and 99:1 respectively. All 12 corporations of the Jammu and Kashmir government had their headquarters in Srinagar with almost 100 per cent of the employees from the Valley. Most major Central government offices were in Srinagar. According to a statement made in the State Assembly in 1988-89, some 43,000 out of 69,000 registered unemployed youth belonged to the Jammu region. Of the State's tourism budget, nearly 90 per cent was spent on the Valley every year. The exclusion of the Dogri language (spoken by 50 lakh people) from the Eighth Schedule of the Indian Constitution was particularly resented because Kashmiri (spoken by less than 30 lakh people) enjoyed constitutional recognition. The recommendation of the Wazir Commission (1983) for the creation of three more districts of Reasi, Kishtwar and Bhau (Samba) in the Jammu region was not accepted, while three new districts — Badgam, Kupwara and Baramulla were created in the Valley.

More important, Kashmir's domination of the political system was rooted in Jammu's under-representation in the State assembly and in the Lok Sabha. The last Delimitation Commission had carved out 87 constituencies for the elections to the Legislative Assembly in 1996. The table reflects the average population and area per constituency.

There is clear dominance of the Kashmir region over Jammu in the Legislative Assembly on the basis of population and area. Kashmir has 4.73 lakh more people than Jammu. On the basis of the average population of 89,000 per constituency in the State, it could claim five more seats than Jammu, against which it has been allocated nine seats, which is 80 per cent in excess of that due.

The JMM argued that in view of Srinagar's total neglect of and discrimination against Jammu in the matter of political and economic development, a separate state of Jammu was the 'only way out' to meet its political aspirations. Jammu, according to this viewpoint, forms a natural region defined by the boundaries of the Ravi on the south and the Pir Panjal on the north and has a distinct cultural and historical identity.

As in the case of the Praja Parishad, the JMM failed to mobilse mass support for its cause. This organisation was founded by a group of intellectuals whose *modus operandi* remained largely confined to oraganising processions and strikes and submitting memoranda to the State and Central governments. Many intellectuals, journalists and politicians of Jammu insisted that it was a product of the Union Home Ministry, which had propped it up as a counterweight to the Kashmiri demand for independence. The limited social base of the JMM further dwindled when it joined hands with the RSS to contest the recent Assembly elections and the political character of this demand increasingly became communalised.

What made the situation more complicated was the double game played by the Bharatiya Janata Parry and the National Conference. For example, deviating from its original demand for a statutoty regional council and statutoty boards for development for the Jammu region, the State unit of the BJP quietly endorsed the trifurcation demand of the JMM-RSS alliance. While L.K. Advani, Union Home Minister and one of the senior most BJP leaders, rejected the demand for the trifurcation of the Jammu and Kashmir State as being an "anti-national" one, the State unit of the BJP persisted in negotiating seat-sharing arrangements with the JMM. Although these did not materialise, the ambiguity in the BJP's stance persisted.

The National Conference too had been speaking with two voices. On the one hand, it strongly opposed the trifurcation demand but on the other, the Regional Autonomy Committee appointed by Farooq Abdullah in 1996 endorsed the communal division of the State by recommending its internal reorganisation into eight provinces. The Report specifically proposed the restructuring of the Jammu region into three provinces, carved along a Hindu-Muslim divide. The district of Doda and the single Muslim-dominated *tehsil* of Mahore from the adjoining Hindu-majority district of Udhampur would form a new Chenab Valley province. The largely Hindu districts of Jammu's, Kathua and Udhampur would make up a Jammu province. Poonch and Rajouri, the Muslim-majority districts, would form the Pir Panjal province. A careful study of the 75-odd memoranda submitted to the Regional Autonomy Committee showed that it had selectively adopted and endorsed the demands of the National Conference supporters, specially from Rajouri, Poonch and Doda. districts of the Jammu region who had earlier sought the creation of two Autonomous Hill Councils — on the pattern of the Leh Autonomous Hill Council — in the Jammu region. These included a demand for the creation of a new Pahari region, separating the predominantly Muslim Rajouri-Poonch from the Jammu Division with an Autonomous Hill Council and a similar set-up for the Chenab Valley region consisting of Doda district, Gool-Gulabgarh *tehsil,* Basantgarh of Udhampur district and Lohai Malhar and Bani of Kathua district. Both demands — for the Autonomous Hill Councils or for carving out new provinces — sought to separate the Muslim-majority areas of the Jammu region from the Hindu-majority areas. Significantly, the BJP, a vociferous critic of the State autonomy proposals that favoured the restoration of Article 370 to its pristine form, remained tight-lipped on the Regional Autonomy Committee's Report. Also, the RSS-backed demand for trifurcation of the State was similar, to the extent that it called for an internal restructuring of the State along a Hindu-Muslim axis.

However, keeping in mind the plural social realities of the Jammu region, they all failed to realise that there are no cohesive or monolithic political grouping of Hindus and Muslims at the grassroots level because their political affiliations cut across ethnic (Dogra, Gujjar and Bakkarwal), linguistic (Pahari, Gojri, Kashmiri and Dogri), caste lines and regional differences. The Jammu Muslims, for example, do not support the BJP's Hindu politics and the demand for a separate state of Jammu, nor are they willing to be assimilated completely into the Kashmiri Muslim identity. At the same time, they do not form a separate and cohesive political grouping, partly because since the pre-Partition leadership of Chowdhary Ghulam Abbas and Allah Rakha Sagar, no political leader had emerged to mobilise them as an independent political force in State politics. Any attempt to super-impose the communal divide will only represent a divisive agenda. It is also bound to fail for two reasons.

First, these are political issues and sharpening the communal boundaries will simply not resolve the problem. For example, the Paharis are spread from Basoli in Kathua to Rajouri and Poonch on the one side and Uri and Keran in the Valley but why does their demand for a Pahari region along the Line of Control exclude areas in the Valley? Also, if the demand is driven by lack of economic development, then the predominantly Hindu hill areas south of the Chenab, in Kathua, have done no better than Rajouri and Poonch.

The solution lies in providing a responsive government, rather than in sharpening communal boundaries. Second, political mobilisation along communal lines is bound to limit the social base of the political groups making these demands. Jammu and Kashmir's political history over the last five decades has proved that without acquiring a mass support base cutting across the ethnic, religious, linguistic and regional lines, such groups are unlikely to achieve their political goals. The rout in the latest Assembly elections of the National

Conference and the BJP, which had sought to exploit the communal card, proves this point. The BJP has retained only one seat in the Jammu region and the National Conference has lost almost 50 per cent of the seats — 29 out of 57 — that it had won in the 1996 elections. Finally, they fail to recognise the fact that to give sanctity to religious nationalism and accord primacy to the political demands of communities based on their religion would not only strengthen the divisive forces within the State but also help Pakistan justify its claim on Kashmir on the grounds of the two-nation theory. Even if they win the battle of statehood for Jammu, they might well lose the war of India's foundational belief in the principle of secularism *vis-a-vis* Pakistan's religious nationalism.

PART — IX

# Significant People

## Chapter 25

# The Concept of Kashmiriat

Kashmir, the very name evokes powerful images and emotions and stirs up deep-felt memories of a past. In the early wake of Indian history, Kashmir was one of the major nurseries of Hindu civilization.

The different names by which Kashmir was known, Kashyapa-pur, Kashir, Kashmir, Kashmira all mean "reclaimed from water". According to—Nilamata Purana the sage Kashyapa reclaimed the Valley by draining out a mountain lake called "Satisar". Hence the region was called Kashyapa-pur.

A Shaivite centre for millennia the Valley was considered the embodiment of Lima, the wife of Shiva. The Vitasta (now renamed Jhelum) was mentioned in the Rig Veda.

Kashmir has an uninterrupted record of history of which, the earliest part, has been recorded by Kalhana, in his work *Rajatarangini.* He admits that he had himself consulted about eleven compositions on history which are no more available . Pandit Jonaraja brought this history up to the fifteenth century A.D., while Srivara and Prajyabhatta took it forward to 1586, when the Valley was annexed by the Mughals. Then, there were the works of Birbal Kacheri, and Diwan Kirpa Ram, one of the governors appointed by Maharaja Ranjit Singh. The Europeans too have contributed to our understanding of the history of Kashmir. Among them, credit goes to Walter R. Lawrence's *The Valley of Kashmir,* which stands out as a monumental work.

The history of Kashmir can be divided into five periods Hindu, -Muslim, Sikh, Dogra and the new phase which begins in 1947.

The Aryan Hindus gave Kashmir its Golden Age. The Valley emerged as one of the great seats of Hindu Learning, producing a distinct Shaivite philosophy. Familiar with the Valley the Vedic Indians, settled along the banks of the Indus, sang in praise of its rivers. There is mention of Kashmir in Rig Veda. It is said that the Pandavas crossed the Valley during their wanderings while they were in exile. Kashmir was thus one of the earliest homes of the Aryans in India.

The Nilamata Purana is a goldmine of information on Kashmir's legends and secured places. The great historian, Kalhana, also throws much light on the legendary past of Kashmir, on the various races which lived in the Valley and its neighborhood, on how Kashmir became part of the Ashokan empire, on the founding of Srinagara, the capital, by Ashoka, on the spread of Buddhism by Majjhantika, one of Buddha's disciples, who was especially entrusted with this task by the Master, and. finally, how Ashoka gave away the whole of the Valley to the Buddhist Sangha as a gift and built 500 viharas. Thus, Kashmir also became a major centre of Buddhism and attracted scholars and students from far and wide.

As against the story of mere kings, the history of the Kashmir mind. of its heart and its sentiments lies not in chronological narrative, but in the timeless Vakyas (Sayings) of Lal Ded, or in the Nurnama of Shaikh Nuruddin. At Charar-i-Sharif both Muslim and Hindu men and women pray and believe that the soul of Nuruddin will be at the eternal service of generations of human beings in their incessant search for comfort, for grace, and for aid from their divine.

In the fourteenth century Padmawati was born at Pandrenthan a few miles south-west of Srinagar.

She went into *tapasya* in a forest, found herself and returned to the world as a naked mendicant, oblivious of any material attachment, and with a powerful message of the inner spirit, to the Original Good in even human being layered by the boundless variations of Original Sin. She challenged ritual with a deeper faith. Truth, she said, did not exist in stone, nor in the tyranny of the priest. She demolished the power of those who made every river and every tree and every simple fact of nature into an object of worship. Her spirit of reformation inevitably spread into language; she disdained the priestly Sanskrit and gave Kashmiri tongue of the people a new dimension. Thirty per cent of Kashmiri proverbs and idioms are said to owe their origins to Lal Ded's Vakyas. Her own life was a splendid example of purity and passion. Her teaching was love service, the unity of man, the discipline of yoga, the intoxication of faith and the rejection of barriers in the name of religion. She became Lalli Arifa for the Muslims and Lalleshwari for the Hindus.

This synthesis of mystical Shaivism and Islamic Sufism went straight to the hearts of the masses. The most beloved of Kashmir's Sufi-saints Shaikh Nuruddin, was born in 1356. Nuruddin's philosophy was weaned at the breast of Lal Ded. He lived in the hearts of both Muslims and Hindus. While Muslims called him their Shaikh, the Hindus referred to him as Nand Rishi. His order of the Rishis became a powerful influence in the Valley for many centuries; Its traces can be found in the 'Rishi' surname common to Hindu and Muslim alike. When Shaikh Nuruddin passed away, among his pallbearers was a Sultan, Zainul Abidin, whose fifty years of rule is still remembered as a golden age of Kashmir. Zainul Abidin lived by the message of his contemporary, a message left for us in the memorable verses of the Rishinama or the Nurnama.

His message of harmony created a reservoir of humanism which became the ideological fountainhead of the modern Kashmir mind. It gave a unique quality to the Kashmiri identity. It provided a conviction which long preserved Kashmir from the unspeakable and unbelievable bloodshed which Indians have inflicted upon each other in the name of religion. The faith of Kashmir can be described as a faith in the beauty of the Kashmiri heart, the Kashmiri soul. As M.J. Akbar puts it, "Perhaps it was no accident that Lal Ded gave respect to Shaikh Nuruddin and Nand Rishi was a contemporary of Zainul Abidin. Kashmir has always flourished best when the Rishi has influenced the Raja. Sadly, that has not always been its fate."

Kashmir absorbed those few who broke the forbidding defensive wall of the Himalayas. The *rawaj* of Kashmir, its culture, enveloped the outsider. The Kashmiri identity was always the dominant reality. It made the Emperor Jahangir remark that he could not distinguish a Kashmiri Muslim from a Hindu.

Kashmir's Geography played a significant part in the preservation of this distinct identity. Its main passes —Zojila and Burzil in the northeast; the Tosamaidan at Pir Panjal; Banihal; or the route through Uri in the Jhelum valley—had the useful merit of being easily guarded. Mahmud of Ghazni might demolish and loot where he wanted on the plains of India, but his armies were incapable of defeating Kashmir's mountains and its weather. Jahangir put it succinctly in his memoirs:

"Kashmir is a garden of eternal spring or an iron fort to a palace of kings—a delightful flower bed, and a heart-expanding heritage for dervishes."

Pandit Kalhana, the first great historian of Kashmir, adds another dimension to the concept :

"The country may be conquered by the force of spiritual merit, but not by the force of soldiers. The inhabitants are afraid only of the world beyond."

Kalhana mentions the legend recorded in the Nilamat Purana about the origins of this lovely land. At the beginning of Katpa, or Creation, the Valley was a lake hundreds of feet deep, called the Sati Saras, or the Lake of Sati, consort of Kashmir's preferred Lord Shiva. In this lake lived the demon Jalodbhav or the One Born in Water, who terrorized the Nagas, snakes who guarded the waters. The word is still used in place names, as in Anantnag. To the human eye, the Nagas either took a plain form, or sometimes appeared as clouds or hailstorms in the age of the seventh Manu, the Sage Kashyapa, father of the Nagas learnt about the brutal oppression of his progeny while on a pilgrimage to the Himalayas. An angry Kashyapa appealed to Brahma the Supreme as well as to other gods. It was not a request which the gods could ignore and they took up position on the mountain peaks surroundings Sati Saras. But the demon was invincible as long as he remained in the womb of water. He simply refused to emerge. The Lord Vishnu then called upon his brother Balabhadra to end the stalemate. He took up his ploughshare and pierced the closed ring of mountains at Baramulla-the waters drained from Sasti Saras; Vishnu engaged the demon and slew him with his disc. The pleased sage settled in the dry Valley, and Kashmir was named after him. But when the gods and goddesses saw the Valley they were so enchanted by its beauty that they too refused to leave. And so the gods settled in the mountains of Kashmir, while the goddesses took the shape of the sparkling, abundant, fertile rivers.

A branch of the Indo-Aryans who took the course of the Oxus and the Jaxertes separated from the main body of migrants eventually settled down in the Kashmir Valley. Pandit Kalhana begins his history, with Gonanda the First, a contemporary and antagonist of Lord Krishna. He lost his life in battle with the Lord, as did his son Damodara. Krishna himself determined the succession, and made Damodara's pregnant wife Yasovati the Queen Regent. When the nobles protested against a woman being given power, Krishna admonished them by reciting a verse from the Nilamat Purana :

Kashmir is Parvati; know that its ruler is a part of Shiva.

After the three Gonanda rulers, twenty-three generations of Pandavas ruled Kashmir, the dynasty being founded by Haranadev, a great-grandson of Arjuna. The ancient temple on the hill of the Shankaracharya in Srinagar is said to date from the Pandava era.

Though the Persians and the Greeks certainly knew of Kashmir, but even Alexander's campaign (327 BC) does not mention its existence. A new power rose in India in the ebb of Alexander's invasion. One of the princes studying in the world-famous university of Taxila during the Greek advance was Chandragupta of Magadh (322-298 BC). He slowly expanded the frontiers of his rule and pushed the Greek viceroys beyond Gandhara. When Taxila revolted during his heir Bindusara's reign, Susima, the king's elder son, was sent to quell the uprising. When he failed, his younger brother Ashoka was shifted from Ujjain to Taxila. Ashoka not only crushed the rebels, but also brought the Valley of Kashmir into the ambit of the Mauryan empire. Ashoka founded Srinagar the capital of Kashmir, which quickly evolved into a flourishing city with "ninety six thousand dwellings resplendent with prosperity." Ashoka constructed a string of famous temples. A son, Jaluka, was born to him after prayers to the Lord Shiva at the shrine of Harmuktaganga. When the emperor turned a Buddhist evangelic, he made Kashmir the northern crucible of his mission. The Buddhist Council held at Pataliputra sent Majjhantika at the head of 5000 monks to the Valley and Gandhara. But while Gandhara became the conduit for the flow of Buddhism into Afghanistan and Central Asia, Hinduism proved more durable in Kashmir. Jaluka established an independent state which promoted the worship of Hindu deities.

It is interesting that the Buddha himself had praised Kashmir as the ideal focal point for the spread of his message; the environment, he said, was made for meditation and for the practice of a religious life. Ananda, the Buddha's constant companion has a disciple called Madhandina who said the Buddha, would take Buddhism to the land of the blue forests, subdue the malevolent Husuta Nagas and sit cross-legged, miraculously covering the whole of Kashmir and making its 60,000 villages a haven of peace. Like Ashoka, Kanishka also gave Kashmir to the Buddhist church. Buddhism did eventually reign over these villages, its essential simplicity a powerful attraction for the ritual-burdened masses. But the excessive zeal of Buddhist monks created the conditions for the restoration of Shaivism.

From Kashmir emerged Buddhist missionaries like Kumarajiva, Yasa, Vimalaksha and Sanghabuti, who reached northern China in AD 381; Gautamasangha, who followed in AD 384; Dharmayasa, Buddhayasa, Vimalaksha, Buddhajiva, all of whom spent years propagating the faith in China; Gunavarman, who took the message first to Java and from there, on royal request to Nanking; whose scholars converted Tibet and the vast plains of the centre of Asia. However, by the start of the sixth century, Kashmir returned firmly to the fold of Shaivism.

After Mihirakula we come to the Karkota dynasty, beginning with Durlabhavardhana in AD 625. The greatest of this line was Lalitaditya, whose rule of thirty-seven years saw an unprecedented expansion of Kashmiri power to Tibet in the east, Badakhan in the west and Punjab and Kanauj in the south.

His first principle was religious tolerance. The king was a Hindu, but the commander-in-chief of his army was a Buddhist, as were many of his ministers. Poetry and the other arts flourished in that congenial environment, the Martand temple was an outstanding contribution to Kashmir's architecture. But after Lalitaditya's death his empire fell apart.

The sordid story of tenth century in Kashmir proves that the Hindu dynasties had rotted to the point of decay. The Muslim incursions into the subcontinent had begun by the turn of the century, pioneered by Mahmud of Ghazni who headed towards Kashmir twice, once in 1015 and a second time in 1021, both times through the Tosamaidan Pass. On both occasions he was checked at the hill fort of Lohkot on the southern slopes of the Pir Panjal range by winter.

Both Changez Khan (1162—1227) and Halaku Khan had slated Kashmir for conquest in their plans. It was however left to another Mongol to take the fury of this particular ill-wind to the Valley. Suddenly, in 1320, Kashmir was routed out of its self-defeating, corrupt complacence by the savagery of 17,000 horse and foot, racing swiftly across the Baramulla Pass under the command of a Mongol Dulacha who chose his weather well: early summer.

Kashmir was ruled at the time by Sahadeva, who at first sought to bribe Dulacha, but the Mongol was not interested in tokenism when he had a defenseless Valley at his mercy. Sahadeva simply abandoned his people and escaped to

Kishtwar. For eight months the Mongols vandalized the grain, the cattle, the gold, and the women.

When Dulacha had left the place, those people of Kashmir met his nemesis at the Banihal Pass, where a fierce blizzard trapped his whole army leaving no survivors.

But the people refused to accept the old order again. They felt crushed and betrayed, and when Sahadeva returned after Dulacha's departure he found a deep and unforgiving anger.

## The Sufis

The memory of Changez and Halaku was still trembling in the stories told to children when another great conqueror rose like a storm:

Taimur, the lame warrior who established himself at Samarqand; Baikh fell in 1369; Khurasan and Herat followed as the Mughal swallowed Persia, and ruled on the principle of total fealty from every conquered subject. One group which refused were the Alawi Saiyyids of the Persian city of Hamadan. Seven hundred of them left their native city to escape Taimur and settled in Kashmir, under the leadership of Saiyyid Hamdani, the great scholar and missionary of the Naqshbandi Order o Sufis. These Sufis mixed easily into the special religious culture of Kashmir: it was a land, as the Buddha had remarked so long ago, created for meditation and faith. Their life style of self-abnegation, simplicity and rejection of the material world struck an immediate chord in the heart of a people who had traditionally honoured such values. Abul Fazl describe this culture in *Ain-i-Akbari:*

The most respected people of Kashmir are the Rishis who although they do not suffer themselves to be fettered by traditions, are doubtless true worshippers of God. They do not revile any other see nor ask anything of anyone. They plant the roads with fruit trees to provide the traveller with refreshments. They abstain from meat and have no intercourse with the other sex. There are 2000 of these Rishis in Kashmir.

Whether Hindu or Muslim, their message was the same in essence that love destroyed hypocrisy, which was at the root of pain, that the purpose of life was worship and peace, not violence.

The Sultanate established by Shah Mir quickly flourished as introduced the basic elements of sensible statecraft like a standing army and a stable tax system. Kashmir now awaited the ruler who could convert its growing strength into imperial power. Shah Mir's grandson Shahabuddin sent his army up to Sind in the south and Afghanistan in the west, but these were punitive rather than expansionist expeditions. Sikandar was sultan when Taimur marched into India in 1398. Taimur's goal was the wealth of Delhi, but Sultan Sikandar sought to buy his peace with booty, and waited at Bhimbhar for Taimur, on the route of the victorious army's march back home. Such weakness encouraged greed and he was informed by an envoy that Taimur would be satisfied with nothing less than 30,000 horses and 1,00,000 silver rupees of the Alauddin Khilji mint. Instead of uniting the people, to defend the country and its wealth, the selfish, shortsighted and frightened Sikand embarked on a savage campaign to raise this extraordinary ransom. While the terrified Sultan stared over his shoulder at the advance scepter of Taimur, his officials seized the wealth of Hindu temples, broke idols, imposed the hated jiziya tax. A vicious anti-Hindu policy was unleashed, from forcible conversions to a ban on music and the wearing of the tika on the forehead. It was the first display of Islamic fundamentalist power in Kashmir. When Taimur learnt that an envoy had made such an unrealistic demand, he rushed emissaries to convey that it was unnecessary; simple allegiance was sufficient. The bigots had acquired a momentum of their own, and their hold over the court became so strong that after Sikandar died it grew further rather than ebbed. The bigots reduced the people of Kashmir to emotional and economic tatters. A mood of revolt was building up, and it was left to Ali Shah's younger brother, Shahi Khan, to articulate the mood and lead the revolt. Ali Shah was defeated and killed at the battle of Thanna, near the Pir Panjal Pass, in the summer of 1420.

By this summer, after two decades of repression, there were only eleven Hindu families left in the Kashmir Valley. Those eleven families who had survived it all called themselves the Malamasis; those who had deserted Kashmir, if only briefly, were given the slightly inferior status of Banamasis.

Shahi Khan was only nineteen when he became Sultan of Kashmir, taking the name Zainul Abidin. He was known among the masses as Bud Shah, or The Great King. He brought fifty golden years of peace, harmony and prosperity to his beloved land.

Zainul Abidin displayed a fine sense of statecraft. He managed the unruly tribe of Khukars. He extended Kashmiri paramountcy over all of western Tibet. For him no one was above the law. Solomon-style stories began to circulate around the king. Architecture, crafts, trade, the arts— particularly music—flourished. The staging of plays returned. The first roads with stone payings were constructed, as well as the first wooden bridge across the Jhelum in Srinagar, known to this day as the Zainalkadal. He refused to touch the state treasury for his personal needs, his income emanating from a copper mine he owned.

Zainul Abidin took a firm decision not to interfere with the faith of its citizens. One of the first policies he adopted was to completely reverse the process of state-sponsored proselytization. A Brahmin Pandit Shriya Bhatt, was appointed officer in charge of expansion of Hinduism in the Valley. Emissaries were sent to persuade Hindus in exile to return. Zainul Abidin abolished Jiziya, the cremation tax, and banned cow slaughter. He personally visited Hindu shrines and places of pilgrimages like Kausar Nag, Naubandana Tirth, and the famous Amarnath. For five days a year he donned the robes of a mendicant and fed devotees during the festivals of Nagayatra and Ganachakra. He understood the meaning of emotional involvement in the state. He gave more substantial benefits to the Hindu Pandits who were inducted into the bureaucracy. They learned Persian, the state language. Historians like Jonaraja and Srivara were given state patronages as much as Persian and Arabic scholars like Maulana Kab (the Sultan's childhood tutor), Mulla Hafiz Baghdad, Mulla Jamluddin ar Qazi Mir Ali. His library acquired great renown and poets and musicians flocked to his court. Schools were established. Education once again became an investment in Kashmir's future. Zainul Abidin was just sensitive to matters of Hindu-Muslim relations. He was always extremely careful in his walk along the tightrope of equality. He was as liberal to the construction of mosques as he was in the reconstruction of temple. The primary responsibility of the state was justice, equality and economic prosperity. Corruption in revenue collection was strictly curbed. Law and order was maintained. Canals and bridges were built; Cities were constructed; floating islands were laid on the Dal Lake. Music flourished. Mulla Jamil, Mulla Udi, Soma Bhatt and Srivara became famous. Of their three wives, two were daughters of the Hindu Raja of Jammu. All his four sons—Adam Khan, Haji Khan, Vasrath Khan and Behram Khan had Hindu mothers; though he himself was a devout Muslim, and took pride in the title of Naib-e-Amir-ul-Momineen.

Zainul Abidin became Badshah: The Great King, a name which soon acquired mythical proportions: labourers and boatmen began to use it to mark the beat of their labours in the belief that even its evocation would ease the pain of their strained muscles. In the words of M.J. Akbar : Badshad's life and his rule were the distillation of that spirit call "Kashmiriyat," a culture of synthesis, understanding and humanism; a the history of the next five hundred and more years proved that Kashmir cannot be ruled except by this spirit.

# Chapter 26

# The Trinity

The present state of J & K constitutes an ethnic triangle, the Hindu (Pandits), the Muslims and the Buddhists. While Hindus are in majority in Jammu, the Muslims are in majority in Kashmir and the Buddhists are in majority in Ladakh. Therefore some people suggest trifurcation on ethnic lines to solve Kashmir problem.

The people of the Valley constitute a racial mix—Aryan, Mongol, Afghan, Persian and others. The Panels are of Aryan stock and are non-martial. The Gujjars and the Bakerwals are nomadic and are mostly Muslims. The Dogras are Rajputs, having greater affinity to the people of Punjab. Finally, the people of Ladakh are mostly of Tibetan origin.

## The Kashmiri Pandits

Kashmir had very few spells of peace after the Muslim advent. Easy adaptability explains the incidence of mass conversion of the Pandits to Islam, by which they became minority in their own homeland. Even in the face of this adversity they did not and could not defend their interests. In fact, when the Muslims offered to reconvert themselves to Hinduism during the reign of Ranbir Singh, the orthodox Pandits opposed this move.

After a long stay in the Valley, C.E. Tyndale Biscoe, a pioneer of public education in Kashmir, said in his book *Kashmir in Sunlight and Shade:* "I must say that an ordinary Kashmiri, such as I have known for thirty years, is a coward, a man with no self-respect and deceitful to a degree." The Chinese pilgrim, Hieun Tsang, held the same view. In his book *Reflections on Kashmiri Politics* Hussain states : "While in India, it was the lowest strata of society which willingly escaped to Islam to avoid caste disabilities, in Kashmir it was the high caste Brahmins that converted to Islam unwillingly to escape Afghan tyranny." Hussain believes that it was state power which led to forced conversions. He argues: "Otherwise, Persian and Pathan Saints and Sufis, who spoke a different language and belonged to a different culture, would not have made such a deep impact on the Valley of Kashmir.

Although reduced to an abject state under Sultan Sikandar. the Pandits failed to throw up a leadership capable of meeting the challenge. In their instinct for personal survival, they even sacrificed the interest of their community and they continued to serve and please their rulers.

In 1950, Kashmiri Pandits passed a resolution eschewing politics and aligning themselves with Sheikh Abdullah's party, the National Conference, though, they never occupied a position in the executive committee of this party. P.L. Handoo, an MP. was merely a special invitee to the meetings of the committee.

After partition the Pandits were the first to oppose the entry of the Punjabis into the Valley. They were afraid of losing their jobs. If Punjabis had settled down in large numbers, the Pandits would not have had to face their present plight. They were also clamouring for the protection of "Kashmiriat" without knowing that it meant nothing to the majority Muslim community. Before the twentieth century, Hindus and Muslims were more integrated in the Valley. There was not much difference in appearance and habits they used to live in close proximity. Both had places of common worship. During birth, death and marriage both followed common customs.

## The Muslims

Over the centuries, there was a division of work between Pandits and Muslims. The Pandits mastered the language of their rulers (Persian, for example). They got petty jobs with the government at the behest of the ruling class. The Muslims confined themselves to agriculture, crafts and trade. With the advent of the British, the Pandits took to English education. The Muslims, refused to learn English and remained backward. Hence, they lost opportunities in jobs in industry and commerce. This led to unwarranted jealousy and hard feelings, though the Pandits did not snatch away the jobs of the Muslims. Again, the Muslims occupied most of the jobs in the state service, although only a small proportion among them was literate. There has been less competition from Muslims for the well-paid higher jobs because highly educated Muslims are still rare.

Since Indian independence and the accession of Jammu and Kashmir to India, huge investments have been made in the state, and a substantial number of families, both Hindu and Muslim, have become extremely wealthy. Their ostentatious life style has been the envy of the new generation, whose members doubt even low-paid jobs. They are therefore, easily lured towards terrorism. Fundamentalist propaganda and madrasa (religious school) education seek to convert every Muslim into a bigot.

During the last decade of the nineteenth century. Walter Lawrence observed: "The Sunni Mussalmans do not strike [one] as zealous or earnest in the profession of their faith, and except in their quarrels with the Shias, they are free from all forms of fanaticism ... they do not keep Friday as a day of rest, and very few Kashmiris make the pilgrimage to Mecca, though the journey is now easy, and does not cost more than Rs. 340. In 1892, twenty-one Kashmiris went to Mecca and this was an unusually large number." Kashmiri Sunnis were Hindus at heart and "Mussalmans" only in name. Fundamentalism has, however, wiped out all memory of the Muslims' Hindu past.

The Kashmiri Muslims are highly emotional. Their loyalty can shift from day to day. They once made Sheikh Abdullah a hero: today his mausoleum has to be protected from vandals. Bakshi Ghulam Mohammad, the Sheikh's successor, was hated, yet when he became chief minister he become the new hero. When the Sheikh was in prison, he was forgotten, but the moment he came out, tens of thousands came on to the streets shouting slogans in his support. Again, when the Sheikh was re-arrested, out went the crowds to hail Bakshi. The Kashmiri is a worshipper of the current gods and fads. At the moment he is for the militants but if the militants appear beaten, the Kashmiri will shift his loyalty to other entities.

Similarly, the Kashmiri politician is adept at speaking in different voices. For example, a familiar charge is that the Sheikh Abdullah could be a communalist in the Valley, a communist in Jammu and a nationalist in New Delhi. In his book *My Frozen Turbulence in Kashmir* the former Kashmiri governor of J&K Jagmohan, has written:

> "Politicians were adept in speaking with two voices. They could be secular as well as communal, democratic as well as dictatorial, accessionist as well as pro-Pakistan. The underlying motivation was not principles but power-power for the person and for the coterie around. If the Central leaders allowed the Kashmiri leaders to rule the State in whatever manner they liked, whether or not it was in the interest of the country as a whole or even in the interest of the 'State, they swore by principles of democracy, socialism and secularism, and accession to India was declared as

final. If on the other hand, any question was raised in regard to exercise of authority. or any personal ambition was checked, accession became temporary and issues of autonomy, or identity and of the personality of Kashmir were raised, and communal feelings roused."

In 1989, Ali Mohammad Sagar, once a minister in the Farooq Abdullah government, admitted that about 60 per cent of the police jobs went to Muslims, whose population strength was 65 per cent. In other jobs they had a stake of 55 per cent. In the light of their low literacy level, Muslims had been enjoying a disproportionate share of the jobs. They continued to accuse the Pandits of stealing their jobs. As for Central Government jobs, the Pandits enjoy a larger share because they have relatively higher education.

With the growth of fundamentalism in the Valley, it was clear that the fate of the Pandits was sealed. So what the Pandit thinks are the greatest achievements of their Kashmiri ancestors are anathema to the converts under the circumstances. As Hari Jaisingh puts it, "To talk of a common culture, a "Kashmiriat", is to live in a make-believe world in these circumstances, for there is little that is held in equal esteem by both. On the other hand, what brings pride to the fundamentalists are the achievements of Islam."

Most Muslims of the Valley have had a history of respecting other faiths. The rich tradition of Sufism alongwith the cult of Rishis had provided for a healthy and multilayered religious homogeneity at the ground level. From the first two decades of this century onwards, the economic differences between the Pandits and Muslims were highlighted in communal terms.

Jammu division had also been a Muslim majority region prior to accession and the Pakistani invasion in 1947, after which, the religious composition changed in favour of non Muslims. A substantial number of Hindu and Sikh traders from Mirpur, Kotli, Sardoli, Muzaffarabad and other "Pakistan-occupied areas" replaced the Muslims in the urban areas of the Jammu region. Presently, Muslims constitute a majority in the districts of Poonch, Rajouri and Doda in spite of their being in a minority in the Jammu region as a whole.

Hari Jai Singh writes, "There is a variety of ethnic groups in the Valley. A thorough understanding of the ethnic differentiation is very important to work out any possible solutions to the Kashmir crisis. Apart from the division between Sunni and Shia sects among the Kashmiri Muslims, there are also caste-like divisions, though less rigid than among Hindus."

Chathley (1995) observes that "the new social groups emerging as a result of economic and political changes have continued to dominate the political scene of the state. A section among them who stick to National Conference have been returning to power in almost every election, even if it be by electoral rigging or manipulations, or unopposed, particularly up to 1970. This process has distorted democratic practice in the state. This has accentuated the process of alienation among Muslim masses, who had been promised a functional democracy by their leader at the time of the accession of the State to India. Understanding the Kashmiri Muslims as a homogeneous group may not help since social groupings have been more on ethnic lines than on religious ones. Even the newly developed colonies in Jammu city show ethnic concentrations. Ethnic differentiations are also reflective in the broad ideology, rank and profile, identification of issues and programmes of action of the dominant militant groups."

As Khushwant Singh writes in the *Hindustan Times* dated July 15, 2000 :

"The Essence of democracy is to accommodate different people's views as far as possible provided they do not hurt other people or interests of the country as a whole. It is clear as daylight that people of Kashmir are not one people but are divided by religion and language and have three distinct opinions about their future. Ladakhis are predominantly Buddhist and want Union Territory status; people of Jammu are predominantly Hindu and do not wish to change their existing relationship with the rest of the country; people of the Valley are predominantly Muslim and want more autonomy to run their own affairs."

We cannot reconcile these three disparate views if we treat Jammu, the Valley and Ladakh as one unit. If Farooq Abdullah and his National Conference want more autonomy, they cannot ride roughshod over the wishes of Ladakhis and Jammuites who do not want it.

Chapter 27

# The Holy Shrine

Hazratbal with its exquisite location on the west bank of the Dal Lake, the dargah is a graceful structure in white marble. A fascinating dome balanced by a minaret, visually and spiritually, is the most harmonious sight. It houses the holy relic, the Moe-e-Muqaddas—a hair of Prophet Mohammed.[1] Hazratbal is a most respected place for Muslims. Nothing else binds Kashmiri Muslims as powerfully as the Hazratbal shrine and even a hint of its desecration would most certainly generate spontaneous and enormous protests.

On December 27, 1963, the mysterious disappearance of the holy relic had led to communal tension in the valley. Property belonging to the former Chief Minister Bakshi Ghulam Mohammad was burnt down, a police station was set on fire and huge crowds defied curfew orders.[2] Not only the valley the incident shook the entire sub-continent. Recalling the disappearance of the holy relic, on "freezing winter night" of December 27,1963, and subsequent events, Sheikh Abdullah in his autobiography— translated by Khushwant Singh for Viking from the Urdu version *"Atish-e-Chinar"* posthumously published, says: That it strained the already over-wrought nerves of Jawaharlal and shaken the seat of power in Delhi.[3] The then Director of Intelligence Bureau, B.N. Mullick was put in charge of the operation and within six weeks on February 4,1964, the relic was traced and kept in the shrine. Initially people questioned the authenticity of the recovered relic, which reappeared as mysteriously as it had disappeared. The Moe-e-Muqaddas had travelled all the way from Medina to Kashmir valley via Bijapur, Delhi and Lahore to rest at this particular place which had come to be known as Hazratbal. Even Aurangzeb had failed to interrupt its passage to this place and all the previous attempts to displace it from there had failed and it had come back to its place of rest. So did the Moe-e-Muqaddas on this occasion also; B.N. Mullick in, *My Years with Nehru: Kashmir*, writes: "we who worked for the cause were only the puppets in the game. Glory to the Moe-e-Muqaddas."[4] He vividly narrates the identification proceedings:

"Syed Masoodi then gave each of the fourteen persons a copy of the Holy Quran and asked to swear by it that they would give only correct verdict. The fourteen took their oaths." The acting Chief Nishan Dez, Noor Din Bandey, then narrated the holiness of the Moe-e-Muqaddas and its history and gave its description from the books for the purpose of identification. He spoke about its holiness and repeated the points of its identification; "the first to give the verdict was Faqir Mirak Shah, the holiest of the holy men in Kashmir, and the stir was caused when he uttered the single word "Haq" meaning right."[5] Thus, the authenticity of the Holy Relic-Moe-e-Muqaddas was established and Pakistan's master-stroke of causing the temporary disappearance of the Holy Relic was foiled by its quick recovery.[6]

The single hair from the beard of Prophet Mohammed, enshrined in Hazratbal is only one of two of these relics in India.[7] The relic is now publically exhibited only on a few select days, including Id and Milad-ul-Nabi, the Prophet's birthday.[8] Earlier it was ritually exhibited ten times a year but was otherwise kept locked in a wooden cupboard.[9] The Ziarat at Hazratbal on the Dal Lake is visited by thousands of Muslims every Friday. It is here that the famous feast of roses is celebrated every spring.[10]

Recounting the history of the shrine, Sheikh Abdullah gives the vivid version: "It is said that the hair of the Prophet was in the possession of a Sheikh who belonged to the inner circle of the Haram-e-Kabba. Differences between him and the ruler of the day and he migrated to India and settled down in Hyderabad acquired the relic at an enormous price. When he was transporting it to Kashmir, the Mughal emperor Aurangzeb heard about it and immediately ordered it to be confiscated and placed at the Dargah of Khwaja Moinuddin Chishti at Ajmer.[11] A dream that night, however, upset Aurangzeb's plans. He dreamt that the Prophet had embarked on a journey towards Kashmir and was disturbed by Aurangzeb's decision, asked him: "Why are you trying to stop me from going to Kashmir?". Aurangzeb got the divine message and immediately ordered that the holy relic be taken to Kashmir under royal protection. When the holy relic reached Kashmir, the entire Jamiat gave it the most reverential welcome. By common consensus, it was placed at Hazratbal and became the symbol of faith and instruction to all the Muslims of the valley.[12] According to Dr. R.K. Parmu, it was during the reign of Fazal Khan 1698-1701, who was God's goodman a reputed builder and an architect, the most important event, both historically and culturally of his regime, was the arrival of Moe-e-Mubarak; of the Prophet Muhammad in Srinagar, in the year 1699. One Khwaja Nur-ud-din Ishbari, an affluent Kashmiri merchant, had bought the hair in Bijapur-Deccan. When holy relic was brought to Srinagar and lodged in its present picturesque site, in the Hazratbal Mosque, overlook Dal Lake, since rendered famous as the custodian of the Hazrat Bal, or the "Prophet Hair", all Kashmiris manifested great joy. All nobles, dignitaries, Maulvis and Ulama, in fact, the entire population, gave the hair an unprecedented, rousing reception, which it richly deserved.[13]

The holy relic-Moe-e-Muqaddas, is kept in a gold embroidered bag in a walnut box is a single hair of Prophet

Mohammed. According to another version it is said to have been brought to India by a Syed Abdullah, who claimed to be a descendant of the Prophet, some 350 years ago. Abdullah was the Chief keeper of the Mosque in Medina, but he fled the place after a family quarrel. He journeyed to India and landed in Bijapur. The Sultan there impressed by the Relic, gave Abdullah a plot of land, on which he stayed for 23 years. When Aurangzeb invaded Bijapur kingdom, he seized this land.[14] After years of penury Hamid met a Kashmiri leader Nooruddin Ashwari who took possession of the relic and that he had had a dream in which the Prophet had directed him to take the sacred relic to Kashmir, and there enshrine it on the banks of Dal Lake. Aurangzeb, hearing of this, thought the thing to be a hoax and had Nooruddin arrested. But later he found the relic to be genuine, he had it enshrined in the Mosque at Ajmer. The Prophet is said to have told the emperor in a dream that relic should go to Kashmir.[15] In the meantime Nooruddin died and Aurangzeb sent the Moe-e-Muqaddas to be enshrined in Naqshaband in 1699. But the mosque was too small to contain the crowds that thronged the place, so it was shifted to Bagh-e-Sadiq, later to be known as Hazratbal.[16]

The sacred hair of the Prophet is kept at Asaar Sharif in the Hazratbal. Perhaps, it is not very widely known that the late Sheikh Abdullah was closely associated with the renovation of Hazratbal and Asaar Sharif which once he described as a "symbol of the unity of the Muslims of Kashmir," cautioning that any harm to it would "amount to their disintegration."[17] Sheikh Abdullah, in the autobiography, *Flames of the Chinar*, recalls the fascinating history of Asaar Sharif and how the Islamic Endowments Committee, chaired by him, renovated it with the best marble brought all the way from Makrana, Rajasthan which was the source of marble for Tajmahal. Calligraphers from Delhi and Lucknow were brought to inscribe verses from the Quran on the marble and the central Chamber which held "Moe-e-Mubarak"—the Prophet's hair, was decorated with a unique Chandelier flown from Czechoslovakia.[18]

Another relic is lodged in Hazrat Baeos Khwaja Dargah near Aurangabad in Maharashtra. It is said to be reminent of the Prophet and is known as "Pehran-e-Mubarak". It is 1,350 years old, and is in this place for the last 700 years.[19] The Prophet gave this "pehran" to a Hazrat Ali who passed it on to Khwaja Hassan Basri in Iraq who in turn gave it to Hazrat Queja Abdul Wahed in about 756 A.D., then it stayed in Khutabad mosque until it came to India. Other relics are believed to be a pair of shoes in the Jama Masjid and another garment in the Sabriya dargah in Daryaganj, both in Delhi. There is also a hair from the beard of the Prophet at Deoband in Saharanpur district of Uttar Pradesh and a scarf at Durloom Arabic University in this town. A tuft of grass sanctified by water from the Prophet's hand is preserved at Bareilly.[20]

Border Security Force on October 15, 1993 had laid a seize of the Hazratbal shrine in Srinagar, not because the holy relic had disappeared but because some terrorists and Pakistani trained saboteurs had gone inside and made it a hide out for the secessionist activities. The purpose of the cordon ostensibly was to protect the shrine and secure the holy relic kept inside Asaar Sharif. Director General of Police M.N. Sabarwal told the reporters on October 16, 1993 that "A criminal conspiracy of the most heinous nature has come to light as the holy shrine of Hazratbal has been misused by militants for activities detrimental to its sanctity, such as display, storage of weapons torture of captives and browbeating of law abiding citizens.[21] The timing of the Hazratbal episode may be the crucial key to figuring out motive behind the renewed series of international chess board moves on the sub-continent with the Kashmir as a convenient pawn. The encirclement of the Hazratbal shrine by Indian Security forces and later the Army, came barely three days before the new-and elected Pakistan Prime Minister was to assume office in Islamabad. It may not be just a coincidence. The occupation of the shrine by militants had also coincided with the stepping up of international pressure by Pakistan, on India regarding Kashmir. The round table conference in Brussels was a bare two days away called by the socialist group of the European Parliament to discuss Kashmir. The UN General Assembly had been in session and Pakistan was going to press for a resolution on Kashmir, which of course, ultimately failed. The Organisation of Islamic Conference had already asked for a UN fact finding team to study alleged human rights violations in Kashmir.[22] This action of the militants had caused great resentment among the people but because of the fear of the gun, they had not publicly voiced their concern to this sacrilege of the stone, Chaudhury's analysis is that New Delhi decided to move in troops to flush out the culprits, apprehending a possible move by ISI backed militants to spirit away the holy relic—as happened in December 1963—and lay the blame on New Delhi's door.

The Government's decision to open Kashmir to the gaze of foreign observers after considerable restraint may be a step due to Western pressure. But it could also be a tactical move to establish the country's credentials through the international T.V. networks as a government that went out of the way to exercise restraint and protect the shrine containing a holy relic, sacred to the Muslim community.[23] The Hazratbal stand off ended early on Tuesday, November 16, 1993, without a single shot being fired after the remaining 65 people, including foreigners and militants holed in the shrine surrendered to the authorities.[24] The Hazratbal shrine was not a hostage like Rubaiya Sayeed to be freed through behind the scene negotiations, A false move could mean tremendous loss of face for the agencies of the Indian State.

In Srinagar not even an attempt was made by the army to show its awesome power. First the High Court at Jammu and later the Supreme Court ordered food supply and at a still later stage blankets were supplied to keep the hostages warm. In this way, the Judiciary stiffened the basic philosophy of extending a humane treatment to those who chose the militant path to protest against the government. The forces showed exemplary sense of perseverance and refused to be provoked. The duration of the siege was punctuated by repeated assurances by the administration that there would be no attempt to storm the shrine to free the hostages and detain the militants.[25] The armed forces and paramilitary outfits had chalked up an impressive victory in preventing any damage whatsoever to the holy place.

Dr. Heptullah, Deputy Chairperson of Rajya Sabha said that Hazratbal Mosque is a most respected place for Muslims. If the terrorists go inside and hide in it, it's a kind of disrespect to that place. This is not a place meant for people with guns to sit around, it's a place for peace.[26]

The Hazratbal operation launched in October, 1993 was undertaken by Indian Government to protect the religious sanctity of the Hazratbal shrine in Srinagar. Undoubtedly, terrorism has no place in a democracy. The militants sitting and hiding in Hazratbal shrine was the Pakistan's strategy to make Kashmir an increasingly internationalised issue, so that world pressure could be brought on India to give up the valley. The government wanted and ultimately succeeded to establish its bonafides by using restraint and a humane approach rather than tough military measures to evacuate the shrine. The security forces displayed commendable-restraint in handling the situation in Kashmir's sacred Hazratbal shrine. However, Pakistan and its inter-services intelligence, has not and will not hesitate in using the sacred shines like Hazratbal for its subversive and nefarious activities.

It is pointless to expect the ISI to use fair means. For this dirty trick department every incident is tailor-made to hurt India and sully its secular image.[27] After the failure of Pakistan at the United Nations Human Rights Commission in Geneva, it was quite obvious that the evil empire called Inter-Services Intelligence, directorate will strike back with vengeance. The former speaker of Jammu and Kashmir Assembly Wali Mohammad too, was shot in the back while thousands of namazis walked around him, just after Friday prayers in Jamia Masjid in Khatikan Talab, Jammu has become a prominent victim of this proxy war. Reports are unambiguous that the murder was committed following a fresh directive from Pakistan's top intelligence officers to militants to eliminate all pro-India Kashmiri Leaders.[28] The Inter-Services Intelligence over which no civilian government, in Pakistan has any control and which organises terrorism in Kashmir uses fundamentalist Islamic groups for the purpose. It has also close links with Islamic groups which practise terrorism world wide.[29]

In India's context, Pakistan unceasing refrain is, "India must be destroyed." Kashmir is only a quasi-core issue, an opening gambit so to speak. The core issue is to destroy India at all costs, by all means. There is not any other issue. The rest are intermediate quasi-core issues till the final result is achieved. In this ultimate goal, the fragmentation, dissolution and final disappearance of India is the final factor.[30] If any proof was still required we have only to hear Ms Benazir Bhutto's ringing statement: "The unfinished work of Jinnah must be completed." In stark effect, the statement conveys that India must be divided again and again to extinction. Another famous Benazir admonition is that India will have to swallow the bitter pill of Kashmir, as Pakistan swallowed the bitter pill of Bangladesh. A ludicrous comparison but a bitter pill of her rhetoric which will have to be swallowed.[31] A careful reading of the statements of Ms. Bhutto ought to bring home the reality. Her Statements are open challenges and what is our response to these challenges which come from the enemies who arc constantly on the prowl to seek and engineer provocations.?

Thus, today, when we have the opportunity to play a decisive role in shaping of history, we are caught in monumental trivialities of our own making. There is no hope for India unless it girds itself, gives itself renewed vision and meets all challenges with fortitude, courage, a sense of self-reliance and confidence, united and strong, once again to be a beacon to the world.[32] It is no more time for behaving small.

## NOTES AND REFERENCES

1. "The story of Hazratbal", *Deccan Chronicle*, October 19, 1993.
2. Ibid.
3. Sheikh Abdullah, Autobiography, *Flames of the Chinar*, (1986) translated from *Aatish-a-Chinar* by Khushwant Singh.
4. B.N. Mullick, *My Years with Nehru: Kashmir*, (1971) p. 166.
5. Ibid., pp. 161-162.
6. Ibid., p. 180.
7. "Hazratbal Crisis ends", *Deccan Chronicle*, November 17, 1993.
8. "The story of Hazratbal", *Deccan Chronicle*, October 19,1993.
9. Rajesh Kadian, *The Kashmir Tangle : Issues and Options* (1992) p. 123.
10. G.L. Kaul, *Kashmir : Through The Ages* (1954) p. 237.
11. Sheikh Abdullah, Autobiography, *Flames of Chinar*, (1986) translated from *Aatish-e-Chinar* by Khushwant Singh.
12. Ibid.
13. Dr. R.K. Parmu. *A History of Muslim Rule in Kashmir* 1320-1819, (1969) pp. 327-328, Also see, Azam, *Wakiati-Kashmir*, p. 156.

14. "Treasured Relics", *The Hindu-Magazine*, p. 1.
15. Ibid.
16. Ibid.
17. "Hazratbal again in the eye of the Storm", *The Hindu*, October 20, 1993.
18. Ibid.
19. "Treasured Relics", *The Hindu-Magazine*, November 21, 1993, p. 1.
20. Ibid.
21. "Militants holed up in Hazratbal Shrine", *Indian Express*, October 17, 1993.
22. Neeraj Chowdhry, "At best a stalemate in Kashmir", *The Economic Times*, October 24, 1993.
23. Ibid.
24. "Hazratbal Crisis ends", *Deccan Chronicle*, November 17, 1963.
25. K.P.S. Gill, "Between Black Thunder and Hazratbal", *The Tribune*, November 18, 1994 pp. 1 & 18.
26. Dr. Najma Heptullah, "Najma apprises Clinton aides of Kashmir Human Rights Issue". *The Economic Times*, October 26,1993.
27. "ISI Show its Fangs", *The Tribune*, March 21, 1994, p. 8.
28. Ibid.
29. "United States and Kashmir", *Indian Express*, October 25, 1993, p. 6.
30. Som Benegal, "Pakistan and Core Issue", *The Tribune*, March 21, 1994, p. 8.
31. Ibid.
32. Ibid.

## Chapter 28

# The Displaced People

The erstwhile Chamba State has been one of the most important hill States with rich cultural and historical heritage. The State played a key role in shaping the boundaries of various States and relationship with other rulers from time to time. The general boundaries of Chamba touch the State of Jammu and Kashmir in the north-west and west and part of Ladakh in the north-east and east. In the west, the Ravi forms the boundary between the Chamba and Jammu.[1] In the Pangi range also the southern flanks are abrupt and precipitous, while, to the north, the spurs subside gradually to the Chander Bhaga. After passing out of the district the range continues its course westward to join the Pir Panjal proper, with which it is in unbroken line, except where it is pierced by the Chander Bhaga at Kashtwar.[2] The Rowa stream forms the boundary to its junction with the Siowa, and later to its junction with the Ravi, separating Chamba from Balaur in Jammu. The boundary on the Padri pass is as shown in the trignometrical survey maps and it follows the create of the ridge. This crest forms a natural boundary between the Chamba District and the Bhadrawah *illaqa* of Jammu and Kashmir.[3]

The Siul, which joins the Ravi lower down than the Chamba town, is the largest tributary of the Ravi. It brings down the entire drainage of the north-western portion of the Chamba Valley. Rising on the top of the Padri Pass, which makes the boundary with Jammu, it flows south-east through a narrow ravine, to a point opposite Himgiri, where it makes a curve around the end of a long ridge, and flows on, at an acute angle to its original course, to join the Ravi at Teleru near Bhalai, about fourteen miles below the Chamba town.[4] The Siowa is the last tributary of the Ravi on the right bank, having any bearing on the Chamba district. It is this tributary which, at this point, forms the natural boundary between Chamba and Jammu territory.[5] Chamba is one of the oldest native States in India, having been founded not later than A.D. 600 and perhaps as early as A.D. 550. It is situated in the bosom of the Himalaya Mountains with Jammu and Kashmir on the north-west and west, on the north-east and east, Ladakh, British-Lahul and Bara Bangahal, on the south-east and south, the districts of Kangra and Gurdaspur.[6]

The Chamba annals State that soon after Ranjit Deo's death in 1781 his son and successor, Brijraj Deo of Jammu, conveyed the suzerainty of Bhadrawah and Kashtwar to Chamba, and on the instigation of Dalel Singh, brother of Mihar Singh, Raja Raj Singh, of Chamba, in 1786, sent an army under the nominal command of his son, Jit Singh, then a boy of eleven years of age, to invade Kashtwar. It advanced by way of Bhadrawah and Balesa, which had come under the control of Chamba in 1783-84 as proved by letters in the Chamba archives, dated 1784, owing allegiance on the part of the Raja Fateh Pal.[7] J. Hutchison, L.R.C.P. & S.E, PH Vogel Ph.D. also confirm that in A.D. 1782 Raj Singh invaded and conquered Basohli.[8] The Balore or Basohli State, as it existed down to the early part of the ninteenth century, corresponded to the Basohli Tehsil of the Jasrota District in Jammu territory—if Bhadu and Mankot be excluded. The State was bounded on the north by Bhadrawah, on the east by Chamba and Nurpur, on the south by Lakhanpur and Jasrota, and on the west by Bhadu and Mankot.[9] Kulu, Balor, Bhadu and Bhadrawah are all from one parent stem, of which the early seat was traditionally at Prayag. At a remote period the family migrated to Mayapuri (Hardwar), and a cadet founded the Kulu State. The Balor

Vansavali claims direct descent for the family from the parent stem at Mayapur, but the Bhadu Vansavali States that the founder of Balor State was a cadet of the Kulu family.[10] The original site of Basohli, however, is said to have been close to the right bank of the Ravi, where ancient remains still exists; and an older town stood there in early times where the Rajas occasionally resided, though the capital was at Vallapura.[11] In A.D. 1786 Chamba also asserted its supremacy over the Native State of Kashtwar.[12] During the occupation of Kashtwar, one Kundan Singh, a cadet of the Bhadrawah family, was appointed Raja. He had previously been refugee in Chamba and had returned with the army to Kashlwar.[13]

The Mani Mahesh temple at Bharmour is said to have been constructed by Raja Meru Verman during the seventh or eighth-century A.D. The temple and images are fine pieces of art and architecture. In the 'Garbh-graha' of the temple there is a magnificent 'Shivlinga' and in front of the temple a bronze image of 'Nandi', the bullvehicle of lord Shiva, is a rare piece of art. The image was constructed by 'Gugga' a sculptor of that time. On the pedestal is an inscription in Kutil[14] script which might have been in vogue in the area during that period.

There is a legend that the image of Nandi, the divine bull, was constructed by Gugga within only one night with the help of his beloved Roopa who belonged to Rihara community. The songs of Roopa Rihari are still sung in some areas of Chamba. According to a popular belief. Lord Shiva blessed the lovers on the condition that they would marry only if the image was completed within one night. They succeeded in doing so but it is attributed more to Roopa Rihari, the beloved. Even upto now, the visitors from Bhadrawah remember 'Roopa Rihari' in their slogans related to Lord Mani Mahesh. It is a matter to be seen that though the local inhabitants, know fully well, that Roopa helped Gugga in making the image but they do not remember her by way of their slogans in her memory. This confirms that the inhabitants of Bharmour area moved to Jammu region during the remote past and still cherish the memory of Lord Shiva of Mani Mahesh and the artists of that area.

Padar area of Jammu was a part of Chamba State prior to 1835 A.D. when it was conquered by Zorawar Singh Kehlooria, the general of Maharaja Gulab Singh of Jammu and Kashmir. At that time, there were only three parganas of Pangi, namely, Saach, Killar and Dharwas. 'Palsar' was the designation of controller of these areas.[15] Ratnoo, a Palsar, whose headquarter was at Padar, was a faithful servant of the ruler of Chamba. During the regime of Raja Charhat Singh (1808-1844 A.D.) he vanquished the Raja of Zaskar and made him to pay tribute to the ruler of Chamba. Earlier Zaskar was under the suzrainty of Ladakh. In Padar area, Raja Chhatra Singh (1664-1690 A.D.) had constructed a fort which was named after the ruler and was known as Chhatragarh. During 1835 AD when Zorawar Singh conquered Padar, the fort was renamed after Gulab Singh and was given the name of Gulabgarh.

The Doda district in the Jammu region, now a hotbed of militant activity, is an integral part of Jammu. It is separated from the valley by the Pir Panjal range. It was predominantly Hindu till a large number of Kashmiri Muslims took shelter there during a famine in the valley towards the end of the 19th century. They now constitute about 25 per cent of the population. Other Muslims of this area are original inhabitants. They speak Bhadrawani and Kashtwari dialects which are similar to Sanskrit.[16] In this world of fluctuations, the refugees-migrants from Chamba to Jammu and Kashmir, settled in Doda district, are once again refugees in their own homeland.

Fifteen kilometres away from the nearest road heads, this obscure sleepy village on the Himachal Border with Jammu and Kashmir, has suddenly become alive with officials, politicians and volunteers wading their way to Makkan Nallah where over 800 Kashmiri migrants from Doda district have been accommodated in tents. Residents of the village living in abject poverty in this extreme mountains terrain greet the stream of visitors with awe and surprise, for they have seldom witnessed so much activity. The migrants, including women and children, hailing from nine villages in Gandoh tehsil, who had fled from their houses on April 19, 1994, and crossed over the Chamba district, have been going through harrowing experiences in the militant-infested Doda district. Migrants, however, are certain about one thing that despite harsh camp life they will not return to their homes, many of which have been burnt or looted by the militants and their supporters in their native villages. "We won't return until militancy is wiped out in Doda district", said a migrant, Om Singh echoing the opinion of the majority.[17] The plight of Hindus of Doda district who had migrated to Chamba district (HP) is miserable in Jammu and Kashmir, asserts Simranjit Singh Maan. The militants have virtually taken control of Doda and the Hindus were being forced to migrate to safer places. About 10,000 Hindus had shifted to Sanwal village in Tissa subdivision of Chamba district. The BSF alongwith local officials were forcing them to go back to Doda, whereas the Hindus were afraid of returning as Doda was completely in the grip of the militants.[18]

The migrants, however, remain apprehensive. A migrant said: we have stopped believing the Jammu and Kashmir government or the administration. The officials who have talked to us here stopped on the road head and never bothered to visit our camps. This speaks of their callousness and general unconcern.[19] Doda district of Jammu and Kashmir with an area of 12,000 sq. km., is one half times more than the entire Kashmir valley.[20] Since the advent of terrorism in Doda district in 1990, communal polarisation has entrenched deeper and deeper after every violent incident. The district has a population ratio of 55 : 45 between Muslims and Hindus with 97 per cent of population living in rural areas.[21] However, Prof. Balraj Madhok asserts that total population of Hindus in Doda district is still about 50 per cent of its total population.[22]

With two of its major towns Bhaderwah and Kishtwar under curfew, terrorists in top gear, exodus of the minority community of Hindus in full swing and an ever widening gap between Hindus and the Muslims, the situation in the mountainous district of Doda can only be described as critical.[23] Doda is being used as a springboard to launch terrorism in the Jammu region along its boundaries touching Kathua, Udhampur and Rajouri and the Chamba district of M.P.[24] Panun Kashmir asserts that selective killings by the militants in the Bhaderwah and Kishtwar belts, forcing Hindus to migrate from Doda district is part of the "religious cleansing" process forming vital aspect the ideological commitment of the militants in Jammu and Kashmir.[25] The high mountain ranges constituting the 150 km border between Chamba and Doda district render the task of the security forces difficult. "Efforts in isolation will have no effect. Pressure will have to be built on the terrorists from both sides of the boundary" asserts a senior official in Himachal Pradesh.[26] The surge of terrorism in Doda district of Jammu region which recently precipitated the exodus of more than 800 persons to the adjoining Chamba district, has signalled dangerous portents for the peaceful State of Himachal Pradesh. The fear of spill-over of terrorism from across the boundary into Chamba district is becoming real.[27] Muslim Gujjars, a nomadic tribe, which roams about with its cattle and the presence of large Muslim settlements in the border region of Chamba add another dimension to the security logistics in the region. The Gujjars who cross over to Chamba every summer where they live in temporary hutments in high mountain ranges, can become soft targets for the terrorists who could intimidate them into providing them with food, shelter and even information.[28] The population of Muslim Gujjars in Chamba district according to 1981 census is 7410, out of total population of 7519 of that tribe.[29] The terrorists have set up a permanent bases atop the mountain ranges dividing the two States. Besides, they also find shelter in the tents of Gujjars overlooking the villages. The terrain is ideal for guerilla warfare.[30] There is sizeable number of Muslims in the border belt.

According to census report 1951, the Muslim population of Chamba district was 5288 and in about a decade it rose to 10,512.[31] The Muslim population of Chamba district according to 1981 census was 17,908,[32] and during the last 15 years it must have been doubled. The majority of the Muslim population resides in Churah tehsil bordering Doda district of Jammu. The fact of homelessness of more than 2.5 lakh people from the valley and the exodus from Doda district is distressing. Mr. Bhim Singh, president of Panthers Party, held talks with Doda refugees and wanted migrants to return to their native village to defeat the designs of the militants who were keen to throw them out the Slate.[33] The rule of law must be established in Doda area and the migrants should be re-assured that the local population would not be hostile to them; such a situation alone is likely to facilitate the return of the Doda refugees to their homes. The cult of gun ultimately destroyes the gunwielder together with his goons.

In a leading article "Striking Back in Doda" *Indian Express* is justified in writing that the exodus of Hindus from Doda district, which began as a trickle last year, is on the verge of reaching alarming proportions. The numbers involved may not excite the international imagination, but that is no reason why the rest of India should acquiesce passively in yet another successful offensive by armed secessionists to push all Hindus out of one more region of J & K.[34] Doda, Kishtwar and Bhadarwah sensitive region lying beyond the Pir Panjal range, close to Chamba, Himachal Pradesh has mixed population of Hindus and Muslims. Like many other areas of Kashmir, this region, too was not affected by militancy. But it also happens to be an area through which the main highway connecting Jammu with Kashmir valley passes through. For this reason, efforts, almost certainly directed by animical forces across the border rather than the militants in the valley, have been made for the past several years to stoke militancy in this area. Indications are that almost all the militants operating there, using the Southwestern part of the valley as their base, are of Afghan or Pakistani origin. Earlier they would cross the Pir Panjal to operate in the origin and return to the valley, but now they have managed to get pockets of support as well as coerce some of the residents of the poverty-stricken area into providing them shelter.[35] The situation in this region of Jammu bordering Himachal Pradesh may be seen in the broader context of 1971 struggle between India and Pakistan. The doctrine of "forget and forgive" may be nice and sweet-sounding to preach, but difficult to digest. Pakistan rightly or wrongly considers India the architect of its bifurcation in 1971. Pakistan has neither forgotten nor forgiven India for this supposed sin. The sense of humiliation at the hands of India and the desire to avenge it have become an integral part of their collective consciousness. Losing sight of Pakistan's motive to revenge may be suicidal for India and invitation to disaster.

The forcible migration of minority community of Jammu and Kashmir and to make them refugees in their own country, involves not only the security of the country, but is also a blatant violation of human rights.

The human rights of every citizen are sacrosanct but they have sometimes to be balanced against foreign intervention which extinguishes the rights of law-abiding Hindu citizens of Jammu and Kashmir.[36] The National Human Rights Commission, will be well advised to maintain the balance by highlighting the plight of the affected people like Kashmiri mirgrants. *The Tribune* in its recent published leading article asserts: that the NHRC set up last year had a genetic defect: It was born under official auspices and have suffered from low credibility. There were also sceptics in India and abroad who expected nothing more from it than to supply a fig leaf to the naked administration.[37] However, Justice R.N. Mishra, Chairman, the National Human Rights Commission clarifies that the commission was an autonomous body with absolutely no government control and has an unimpeded access to the common people.[38] Oleg Malghinov, first deputy head of the Russian Foreign Ministry's Department on International Humanitarian Cooperation and Human Rights, has justifiably said in no uncertain terms that Russia believes that Kashmir, is not a human rights issue but a political problem which is being manipulated by Pakistan and Kashmiri separatists for achieving their own objectives that include the disintegration of India.[39] Disintegration of India will be the first step towards the disintegration of the Indian sub-continent.

While the rest of the world approached the 21st Century with plans to increase interdependence and with determination to transcend international boundaries and search for common values, India and Pakistan will celebrate the 50th anniversary of the conflict in Kashmir. The strangest and most puzzling aspect of this conflict is that until the country was partitioned, no one predicted that it was going to be Kashmir of all things which would become the unsolvable problem of the sub-continent.[40] Terrorism in the State of Jammu and Kashmir appears to be inspired by Islamic fundamentalism and actively abetted by Pakistan, is nothing short of an undeclared war against the territorial integrity of India. However, in the interest of their respective people, it is expected, that India and Pakistan would sit around the negotiating table to work out a mutual beneficial solution to the Kashmir problem and to save the Indian sub-continent from disintegration, bearing in mind that given the will and sincerity of purpose there is no knot that cannot be possible to be untied. His Holiness the Dalai Lama, is hopeful that the twentyfirst century will be friendly, more harmonious and peaceful.[41]

The usual aim of terrorists is to wreck vengeance against whom they regard as their enemies, oppressors and usurpers and otherwise obstacles in the achievement of their goals. It matters little to those elements that their aims are unethical, illegal and disruptionist. Social analysts rightly assert that the ultimate battle against terrorism will have to be fought by the people.

The people seem to be fed up with the militants, their associates-mercenaries and increasingly not to have compromise with the cult of the gun.

On situation created by migrants of Doda District to Chamba, Virbhadra Singh, Hon'ble Chief Minister, Himachal Pradesh is of the view that the State Police and other security agencies were fully prepared to thwart any attempt of terrorists to infiltrate into Himachal and that Himachal Pradesh Police was trying to have a perfect co-ordination with Punjab and Jammu and Kashmir Police. The Himachal Pradesh government has asked the centre to provide sophisticated and modern weapons to the State Police to meet the increased threat of Pakistan from across the J & K border.[41] Virbhadra Singh asserts that the migrant from Bhadarwa and Kishtwar are properly and well looked after in HP and will soon return to their homes on restoration of normalcy. It is hoped that the forces of militancy, especially those having extra-territorial loyalty, will be dealt with iron hand, paving way for responsive system creating new bridges of understanding. Kashmir problem, of course, is the outcome of partition of the country on the basis of religion. The country needs to generate a thinking process on the individual and collective basis. The right of thinking in no circumstances can be abdicated. The people who deal daily with current problems must focus on the immediate problem but at the same time must look at the long-term effect on the humankind, on the human society and about the long-term future of mankind; It is necessary to combine temporary and long-term handling of problems.[42] In the ultimate analysis the people may come to the conclusion that partition of the country on the basis of two nation theory was not only a mistake-blunder but a sin. The partition has not brought peace to the sub-continent. The unification of the India and Pakistan would not only solve the problems of Doda migrants, living in Chamba district, Kashmir problem, but will take the subcontinent towards poverty alleviation. Thus, the united sub-continent shall emerge a world power to reckon with. That being the truth will ultimately prevail. But it matters that falsehood has not too long innings. It is never too late to observe what Quran Sharief ordains: "Truth in word and deed is our fullest satisfaction and reward." That will give meaning to the prophecy of His Holiness The Dalai Lama that the 21st Century will be more peaceful and full of co-opertion. He elaborates: This blue planet of ours is the most delightful habitat. Its life is our life; its future, our future. The Earth itself is not a sentient being, it does indeed act as our mother, and, like children, we are dependent upon her. Now mother nature is telling us to co-operate. Our mother is teaching us a lesson in universal responsibility. Unless we all work together, no solution will be found.[43]

## NOTES AND REFERENCES

1. T.S. Negi, *Himachal Pradesh District Gazetteers Chamba* (1964) p. 375.
2. Ibid., p. 6.
3. Ibid., p. 7.
4. Ibid., p. 15.
5. Ibid., p.16.
6. J. Hutchison J.P.H. Vogel, *History of the Panjab Hill States,* Vol. 1, p. 268.
7. T.S. Negi, *Himachal Pradesh District Gazetteers-Chamba* (1964) p. 139.
8. J. Hutchison J.P.H. Vogel, *History of the Panjab Hill States,* Vol-1, p-316, also see. The date of the conquest of Basohil is recorded on a marble slab in the pavement in front of the Lakshmi Narayana Temple at Chamba.
9. Ibid., Vol.11, p. 587.
10. Ibid., p. 588.
11. Ibid., p. 589.
12. Ibid., Vol-I, p. 316.
13. T.S. Negi, *Himachal Pradesh District Gazetteers-Chamba,* 140.
14. J.P.H. Vogel, Ph. D. *Antiquities of Chamba State,* 1911 p. 144.
15. J. Hutchinson and J. P.H. Vogel, *History of The Panjab, Hill States,* (Reprint 1982) p. 323 wherein it has been mentioned: In A.D. 1835 Gulab Singh of Jammu sent an army under Wazir Zorawar-Singh, Kahluria, one of his ablest generals, to invade and conquer Ladakh. After the conquest a force under Wazir Lakhpat Rai was detached from the main army to annex Zanskar, which still held out, and having done this the force crossed the Umasi Pass and passed through Padar on the way back to Jammu. It is believed that Gulab-Singh had no intention of encroaching on State territory, but the Padar people were suspicious, and some opposition was

offered to the passage of the Dogra army. This, however, did not amount to much, and the main body passed on, leaving only about thirty men in Chatargarh to keep up communications. Thereupon Ratanu, the Chamba official, stirred up the people, seized the Dogra soldiers, and sent them to Chamba. Charhat-Singh at once disowned the act of his official, but the mischief had been done, and in the spring of 1836 Zorawar-Singh came in person with a large force to avenge the insult. Ratanu had the bridge over the Chandra-Bhaga broken down, and in this way kept the Dogras at bay for three months, but at last, having with the help of some villagers, passed a jhula across the river a few miles lower down. Zorawar Singh succeeded in transferring a portion of his force to the other bank, and thus, advancing under cover of night, effected an entrance into Chatargarh by the bridge over the Bhutna Nala, which had been left intact. Chatargarh was razed to the ground, and the name of the place changed to Gulabgarh; and several of the Padar people were hanged or mutilated. The country was then annexed to Jammu".

16. Balraj Madhok, "Political Answers in Jammu & Ladakh," *The Times of India*, May 6,1994,p.8.
17. Rajesh Deol, "Assurances Fail to sell 'Return' to Migrants", *Indian Express*, June 7,1994, p. 1.
18. Simranjit Singh Maan, "Doda refugees in Pitiable State", *The Tribune*, June 7, 1994,p.4.
19. Rajesh Deol,"Assurances fail to sell, 'Return' to Migrants", *Indian Express*, June 7,1994,p. 1.
20. S.M.K. Kazmi, "Doda offers terrorists what the valley denies", *Indian Express*, June 5, 1994,p.1.
21. Ibid.
22. Balraj Madhok, "Political Answers in Jammu & Ladakh," *The Times of India*, May 6, 1994, p. 8.
23. S.M.K. Kazmi, "Doda offers terrorists what the valley denies", *Indian Express*, June 5, 1994, p.1.

24. Ibid.
25. "Communal Clashes rock Bhaderwah", *The Tribune*, June 8, 1994, p. 1.
26. Rajesh Deol, "Chamba faced with spill-over of terrorism", *Indian Express*, June 8, 1994, p.1.
27. Ibid.
28. Ibid.
29. "*Statistical Outline of Himachal Pradesh*, (1990) p. 24. Published by Economics and Statistics Department, Himachal Pradesh, Shimla.
30. Rakesh Lohumi, "Migrants Unwilling to return", *The Tribune*, June 9, 1994, p.16.
31. T.S. Negi, *Himachal Pradesh District Gazetteers-Chamba*, (1963) p. 172.
32. *Statistical Outline of Himachal Pradesh*, (1990) p. 24. Published by Economics and Statistics Department, Himachal Pradesh, Shimla.
33. T.S. Negi, *Himachal Pradesh District Gazetteers-Chamba*, (1963) p. 172.
34. "Striking Back In Doda," *Indian Express*, June 8, 1994.
35. "Outlook in Kashmir", *The Times of India*, June 10, 1994, p. 10.
36. "NHRC Asserts Rights", *The Tribune*, June 8, 1994 p. 10.
37. Ibid.
38. "Rights Panel to Probe Violations in Kashmir", *The Times of India*, June 8, 1994, p.5.
39. "Positive Signals from Moscow", *The Tribune*, June 10, 1994, p. 8.
40. *Pak: Tricky past to Grim Future*, (1994) edited by William E. James and Subrorto Roy.
41. H.H the Dalai Lama, "Reflections on the Challenges of the 21st Century", *Tibetan Bulletin* (May-June, 1994), p. 19.

41. Virbhadra Singh "HP asks Centre to provide modern weapons", *Indian Express*, June 16, 1994, p.1.
42. Charles G. Rose, in *Religious Values and Human Society* (Reprint. 1988) p. 16, Fourteenth Dalai Lama, His Holiness Tenzin Gyatso.
43. Tenzin Gyatso, *The Global Community and the Need for Universal Responsibility*, (1992) p. 21.

# Bibliography

**Books and Journals**


Abdullah, Sheikh, *Autobiography, Flames of the Chinar* (1986) translated from *Aatish-a-Chinar* by Khushwant Singh.

Adel, Daljit Sen, *China and Her Neighbours*, (1984).

Akbar, M.J., *The Shade of Swords* (2002)

Arora, Vasantha, "Bush Urges on Trade Differences", *In India West*, August 18, 1991.

Bamzai, P.N.K., *A History of Kashmir* (1973).

Basham, A.L., *The Wonder That was India*, (1994).

Bazaz, Prem Nath, *Kashmir in Crucible* (1976).

Bazaz, Prem Nath, *Kashmir on Crucible* (1967).

Bhutto, Z.A., *If I am Assasinated*, (1979).

Biscoe, C.E., Tyndale *Kashmir in Sunlight and Shade* (1971).

Bowles, Chester, *Promises to Keep*, (1972).

Brecher, *India and the World Politics*.

Bright, Jagat S., *Kashmir Forever* (1958).

Butt, Masood, Muslims of Tibet, *Tibetan Bulletin*, (January-February 1994).

Capra, Fritjof *The Turning Point*, (1982).

Chakravarti, K.P., "Words and Phrases under the Constitution (1986).

Chitkara, M.G., *Indo-Pak Amity* (1994).

Chitkara, M.G., *Indo-Pak Amity: A New Concept*, (1991).

Cloughley, Brian, *A History of the Pakistan Army*, Oxford University Press, Karachi, (1999).

Dasgupta, C., *War and Diplomacy in Kashmir* (2002)

Diwakar, R.R., *Mahayogi* (1954).

Gajendragadkar, P.B., *Law, Liberty and Social Justice*, (1954).

Gandhi, Rajmohan, *Muslim Mind* (1966).

Golwalkar, M.S., *Bunch of Thoughts*, (1966).

Gul. Moh. Wani, *Kashmir Politics*, (1993).

Gyatso, Tenzin, *The Colobal Community and the Need for Universal Responsibility* (1992).

Haksar, P.N., Foreword, *Problems of Living in Nuclear Age*, (1985) ed., by K.S. Subramanyam, M. Zuberi and Raja Ramanna.

Harperin, H., Morton *China and the Bomb*, (1965).

Hibbs, Mark, "Regional Nuclear Gambit Checked, U.S. Has Few Cards to Move India", *Nucleonics Week*, April 2, 1992.

Hodson, H.V., *The Great Divide* (1970).

Hodson, H.V., *The Great Divide* (Hutchinson, 1969).

Hussain, Yusuf, *Indo-Muslim Polity*, (1971).

Hutchison, J., Vogel, J., "*History of the Punjab Hill States*" Vol. 1.

Jagmohan, *My Frozen Turbulence in Kashmir*, (1991).

Jaisingh, Hari, *Kashmir : A Tale of Shame* (1996).

Jha, Prem Shankar, *Kashmir* (1947), Delhi: Oxford University Press.

Kabir, Humayun, *The Indian Heritage*, 1955 (Reprint 1964).

Kadain, Rajesh, *The Kashmir Tangle : Issue and Opinion*, (1992).

Kant, Krishan, "The Nuclear Option-No Alternative to Bomb", In *Indian Security*, (1990) ed. By Maj-Gen Rajendra Nath, Shyam Khosla and Ashok Malik.

Kaul, G.L., Kashmir: *Through the Ages* (1954).

Kennedy, John F., *The Strategy of Peace*, (1961).

Khan, M., Ishaq *Kashmir's Transition to Islam* (1994).

Khanduri, Brigadier C.B., *Field Marshal Cariappa—His Life and Times*, New Delhi: Lancer, 1995.

Khilnani, Sunil, *The Idea of India* (1997).

Korbel, Jospeh, *Danger in Kashmir* (1954).

Krishnan, T.V. Kunhi, *The Unfriendly Friends : India and America*, (1974).

Lama, the Dalai Afterwords to: *Indo-Pak Amity*: A New Concept by M.G. Chitkara.

Lama, The Dalai *Guidelines for Future Tibet's Polity and the Basic Features of Its Constitution*, (1992).

— *Tibet, China and the World* (1989).

Lamb, Alastair, *The Kashmir Problem*, (1968).

Limaye, Satu P., *U.S.-Indian Relations*, (1993).

Lohalekar, Devidas, *U.S. Arms to Pakistan*, (1991).

Mahajan M.C., *Accession of Kashmir to India : The Inside Story*, Sholapur.

Mahajan, Mehar Chand, *Looking Back* (1963).

Maheshwari, Shriram, *Indian Administration*, (1991).

Malik, B. N., *The Chinese Betrayal*, (1971).

Menon, V.P., *The Story of the Integration of the Indian States*, (1956).

Morgenthau, Hans J. (ed.), *Politics among Nations*, (1969).

Mullick, B.N., *My Years with Nehru's Kashmir* (1971).

Naqash, Nasir. A. and Shah, G.M., *Kashmir: From Crisis to Crisis* (1997).

Naqvi, Javed, "India Withdraws Nuclear Reactor Offer to Iran", *India West*, November 20, 1991.

Negi, T.S., in *Bureaucracy and Social Change* (1994) by M.G. Chitkara.

Nehru, Pt. Jawaharlal, Introduction to P.N.K. Bamzai, *A History of Kashmir* (1973).

Palkhivala, N.A., *We the People*, (1988).

Palmer, Norman D., "Ups and Downs in *Indo-American Relations*", American Academy of Political and Social Science, (Philadelphia, Vol. 294 (July 1954).

Pannikar, K.M., *The Founding of the Kashmir State* (193).

Parakal, Pauly, *Peking's Betrayal of Asia*, (1976).

Parmu, Dr. R.K., *A History of Muslim Rule in Kashmir*, 1320-1819, (1969).

Phillips, and Wade, *Constitutional and Administrative Law*.

Phrakal, Paurly, *Peking's Betrayal of Asia* (1976).

Prabhakar, Gulab Mishra, *Indo-Pakistan Relations* (1987).

Raina, Dinanath, *Unhappy Kashmir*, (1990).

Rampa, T. Labsong, The Third Eye, Illustrated by Tessa Theobald, (1969).

Rao, H.S. Guruo Raj, *Legal Aspects of the Kashmir Problem* (1967).

Richardson, 1952: 71, as Quoted by Deborah E. Klimburg Salter, in "*The Silk Route and the Diamond Path*", (1982).

Rose, Charles G., in *Religious Values and Human Society* (Reprint 1988).

Roychowdhury, Shankar, *Officially at Peace* (2002).

Saha, Meghnad, Birth Centenary (1992-93) Souvenir, Department of Physics University of Allahabad.

Saklani, Lt. Gen (retd) D.D., *Kashmir Saga* (1999).

Singh, K. Natwar, "A Spirited Fighter Even at 74." *The Sunday Tribune Book*, February 6,1994.

Singh, Mahendra, *Indo-US Relations* (1982).

Singh, N.B., "Air Power and Regional Security", in Indian Security, (1990).

Singh, Naunihal, *The World of Terrorism* (1989).

Singh, Sampooran, *India and the Nuclear Bomb* (1971).

Spector, Leonard, *Nuclear Proliferation Today*, (1984).

Srivastava, B.K., "Indo-American Relations Retrospect And Prospect", International Studies, Vol. 14.

Tendulkar, D.G., *Mahatma*, Vol. 8 (1990).

Thomas, Lowell Jr., *The Silent War in Tibet*, (1960).

Tsering, Bhuchung K., "Proving Truth From Facts", *Tibetan Bulletin* (May-June 1993).

Wani, Gul Mohd., *Kashmir Politics* (1993).

Yurkov, Steophan, *Peking Plans for Asia*, (1982).

## Newspaper Articles

Bidwai, Praful "Verdict For Secular Democracy", *The Tribune*, March 21, 1994.

Gupta, J.V. "Demolition, Emplosion of Hindu Sentiments", *The Tribune* February, 1993.

"It's Terroristan", *The Tribune*, 14th August, 2000.

Khazanchi, Ramesh, "Follies of Plebiscite in Kashmir", *The Times of India*, March 9, 1994.

Lawn, Bernard, "New World Order and Globalism", *The Tribune*, December 23, 1993.

Rustamji, K.F. "Towards Confederation?", *The Tribune*, January 13, 1993.

"Some Rights other Wrongs", *Indian Express*, February 11, 1994.

Sukant Gupta, "Tibetan's never-ending Struggle", *The Tribune*, March 19, 1994.

"Testing Time in Kashmir", *The Tribune*, February 1, 1994.

# Index

N



O

❑❑❑